Twentieth-Century Sentimentalism

TWENTIETH-CENTURY SENTIMENTALISM

Narrative Appropriation in American Literature

JENNIFER A. WILLIAMSON

Rutgers University Press
NEW BRUNSWICK, NEW JERSEY, AND LONDON

LIBRARY OF CONGRESS CATALOGING-IN-PUBLICATION DATA

Williamson, Jennifer A., 1978–
  Twentieth-century sentimentalism : narrative appropriation in American literature / Jennifer A. Williamson.
    pages cm. — (American Literatures Initiative)
  Includes bibliographical references and index.
  ISBN 978-0-8135-6298-8 (hardcover : alk. paper)
  ISBN 978-0-8135-6297-1 (pbk. : alk. paper)
  ISBN 978-0-8135-6299-5 (e-book) (print)
  1. American literature—20th century—History and criticism. 2. Sentimentalism in literature. I. Title.
PS228.S38W55 2013
810.9'384—dc23

2013010361

A British Cataloging-in-Publication record for this book is available from the British Library.

Copyright © 2014 by Jennifer A. Williamson

All rights reserved

No part of this book may be reproduced or utilized in any form or by any means, electronic or mechanical, or by any information storage and retrieval system, without written permission from the publisher. Please contact Rutgers University Press, 106 Somerset Street, New Brunswick, NJ 08901. The only exception to this prohibition is "fair use" as defined by U.S. copyright law.

Visit our website: http://rutgerspress.rutgers.edu

Manufactured in the United States of America

A book in the American Literatures Initiative (ALI), a collaborative publishing project of NYU Press, Fordham University Press, Rutgers University Press, Temple University Press, and the University of Virginia Press. The Initiative is supported by The Andrew W. Mellon Foundation. For more information, please visit www.americanliteratures.org.

For my mother, Gail

Contents

	Acknowledgments	ix
1	Introduction	1
2	Grace Lumpkin's *To Make My Bread*: Standing Together, Side by Side	23
3	Josephine Johnson's *Now in November*: Not Plough-Shares but People	59
4	Caretaking, Domesticity, and Gender in John Steinbeck's *The Grapes of Wrath*: "His Home Is Not the Land"	87
5	Margaret Walker's *Jubilee*: "Forged in a Crucible of Suffering"	112
6	Octavia Butler's *Kindred*: "My Face Too Was Wet with Tears"	127
7	Toni Morrison's *Beloved*: "Feeling How It Must Have Felt to Her Mother"	147
8	Conclusion	186
	Notes	203
	Works Cited	213
	Index	227

ACKNOWLEDGMENTS

I am deeply grateful to many people for supporting me in the process of completing this book. I would like to thank my advisors, friends, and colleagues at the University of North Carolina at Chapel Hill and Duke University for talking through this material and offering critical support. I hope they can see their impact on this project: William L. Andrews, Philip Gura, Fred Hobson, Wahneema Lubiano, Harry Thomas, Kelly Bezio, Ben Bolling, Angie Calcaterra, Ashley Reed, and Meredith Farmer. I also thank Linda Wagner-Martin for her constant support, guidance, and advice and without whom this book project would not have been possible. Thanks to *Modern Language Studies*, in which a version of chapter 5 was first published in Winter 2011.

And with deepest affection, I send thanks to all of my family for their faithful and loving encouragement. Special thanks go to my father, who has supported and cheered me on throughout this process, and to Aunt Martha, friend of my heart.

Twentieth-Century Sentimentalism

1 / Introduction

Contemporary beliefs about sentimentalism or "the sentimental" are that sentimentalism is an outdated mode of appealing to readers and to the general public. This opinion is largely influenced by the cultural sway of twentieth-century modernism, which asserted that sentimentalism portrays emotion that lacks reality or depth, falling flat in its attempts to depict real life and achieving only feminine melodrama. However, narrative claims to feeling—particularly those based in common and recognizable forms of suffering—have remained popular throughout the twentieth and twenty-first centuries. Contemporary authors continue to portray the struggles of working-class families to survive economic hardships as well as immigrants who seek to overcome obstacles and rise above poverty and intolerance. They depict women who suffer at the hands of abusive lovers or make constant self-sacrifice to care for others. They describe African American men and women who strive to transcend historical and present-day violence, racism, poverty, and discrimination. There continues to be a fascination with the suffering of vulnerable individuals whose identities render them cultural "Others." Authors writing sentimentalized depictions of suffering not only generate sympathy for their subjects but continue the nineteenth-century project of arguing for their inclusion in American culture and connecting them to American sentimental ideologies of the "national family."[1]

Because of its roots in the nineteenth century, contemporary authors self-consciously struggle with sentimentalism's seemingly outdated gender, class, and race ideals. However, its dual ability to promote these ideals and extend identification across them makes it an attractive and effective mode for engaging with political issues and extending social influence. Common sentimental themes such as vulnerable womanhood, motherhood and familial responsibility, caregiving and domesticity, death and the fear of separation, and Christian salvation to establish sympathy for Othered members of society were formed in the nineteenth century but continue to hold resonance in the contemporary era. Sentimental literature not only helped mark private and public spaces, but it also redefined the family as more than just a biological or economic unit—by focusing on the bonds of feeling and sympathy that transcended kinship obligations, it bound the family in terms of affection and love. Like their nineteenth-century predecessors, contemporary authors expand definitions of family and kinship in order to develop sympathy for those who have been cast as outsiders and Others. Although the middle-class (white) nuclear family remains the atomic unit of American national identity, contemporary writers continue to demonstrate the ways in which Othered individuals and groups parallel that familial structure, suffer in like ways, and create sympathetic, affectional bonds that connect these units into a larger, cultural family.

Thus, the nineteenth-century American sentimental mode appears in more recent literature than previously thought, revealing that the cultural work of sentimentalism continues in the twentieth century and beyond. From working-class literature that adopts the rhetoric of "feeling right" to promote a proletarian ideology to neo-slave narratives that wrestle with the legacy of slavery, this study explores the ways contemporary authors engage with familiar sentimental tropes and ideals. Contemporary authors modify the sentimental mode through narrative appropriation—adopting the perspectives and voices of Others and figuring them as legitimate objects of reader sympathy. Many current sentimental works appropriate the subjectivity of the Other in a form of colonial or postcolonial sympathy that assumes or critiques a universal Western perspective that believes its power of sympathy to be so strong that it can effectively inhabit the Others it seeks to help and improve. Through these methods, authors such as Grace Lumpkin, Josephine Johnson, John Steinbeck, Margaret Walker, Octavia Butler, and Toni Morrison apply the rhetorical methods of sentimentalism to the cultural struggles of their age.

Nineteenth-Century Sentimentalism

Nineteenth-century sentimental novels relied on depictions of the inherent goodness of human beings, the importance of emotional connection to others, and the power of feelings as a guide to right conduct for a vulnerable female protagonist as well as for the reader. They helped create the American Culture of Sentiment and placed women at its center by focusing on their extreme vulnerability and their inherent moral qualities—and, thus, their ability to guide others to religious and moral righteousness.[2] As Jane Tompkins, Philip Fisher, Shirley Samuels, and many other scholars have argued, sentimental novels do more than just tell tragic tales of women in distress or who find comfort in their Protestant Christian beliefs. Such novels enact a form of cultural work by relying on emotional appeals to generate sympathy in readers. This sympathy serves a key rhetorical function that allows a text to generate compassion for its subjects and subject matter to promote emotional and moral education for the reader. Sentimental novels attempt to teach readers to "think and act in a particular way" (Tompkins, *Designs*, xi). The function of the events, scenarios, and symbols in the texts are "heuristic and didactic rather than mimetic ... they provide a basis for remaking the social and political order in which events take place" (xvii). Working as a set of rules for how to "feel right," sentimentality is "a set of cultural practices designed to evoke a certain form of emotional response" in the reader; this empathy enables the text to produce "spectacles that cross race, class, and gender boundaries" (Samuels, *Culture*, 4–5). Thus, Harriet Beecher Stowe's *Uncle Tom's Cabin* (1852) can convince its assumed audience of white, middle-class readers to sympathize with the separations and suffering of enslaved African Americans in order to argue against the institution of slavery, while Fanny Fern's *Ruth Hall* (1855) witnesses the sexual politics and structures of male authority that inhibit women as it argues for women as cultural consumers and economic participants. As the reader sympathizes with the suffering and moral education of characters in a novel, she transposes those lessons upon her own life and onto the real world, creating a metaphor through which she views her role in society and her potential for transforming that society.[3]

Rather than attempt to depict or reflect a literal version of reality, nineteenth-century sentimental authors were casting the symbolic details, characters, and ideas of their historical moments in a rhetorically transformative mode. In so doing, they created representations that became culturally embedded and symbolically concrete. Not only did sentimental novels deliberately employ clear, simple language and familiar themes to make use of the social and cultural resonance an author expected a particular trope to hold for the reader—the use of stereotype was a form of cultural shorthand for conveying moral purpose in parallel ways to religious texts such as *Pilgrim's Progress*—but those symbols eventually became deeply embedded within American culture. Thus, nineteenth-century sentimental fiction accomplished a social transformation by which "the unimaginable becomes, finally, the obvious" (Fisher, *Facts*, 8). Although contemporary readers may now scoff at depictions of orphans, abandoned wives, fallen women, tubercular girls on their deathbeds, and angelic Little Evas, the symbolic meaning of a nuclear family, living in middle-class comfort, headed by a benevolent fatherly provider and motherly moral guide with clean, obedient children, remains in full force, as does the repeated vulnerability and risk to those—particularly women—who lose familial connection or exist outside of established social norms.

It is this potential loss of familial and social connection that drives the plot tension of sentimental texts. While the development of the individual and the self-in-society have long been recognized as significant (masculinized) themes of American literature, sentimental literature values and operates within a different social structure. Instead, according to Joanne Dobson, sentimental literature "envisions the self-in-relation; family (not necessarily in the conventional biological sense), intimacy, community, and social responsibility are its primary relational modes" ("Renaissance," 267). The core of the sentimental text "is the desire for bonding, and it is affiliation on the plane of emotion, sympathy, nurturance, or similar moral or spiritual inclination for which sentimental writers and readers yearn" (267). Whereas traditional texts derive their tension from the possibility that masculinized qualities of individuality, freedom, and independent selfhood are threatened, the tensions of sentimental texts are created through a feminized identity construct in which familial and affectional bonds are threatened through death or separation—divine consolation is the only reparative for earthly loss—and human connections are idealized. The driving force in sentimental texts is the fear of loss, emotional connection, and the formation of utopian relationships that are grounded in affection and sympathy.

It is particularly significant to note that through a focus on sympathetic connection as a transformative social force, the loss of familial connection (and death, which is a form of family separation) as one of life's deepest tragedies, and the idealization of affectional bonds, sentimental novels redefined the social structure of the family. Cindy Weinstein, in *Family, Kinship, and Sympathy in Nineteenth-Century American Literature* (2004), argues that the central project of all sentimental novels is the "making of a family" but that this construction is based on "an institution to which one can choose to belong or not" (8). Rather than define families on the basis of biology (or, to use Weinstein's term, *consanguinity*), sentimental novels emphasize affection and adoption in the re-formation of the American family. Orphans, vulnerable children, and women move through difficulties in each novel, during which they form sympathetic kinship groups with new friends and adoptive families. These groups represent the ideal, sentimental family based on choice and affection, rather than biological imperative or economic obligation. Although many critics have credited the sentimental novel with producing the contemporary middle-class, nuclear family structure, Weinstein argues that sentimental texts also "fiercely challenge the patriarchal regime of the biological family by calling attention to the frequency with which fathers neglect the economic as well as emotional obligations owed to their children" (8–9). To make up for frequent paternal failure, the texts "advance a theory of mother love," but most sentimental plots also require a protagonist child to be motherless (9). Thus, the sentimental novel must expand, through sympathy, the possibilities for who counts as family: as Weinstein draws it, "To extend the meaning of family is to extend the possibilities for sympathy" (9).[4] This process of extending the definition of family to friends and adoptive families—to those with whom one forms affectional or sympathetic bonds—has radical transformative potential. The family has long stood as an ideological symbol for the national, political body, representing the units by which society is both formed and ordered. Extending the definition of family through sympathy—a process that crosses the gender, race, and class boundaries that delineate lines of Othering and nationalized social exclusion—also enables the transformation of the national family and national identity.

The Rise of Anti-Sentimentalism in the Twentieth Century

Because of its use of familiar imagery and simple language, because many of its tropes have become so commonplace, and because of its focus on feminized familial connection rather than masculinized individualism, nineteenth-century sentimental literature has often been labeled by contemporary critics as, plainly and simply, "bad" writing. Nathaniel Hawthorne may be the earliest, most famous critic of sentimentalism, writing in 1855: "America is now wholly given over to a d——d mob of scribbling women, and I should have no chance of success while the public is occupied by their trash" (qtd. in Person, *Introduction*, 24). His assessment continued to be reiterated as a shorthand appraisal of sentimental literature or women's writing in general. Throughout the twentieth century, the term *sentimental* has been used as a label for melodramatic, flat representations that are deemed unrealistic, unsophisticated, and unliterary. Furthermore, calling a work "sentimental" became a way to judge it, negatively, as feminine—whether written by a woman or a man—because of its association with emotion and other woman-linked themes such as domesticity or religion.

Perhaps the pinnacle of anti-sentimental critical assessments occurred with the publication of Ann Douglas's *The Feminization of American Culture* in 1977. Although one of the first scholarly works to take sentimental fiction as a serious critical subject, it sees sentimental culture and fiction as failures because they use language that has "gone bad," insofar as it has "utterly capitulated to the drift of its times," and because they promote passive, domesticated Christian virtues that flatter women into accepting less powerful social roles within newly forming urban capitalistic societies dominated by men (255). Douglas's criticisms have been subsequently countered by a focus on sentimentalism's "cultural work," but it is important to note that her judgment about the quality of writing is based upon a modernist critical perspective that changed the way literature was valued and cast sentimentalism as a particular violator of its aesthetic precepts.

Despite the phenomenal popularity of the sentimental novel and the cultural pervasiveness of sentimentalism in the nineteenth century, prevailing critical views hold that the twentieth century became increasingly hostile to the sentimental as a literary and political mode. Realism, naturalism, modernism, and postmodernism set themselves in opposition to romanticism and sentimentalism, figuring the latter forms as feminized as well as lacking qualities necessary to understand contemporary life and the modern individual. Sentimentalism became viewed as the product of a bygone era, and twentieth-century writers consciously sought to move away from highly structured, moralistic presentations of social and religious life, de-emphasizing an individual's ability to enact social change through moral rightness. Instead, modern authors tended to portray individuals with complex psychology who were subject to social and environmental forces that had overwhelming power to affect the course of their lives.

Rather than depict life in symbolic or idealized terms, realist fiction sought to represent faithfully the lives of ordinary people. Writers of realism engaged with and opposed the overtly symbolic and political stance of sentimental writing and reform novels, often figuring such debates in gendered terms. Naturalist fiction even more strongly opposed literary traditions labeled as feminine, including the sentimental novel. Such texts often depict the masculinized urban industrial world, city sprawl, and scenes of slum life through the experiences of the middle and lower classes. By portraying their modes of writing and their relationship to the social conditions of the new century as more real, more authentic, and more objective than sentimental writing, these writers argued that the sentimental novel no longer effectively captured either American experience or its cultural conditions. Despite realism and naturalism's need for sentimentalism by which to define themselves against, authors of these genres self-consciously argued that sentimentalism had no place in the modern era.

Like proponents of realism and naturalism, critics view modernism as inherently anti-sentimental, disdaining the overtly moral and feminized novel of the previous era. Modernism—developed as a rejection of conservative realist values—encompasses the work of artists and writers who felt that traditional forms of art, literature, religion, social organization, and daily life were outdated because of changes in the economic, social, and political structures of the rapidly industrializing twentieth-century world. Although not a broadly antireligious movement, many modernists questioned the existence of an all-powerful, compassionate Creator, and one feature of modernist writing was to interrogate the accepted beliefs of the previous age. As an artistic movement intent on capturing the zeitgeist of the new era, modernism not only sought to embody the energies and experiences of the fast-paced industrializing twentieth century, but it also worked to dismantle previous understandings of art, literature, and society that loomed large at the start of the new age. One of its largest targets was sentimental literature, which had adapted Enlightenment values of sensibility in the nineteenth century and shaped the world through a feminized, religious, middle-class lens of Victorian mores.

The legacy of the modernist movement continues to affect literary criticism as well as popular understandings of art and literature today because texts are judged within a largely masculine tradition that values attempts to achieve "a timeless, universal ideal of truth and formal coherence" (Tompkins, *Designs*, 200). Sentimental texts fare poorly within this critical perspective and are often evaluated as lacking artistic value, only able to be judged as an artifact of popular, trite women's culture, thus enabling a dominant scholarly narrative that twentieth-century authors all but turned away from sentimental forms and tropes, abandoning them under the censure of modernism's growing influence.[5]

From Marxism to Sentimental Proletarianism: "All That Feel the Same, They Are Together"

By the mid-1930s, communist ideologies about social welfare and universal human responsibility to a collective well-being were broadly circulating in the United States because of an influx of radical left thinkers as well as the stranglehold of the Depression.[6] Communism as a political movement was closely linked to the contemporary arts and literary scene throughout the 1920s, 1930s, and early 1940s. *Proletarian literature* was the term officially adopted by the American Communist Party to describe writing from the late 1920s and the 1930s that addressed concerns of the working class, the destructiveness of capitalism, and the potential for revolution. From the outset, Marxist literature and criticism were infused by communist class ideologies, integrating literary aesthetic with political theory. However, as the 1930s progressed, modernism's influence began to affect the views of Marxist critics, spurring debate and creating a divide between those who focused on Marxist philosophy and those who increasingly emphasized Marxist aesthetics.

It might at first seem that Marxist critical emphasis on a text's relationship to historical and material conditions as well as its political and social intent would have brought about a renewed appreciation for nineteenth-century sentimental writing because of its strong association with social reform. However, Marxist critics belittled women's writing of the previous century—as well as the "sentimental"—for a number of reasons. For one thing, Marxists opposed sentimental fiction's strong emphasis on Protestant Christian values and the social structures based on Christian belief systems that the novels often promoted. Marxism questioned religion as a bourgeois social institution that—along with legal, philosophical, and political systems—keeps unequal economic power structures in place. Even more damning from a Marxist perspective was sentimental fiction's focus upon, promotion of, and—many scholars argue—creation of the American middle class. By repetitively insisting that women occupy certain kinds of spaces and perform specific behaviors and social identities, sentimental novels "both recommend and perform a middle-class... way of being in the world" (Baym, *Woman's Fiction*, xxii).

Like the modernists and realists, Marxist writers and critics also participated in a gendered devaluation of sentimental writing. As proletarian writers responded to early twentieth-century economic crises and promoted social reform, they tried to capitalize on the rising influences of literary naturalism and realism to argue through fiction, poetry, and reportage that social and environmental factors—systemic abuses sanctioned and promoted by capitalism—lay at the root of working-class human misery. Such realism, however, was heavily masculinized: writers focused on male-dominated work spaces such as factories, mines, and fields, and the oppressed or triumphant worker was typified by a muscled, sweating, laboring male body that served to represent all workers and all parts of the working class. Sentimental fiction's emphasis on the middle-class, bourgeois domestic space was considered feminized and trivial and was placed in opposition to the serious, masculinized, working-class struggle of proletarian texts.

This push for hard-hitting literary realism, however, left many proletarian writers open to charges of overdoing their depictions and of emotional falseness in their characters and plots. They were accused of writing sappy melodramas instead of what modernist and subsequent critics designated as "Literature." Critics who registered some alignment between using realist scenes to stir the reader to revolutionary awareness and sentimental fiction's ability to move the reader on an emotional level actually denigrated attempts to move through feeling as "sentimental proletarianism," equating it as mere emotional propaganda. As with the modernists, the term *sentimental* becomes Marxist shorthand for feminized and maudlin attempts to influence readers into an emotional state. Criticisms of proletarian writing, as it emerged both in the 1930s and later in the century, often used the term *sentimental* as a label for works they found to be overwrought and emotionally contrived. Writing for the *North American Review* in 1939, R. W. Steadman dismisses proletarian writing almost as a whole, citing the "tragic triviality" and "sentimentalism" of poems and fiction produced by nearly every major writer of the genre ("Critique," 146, 148). Literature, according to the increasingly modernist critical establishment, "requires not merely observational accuracy; it requires also emotional honesty," and the proletarian emphasis on depicting working-class suffering while promoting a Socialist message cannot, according to modernist philosophy, achieve both (152).

The irony, perhaps, of such critical charges is that they are, in some cases, unintentionally accurate, particularly when considered through today's new understandings of the nineteenth-century sentimental rhetorical mode. Early and mid-twentieth-century critiques of proletarian writers as "sentimental" were intended to point out their work's lack of emotional realism and the ways it doesn't live up to modernist literary principles. Such criticisms also highlighted the supposedly feminized qualities of the writing. These indictments did not, however, recognize the "sentimental" in these works as the deliberate use of a political, rhetorical strategy associated with emotional sympathy and affectional bonds. Yet some proletarian writers who stood accused of the grossest violations against what counted for "good literature" had indeed employed sentimentalism as a deliberate rhetorical strategy. Like the nineteenth-century authors vilified by the modernists for their maudlin sympathies and common appeal, they employed their pens to reform moral views and advocate for improved social conditions.

Drawing upon nineteenth-century models and familiar sentimental tropes of the mother spurred to protective action, the young woman vulnerable to an indifferent male-dominated world, feminized sexual exploitation and tragedy, and feeling-influenced moral education, a modern sentimentalism reemerges in 1930s fiction as a means of influencing readers to identify with the proletariat and to argue for improvements to labor conditions as well as to the lives of the working class. While revealing dangerous and unhealthy conditions in factories, mines, and farms, such writers focus also on the home and family to show the integral connection between domestic and industrial spheres. This revised sentimentalism appears more frequently in female-authored fiction: women writers use the sentimental mode to emphasize the cornerstones of motherhood and family as intrinsic to the proletarian community as well as the imagined human community at large.

The sentimental mode allows proletarian authors such as Grace Lumpkin, Josephine Johnson, and John Steinbeck to refigure members of the working class as legitimate recipients of middle-class sympathy and as members of the American national family. During the 1930s, members of the working class were fighting against exploitation by their employers and by a middle class that benefited from the products of their labor. To achieve reforms, they had to convince the middle class that they deserved government protection. Where logical, political, and economic arguments for reform failed, these authors appealed to the sympathies of middle-class readers by positioning members of the working class as outsiders who can be understood because of their dedication to family and because of their suffering. Applying familiar sentimental tropes to working-class bodies and figuring the traditionally masculine proletarian worker in a "feminized" sentimental form, these authors argued not only for extending sympathy to the working class but that such sympathy would lead to a radical political awakening. By drawing upon the emotions of their readers, Lumpkin, Johnson, and Steinbeck call attention to the humanist principles at work within sentimentalism and suggest that the recognition of others' suffering leads to a motivation for proletarian action.

Significantly, most of the authors who wrote sentimental proletarian fiction were not themselves working-class, although many witnessed these struggles through reportage; they were members of the Communist Party USA (CPUSA), participated in strikes, and lived among the working class for periods of time. Not only did real-world circumstances empower middle-class individuals to write these stories by providing access to education, funds, and the types of employment or leisure time in which to write novels that were generally denied working-class writers, but their desire to speak for the economically disenfranchised led to their speaking through the voices of the working class. By appropriating the voices of the working class and attempting to combine both the sentimental and the realistic modes in the telling of their stories, proletarian authors speak on behalf of and through the disenfranchised to create a sympathetic bridge with the skeptical, modern reader. Furthermore, unlike nineteenth-century sentimental writers, contemporary authors no longer assumed or wrote for an entirely white, middle-class readership. Proletarian authors sought to inform and include a working-class readership while neo-slave narrative authors deliberately appealed to and included African American readers. However, as proletarian authors and neo-slave narrative authors sought sympathetic identification from white, middle-class readers for the working class and minorities, it was necessary to appeal to the dominant culture and target a broad readership. This function of sentimentalism remains in the twentieth-century novels discussed.

The Negro Family and the Case for National Action

When the Moynihan Report was published in 1965, it made explicit a number of American ideologies about the relationship between race, gender, class, family structure, and the national body.[7] Concerned about an increasing gap in African American achievement as well as rising welfare rates, Daniel Patrick Moynihan writes, "At the heart of the deterioration of the fabric of Negro society is the deterioration of the Negro family." While only briefly nodding at the obstacles created by a history of slavery, segregation, and unemployment—and without a clear discussion of institutionalized discrimination—Moynihan's primary focus is on the ways African American families are fundamentally different from white families, and he seeks to explain why. In a pivotal point for American culture, he, a sociologist, argues that African American families are failing primarily because of matriarchal family structures. Moynihan cites a problematic reversal of gender roles whereby African American husbands are emasculated by their wives: "Negro husbands have unusually low power. . . . Whereas the majority of white families are equalitarian, the largest percentage of Negro families are dominated by the wife." Furthermore, according to Moynihan, the frequent absence of fathers and the domination of mothers result in disproportionate attention to female children and in low-achieving boys who are unable to adapt to white patriarchal culture.

Although Moynihan's report was controversial even at the time of its publication, these images—of a domineering female-headed African American family and black welfare mothers—became dominant in American cultural consciousness and remain in common circulation today. Shifting the discussion to African American family structure removes focus from institutionalized racism and social configurations that privilege white nuclear households. What was occurring was a resurgence of the sentimentalized ideology of the white, middle-class nuclear family, headed by a benevolent male provider and a female moral guide that produced good children (citizens) for the national family. There is no coincidence that this renewed appreciation for the white nuclear family—and the unfavorable racialized, gendered comparison—occurred in the midst of the 1960s civil rights era as well as the second wave feminist movement, in which African Americans were fighting for equal rights and women were achieving new social freedoms.

African American women, however, were in a very different position from the working-class women of the 1930s, who needed to show that they, too, aspired to sentimental, middle-class ideals and were only prevented from meeting them due to capitalist failures. Instead, African American families faced a much longer, racialized history of being held to sentimental ideals and prevented from meeting them. Whereas proletarian writers adopted sentimentalism as a rhetorical strategy in the midst of a social revolution to argue for inclusion in the national family as well as socioeconomic change, African American writers adopted sentimentalism both in the nineteenth century and beyond to respond to the ways in which they have continued to be integral to the definition of the American family and caught up in an ongoing cultural debate.

When sentimental families were being shaped in the nineteenth century, African Americans were often excluded by their racial identities as well as their social circumstances—sentimental heroines were always white and had to adhere to principles of class and sexual purity that were largely unavailable to enslaved African American women. In the later part of the nineteenth century, free blacks and middle-class African Americans sought to demonstrate the ways they both met the ideals of sentimentalism and the ways sentimental ideals failed. Neo-slave narratives emerged in the twentieth century as an artistic and cultural response to the African American history of slavery and the civil rights struggle as well as this resurgence of sentimental ideals. Particularly as the genre developed into the 1980s, during which time female authors of neo-slave narratives more fully explored the relationship between the tangled history of slave narratives, American literature, and sentimental ideals, neo-slave narratives demonstrate a return to the use and critique of sympathy as a rhetorical tool. The history of sentimentalism and African American writing remains complex and intertwined because of the ways in which they formed as responses to each other well into the twentieth century.

At their inception, sentimental novels and slave narratives emerged as parallel but connected literary forms. Slave narratives developed as a largely autobiographical genre, focused on establishing a text's veracity in order to reveal the atrocities of the institution of slavery and, simultaneously, to argue for the humanity of the enslaved. Accounts of slavery and autobiographical narratives were published in a variety of formats from the eighteenth century through the beginning of the twentieth century.[8] However, the genre exhibited a stylistic evolution, as William L. Andrews outlines in *To Tell a Free Story: The First Century of Afro-American Autobiography, 1760–1865*, that developed from arguing that the black former slave is a "brother and man" to whites (and especially to white readers) to, later in the nineteenth century, more individualistic portrayals of selfhood in which authors seek to prove themselves to be moral, spiritual, and intellectual peers of whites (1, 3). Even as the authors of slave narratives sought to argue for the humanity of the enslaved or to demonstrate the ways white culture marginalized black identity, the authenticity of the text was of constant concern because skeptical reviewers were quick to point out what they termed were exaggerations or lies in order to undermine abolitionist arguments and support counter-narratives that presented slavery as a benign institution. When authors began to incorporate novelized features into the narratives—such as the addition of dialogue or third-person narration—to dramatize their stories and increase the impact of their messages, they encountered challenges to the truthfulness of their stories. Thus, Andrews points out: "The reception of [an author's] narrative as truth depended on the degree to which his artfulness could hide his art" (3).

Sentimental novels, on the other hand, were published as fiction and made no claims to conveying autobiographical truthfulness. Furthermore, such novels were written with an artfulness that was, of necessity, easily recognized by readers. This ability to identify the tropes and devices by which sentimental novels function allowed readers to decipher the moral messages encoded within the narrative. Ironically, despite accusations against sentimental novels and sentimentalism for an inability to portray "real feeling" and a melodramatic mimicry of emotion, the sentimental novel's goal of "veracity" was the desire to achieve truth through its portrayal of emotional experience and its moral imperative. While scholars have argued that the moral and social messages inhabiting sentimentalism ranged from critiquing the social outcomes of coverture (Davidson) to establishing a new form of social republic (Barnes), as the nineteenth century progressed, sentimental authors also sought to contribute to the public discussion of slavery. Furthermore, with the rising popularity of the slave narrative, sentimental novels were heavily influenced by the genre, as evidenced by Harriet Beecher Stowe's *Uncle Tom's Cabin* (1852), Mary Langdon's (Mary Hayden Green Pike) *Ida May* (1854), and (on the pro-slavery side of the debate) Caroline Lee Hentz's *The Planter's Northern Bride* (1854).

Such influence extended in two directions. As sentimental novels become blockbuster sellers, slave narrative authors began to incorporate fictional elements and sentimental features into autobiographical accounts of slavery. Many antislavery groups adopted the tactic of "moral suasion," focusing rhetorical appeals on the basic goodness of human nature in order to convince people that slavery was wrong for moral reasons. Such groups were aware that they could capitalize on growing reader interest in the lives of former slaves, not only to expose the hardships and evils of slavery, but also to adopt principles of instruction based on sympathy and religious (moral) correctness that was an integral part of sentimental fiction and the Culture of Sentiment. Embarking on a campaign of moral suasion, abolitionist presses flooded the North and South with "antislavery fiction and poems, accounts of fugitive slaves, reports of slave kidnappings, criticism of colonization plans, and stories of free blacks" and published hundreds of book-length accounts of life under slavery written by fugitive slaves (Risley, *Abolition*, 42).[9] Indeed, abolitionists believed that the power of sympathy awakened by the sentimental novel could be just as forcefully wrought in the slave narrative because of its claims to real-life experience and, thus, offers a truth of suffering that inspires even greater sympathy. When Frederick Douglass published *My Bondage and My Freedom* in 1855, a reviewer declared: "We have read nothing since *Uncle Tom's Cabin*, which so thrilled every fiber of the soul and awoke such intense sympathy for the slave as this touching autobiography. It is a sad thought, that what Frederick Douglass suffered in slavery, three million of human beings are this day suffering" ("Miscellaneous"). The symbiosis between slave narratives and sentimental novels indicates an awareness of the usefulness of sympathy as a method for reaching readers as well as a convergence of political and cultural interests—sentimental novelists often promoted abolition, while slave narrative authors were frequently supporters of the women's rights movement. Both slave narratives and sentimental novels also struggle with the forms of power encoded within their ideological systems. Though often upholding white patriarchal power by teaching women to maintain familial relationships, sexual purity, religious piety, and strict rules of social decorum, sentimental novels also subvert existing power structures by arguing for women's individual legitimacy and placing them, and the domestic realm, at the center of the new social order they promote. Slave narrative authors not only capitalized on the use of emotional appeals to challenge existing white patriarchal structures and argue for their own human legitimacy, but they also examined the ways sentimental novels that value domesticity, chastity, and gentility—qualities available only to middle-class whites—exclude African American women from sentimental female ideology and maintain racial ideologies that promote white dominance.[10]

In the twentieth century, many African American authors returned to the subject of slavery in their texts, publishing novels that depict fictional re-creations of life in American slavery or that draw parallels between contemporary social and economic conditions and nineteenth-century slavery. Bernard W. Bell, in his 1987 study *The Afro-American Novel and Its Tradition*, coined the term "neo-slave narrative" to describe "residually oral, modern narratives of escape from bondage to freedom" (289); the term is now applied to a broad range of texts that are influenced by the slave narrative genre. This genre has grown to include works set during the time of slavery as well as any time from Reconstruction to the Jim Crow era to the present. There exists a variety of textual experimentation among neo-slave narratives, so that while they gesture toward the generic conventions of nineteenth-century slave narratives, many also experiment with style, form, chronology, point of view, and structure. However, regardless of their structural differences, "these texts illustrate the centrality of the history and the memory of slavery to our individual, racial, gender, cultural, and national identities" (Smith, "Neo-Slave Narratives," 168). As works of literature written in the twentieth century, with the benefit of both the passage of time and critical trends such as postmodernism that encourage self-reflexive art, neo-slave narratives are written from "a perspective informed and enriched by the study of slave narratives, the changing historiography of slavery, the complicated history of race and power relations in America and throughout the world during the twentieth century, and the rise of psychoanalysis and other theoretical frameworks" (169).[11] Authors of neo-slave narratives are as concerned with the effects of slavery on those who directly experienced it as they are with the generations who deal with its legacy.

Authors of twentieth-century neo-slave narratives explore a variety of themes in their works such as definitions of freedom and bondage, the cultural role of religion, white supremacy and white privilege, interconnections of race and gender, black masculinity, external control of black women's bodies, definitions of family, orality and literacy, living histories, and traumatic recurrence. Because African American women were subjected to additional, extreme marginalization under slavery and under the definitions of womanhood offered by sentimentalism, many authors of twentieth-century women's neo-slave narratives do more than just examine the legacy of slavery in a contemporary context. They also take on the legacy of sentimentalism as it is intertwined with the slave narrative, adopting the sentimental mode in order to remind contemporary readers of the suffering experienced by enslaved persons and to show the impact of that suffering on later generations. Simultaneously, such authors critique sentimentalism's gender and race tropes, showing that oppressive ideologies that have survived into the modern era were developed during slavery. In so doing, writers of women's neo-slave narratives, which appeared after the publication of the Moynihan Report (1965), were responding to contemporary devaluations of black womanhood and community as well as revealing that (white) perspectives of African American identity were shaped by a bifurcated cultural legacy of slavery versus white supremacy.

Margaret Walker began writing her novel *Jubilee* long before the debates of the Moynihan era, but it was finalized and published during that period. Her neo-slave narrative is a more direct rewriting of the sentimentalized slave narrative that addresses contradictions in sentimental ideals as well as the painful history of American slavery and casts African American women as the moral and spiritual guide of African American healing, reconciliation, and cultural advancement. Octavia Butler's *Kindred*, however, faces more complex representations of American race relations in the post-Moynihan era, in which African Americans not only must address a history of racial Othering, but they must also address the ways they have become divorced from their own past in an effort to struggle forward. Toni Morrison's *Beloved*, meanwhile, not only takes on the issue of African American suffering but also addresses the value—and dangers—of matriarchy as well as the value of sympathy as a rhetorical tool. These authors appropriate the slave narratives and slave histories of the past as well as nineteenth-century sentimental ideals that continue to hold resonance today in order to critique an ongoing marginalization of African American women and families. They not only argue for the cultural value of acknowledging past suffering in order to move forward, but they critique the ideologies that continue to exclude them from full acceptance into American society (and the American family). African Americans, they argue, are not only excluded by their identities, but they are marginalized by the very suffering that is supposed to render them sympathetic to the dominant social group because the sympathetic identification has failed and is treated like an open wound that demonstrates difference instead of creating affectional kinship bonds.

The chapters of *Twentieth-Century Sentimentalism: Narrative Appropriation in American Literature* demonstrate that sentimentalism not only survived well beyond the turn of the century but that it remains a popular genre that appeals to common readers and continues to do "cultural work."[12] Although contemporary writers often grapple with the cultural norms established by sentimental texts, they work from a foundation of race, gender, and class conventions that were popularized by nineteenth-century novels. Many widespread beliefs about the nuclear family, about domesticity and middle-class life, about mothers, about gender—women's "natural emotional sensitivity" and men's "inherent need to provide"—and about the behaviors and personal traits of whites and blacks were formed during the nineteenth century, shaped by the characters and events in sentimental fiction. While modern authors often complicate these beliefs, they are aware that their readers not only are familiar with them but continue to feel emotionally connected to them because they have been absorbed into constructions of American identity. While nineteenth-century sentimentalism was primarily associated with reform because of the way it promoted changes in the American cultural landscape, contemporary sentimentalism is appealing because it is soothing, crossing many divisive modern boundaries and reflecting familiar beliefs. Because of the influences of modernism and other critical schools, audiences demand realism and refuse the stilted constructions of past sentimentalism, while also preferring to engage with sympathy and emotional connection as a driving human force. Thus, contemporary authors work within a sentimental matrix that infuses cultural products with self-consciousness: one is both living in a culture shaped everywhere by sentimentalism and skeptical of it.

The working class and people of color, I argue, remain the primary inheritors of the contemporary sentimental tradition because of its association with defining white, female, middle-class identity—and, therefore, defining its opposite. Bringing together proletarian literature and neo-slave narratives highlights two significant moments in twentieth-century history, culture, and literature—one in which the working class adopts the sentimental mode to argue for inclusion in the American national family and the need for social reform to make that inclusion possible, and one in which African Americans adopt the sentimental mode to argue for recognition for their place in the American national family while simultaneously critiquing sentimental ideals and failures of sympathy as the very means by which African Americans have also been excluded by the culture from which they seek acknowledgment.

Throughout the past century, cultural shifts due to economic changes, world wars, civil rights battles, sexual revolutions, feminism, and changing immigration patterns created new arrangements of insiders and outsiders. Sentimentalism remains a useful method of promoting sympathy across boundaries during and after these cultural upheavals, encouraging reforms and offering sympathy to newly visible Others to reconnect them to the dominant group. Although the laboring class has always existed, the rise of industrialization and urbanization in the mid- to late nineteenth century created new middle- and working-class structures that differed from previous social formations. After a period of prosperity, the 1929 crash and the Great Depression brought attention to the plight of the working class. Authors who adopted sentimentalism to write about miners, factory workers, and farmers were arguing not only for social reform but also for their inclusion in American society, showing working-class familial structures and struggles and revealing them as a reflection of the American Dream—but these families were more often the result of the failed dream. Similarly, the United States has a shameful history of slavery and colonialism, so its past has always been multiracial. Nineteenth-century sentimental fiction focused on abolitionist debates and presented African American identity from an antebellum perspective. In the twentieth century, slavery has been abolished, but African Americans have experienced decades of institutionalized racism and continue to work toward cultural equality. Although African Americans are not new outsiders, the way in which their status as Others is established continues to evolve. Thus, contemporary authors can trace African American marginalization to slavery while also acknowledging the nuances of modern conflict. Sentimentalism allows such authors to outline the history of racism as well as reform efforts, developing sympathy for the Other while also showing the ways sentimentalism often maintains white dominance.

Twentieth-Century Sentimentalism: Narrative Appropriation in American Literature brings together six novels that illustrate contemporary sentimental appropriation. The first three texts are examples of significant proletarian fiction from the 1930s and demonstrate the ways in which the sentimental mode was adopted to extend sympathy for the working class, a new subject for the traditionally middle-class, white sentimental novel. Sentimental proletarian writers teach the middle-class reader to "feel right" by recognizing the legitimacy of working-class families and sympathizing with their struggles, a sympathy that is directed toward revolutionary action. Although the authors of proletarian sentimentalism were not themselves members of the working class, they acquired information about working-class experiences through reportage and interviews. Like their nineteenth-century counterparts whose authors turned to the novel to argue for social reform, these texts are the result of efforts to demonstrate the plight of the working class and reach readers more effectively than is believed possible through nonfiction.

Whereas proletarian authors sought to extend sympathy to those who were Othered by class, authors of neo-slave narratives not only contend with racial Othering, but they also address the historical links between slave narrative and sentimental fiction genres. The last three texts in this study are prominent examples of neo-slave narratives that experiment widely with form, ranging from historical fiction to science fiction to a postmodern ghost story. As twentieth-century authors address contemporary racial conflicts and the legacy of slavery, they also attend to the ways that sentimentalism not only contributed to the development of African American letters but also played a role in maintaining the racial Othering that persists today. Just as slave narrative authors of the nineteenth century adopted sentimental forms while critiquing the sentimental marginalization of black identity, these novels investigate the relationship between suffering and sympathy as well as constructions of the African American family and gender roles. Neo-slave narrative authors draw from family oral history accounts of slavery as well as published slave narratives to construct their reimaginings of slave experience in the modern era. In their various generic experiments, these authors play with the relationship between time and history as well as cultural memory.

In chapter 2, I examine Grace Lumpkin's 1932 novel *To Make My Bread* as an important example of proletarian sentimental fiction. I argue that Lumpkin's novel adopts the sentimental mode, both upholding and critiquing nineteenth-century gender and class ideals in order to confer sympathy upon the working class and endorse a Marxist awakening. By revealing the suffering of the working class, by showing that women are prevented from being ideal mothers because of their class, and by turning the entire working community of the factory into a family, Lumpkin argues that the proletarian worker is a member of the human community for whom reform is needed.

Similarly, in chapter 3, I analyze Josephine Johnson's Pulitzer Prize–winning novel *Now in November* (1934) as a proletarian sentimental novel that argues for sympathy for the working class through the lens of the family. Set on a farm instead of in a factory, Johnson's novel is narrated from the perspective of the middle daughter, who recounts her family's domestic and agricultural hardships, worrying over their survival and observing the ways that they are systemically prevented from achieving stability. Johnson's novel, like nineteenth-century sentimental texts, reorganizes the family around a feminine moral center and examines the consequences of gendered transgressions. *Now in November* advances a proletarian humanist argument by dismantling fundamental capitalist mythologies. Significantly, Johnson—like some other women proletarian writers—reveals that outside forces affect what happens within the home, but rather than emphasize men's traditionally violent response to this suffering, she creates a portrait of sentimental men who suffer over their inability to provide.

In chapter 4, John Steinbeck's *The Grapes of Wrath* (1939) provides an example of the male sentimental proletarian novel. Here Steinbeck portrays domestic caregiving as a necessary force for survival in an age when patriarchal, capitalist individualism has failed. Drawing on sentimental nostalgia for the home, Steinbeck expands the definition of family by broadening the boundaries of domestic space. By following the nomadic journey of the Joads as they are forced from their Oklahoma farm, creating a new home each time they set up camp, Steinbeck turns the entire American landscape into the domestic realm. Further, by revealing the ways that men as well as women serve as caregivers and develop kinship groups, Steinbeck brings men back into the home and crosses traditional gender boundaries to demonstrate that working-class survival is a human enterprise.

After exploring the ways that proletarian literature adopts the sentimental mode, I move to the genre of American neo-slave narratives. Beginning in chapter 5 with *Jubilee* (1966), I argue that Margaret Walker's novel mimics the religious, emotional education of nineteenth-century sentimental novels. *Jubilee* suggests that African American suffering under slavery is part of a larger Christian destiny, and Walker's protagonist, Vyry, develops a Christlike philosophy of suffering, forgiveness, and redemptive love that provides agency through her acceptance of suffering. The novel is historical fiction, based upon the life and oral history of Walker's grandmother, so its epic scale and implied historical veracity give a religious momentum to the narrative events, moving not just from slavery to freedom but from ignorance to enlightenment in parallel with figures such as Moses, Christian from *Pilgrim's Progress*, and Ellen from *The Wide, Wide World*. Drawing upon a history of sentimentalism that connects suffering to moral redemption and places women at the center of a new world order, Walker draws the new, post-slavery world with an African American mother at its center. Only the African American woman who suffers and embraces sentimental ideals, interpreting a divine purpose from that suffering, is able to lead her family—and by extension her community—into peace and prosperity.

In chapter 6, I examine Octavia Butler's *Kindred* (1979), which departs from historical realism and adopts the genre of science fiction fantasy in order to shorten the distance between the past and the present. By doing so, *Kindred* directly links twentieth-century racial attitudes and cultural perspectives to their formation in slavery while also revealing the ways in which members of American society—both black and white—have developed a cultural amnesia that allows them to forget the origins of their beliefs as well as the humanity of their ancestors. Butler makes these choices to reawaken sympathy for the enslaved and to remind modern individuals of their shared humanity. As the protagonist, Dana, jumps back and forth between 1970s California and antebellum Maryland she learns to sympathize with her ancestors by her own direct experiences of suffering. Dana's shift in subjectivity—from observer of slavery to subject of slavery—confronts modern readers about their shared slave history and its ongoing legacy.

Finally, in chapter 7, I discuss Toni Morrison's critique of sentimental sympathy in *Beloved* (1987). Morrison is able to draw Sethe, a woman who killed her own daughter, as sympathetic precisely because this postmodern narrative reveals her obsessive focus on loving and protecting her children in alignment with sentimentalism's prioritization of the mother-child relationship. Sethe's acts are described as an extreme expression of sentimental motherhood, as she draws the boundaries of family through biology, affection, and action. Morrison also turns this critique of sympathy toward the African American community, pointing to problems of sympathy that inhibit them from overcoming or healing from their traumatic past. Although the novel does not advocate forgetting the past—as its emphasis on "rememory" and the return of Beloved attest—the novel emphasizes that the ongoing suffering of those who have experienced trauma must be acknowledged and addressed for healing to occur. Even more important than why Sethe killed her daughter is the effect that killing has on her community and the community members' capacity to extend sympathy to her despite their inability to understand her choice. Morrison's novel questions whether or not a community can extend sympathy to those who have suffered *differently from them* and facilitate healing. The fractured community and the promise of its reconciliation offer a recognition of the limits of a sympathy that requires its recipients to experience continuous and homogenous forms of suffering.

2 / Grace Lumpkin's *To Make My Bread*: Standing Together, Side by Side

> *For so long each had been alone with his family striving after enough food to keep from starving.... Now they were going to stand together, side by side...*
>
> —GRACE LUMPKIN, TO MAKE MY BREAD (333)

Published in 1932, inspired by the events of the 1929 textile mill strikes in Gastonia, North Carolina,[1] Grace Lumpkin's *To Make My Bread* was praised by reviewers as both a "beautiful and sincere novel" and "very good, very effective propaganda" (Vorse, Review, 104; Cantwell, Review, 372). In his critique of the novel, Roy Flanagan observes that "Miss Lumpkin writes well and honestly, and her book provides horrible but salutary instruction from beginning to end" (Review, 560). Another reviewer in the *New York Times* defends Lumpkin against common criticisms leveled against proletarian writers for being overly didactic by arguing that "[i]t is the sort of propaganda novel to which no sneer can be legitimately attached—which is to say that its meaning rises out of people in dramatic conflict with other people and with the conditions of their life.... Here, she says, is this family; this is what happened to them when they were torn from their roots and set down in alien surroundings" ("A Novel of the Southern Mills," BR7). Robert Cantwell, the novelist who had called *To Make My Bread* "very effective propaganda," concludes his review in the *Nation* by stating, "I cannot imagine how anyone could read it and not be moved by it" (372). Thus, the novel was successful not just in its portrayal of working-class experience but also in its ability to affect readers on an emotional level.

Lumpkin was a descendent of the southern aristocracy and a member of the middle class, although she experienced periods of poverty during her lifetime. She closely observed and interacted with sharecroppers, mill workers, Appalachian mountain folk, and participants in the Gastonia strikes, but she was a witness and not a member of the groups whose stories she tells.[2] Although Lumpkin may have included a representation of herself—and those who generally occupy her subject position—as Miss Gordon, the misguided, middle-class demonstration agent who feels sorry for the poor, she chose not to write *To Make My Bread* from a middle-class perspective. Rather than objectify the working class and extend sympathy outwardly toward them (following the standard operation of nineteenth-century sentimental texts), Lumpkin narratively appropriates and inhabits the position of Other in order to overcome the limits of earlier forms of sentimentalism and address the gendered challenges of writing proletarian fiction. *To Make My Bread* serves as an example of both colonial and postcolonial sympathy, in that Lumpkin inhabits the subjectivity of the working-class Other for whom she seeks to develop sympathy. She adopts this mode as a way to create space within proletarian literature for the female voice.

Traditionally, proletarian literature required that its subjects and voices be male; female writers had a difficult time addressing the concerns of working-class women or being taken seriously as proletarian writers. Critics such as Constance Coiner, Barbara Foley, Jacquelyn Dowd Hall, Charlotte Nekola, and Paula Rabinowitz have demonstrated that women writing revolutionary fiction in the 1930s were caught in the competing demands of Marxism, which dictated that all class struggle was the same for men and women, and the masculinized dictates of proletarian realists who demanded that authors write from real-life experiences drawn from the male-dominated industries of fields, mines, mills, and factories. Rabinowitz argues that female intellectuals in the Communist Party found few accepted outlets for expression within the emerging proletarian genre because of the association of a feminine literary tradition with the middle class and the assumption that appropriate topics for proletarian literature excluded women's issues: "[T]he aesthetics of 1930s literary radicalism stressed the importance of external social forces in shaping literary work. This shift of emphasis denied a feminine literary tradition to the 1930s woman writer and separated her from her bourgeois female literary precursors" (*Labor and Desire*, 178). Male writers and theorists dominated literary scholarship, serving "as artistic and intellectual gatekeepers," who, according to Hall, "often misrecognized the work of radical women writers who saw gender—intertwined with race and class—as a symbol of human powerlessness and a key determinant of people's lives. That misrecognition sometimes took the form of overt dismissal and condescension" ("Women Writers," 31).

Authors who wrote from women's experiences and described working-class women's domestic concerns—women's exhausting double shift of labor inside and outside the home, managing child care, cooking and cleaning, marital rape, birth control, the dangers of childbirth, domestic abuse—were often criticized for valuing women's issues over class issues. If the "proper" proletarian novel was about men who worked in factories, mines, and fields, and participated in strikes in those arenas, how could women write such fictions?

Foley has pointed out that a majority of women proletarian authors drifted into obscurity—only to be "rediscovered" in the late twentieth century through feminist recovery—because the left press "adopted a male gaze" and "presupposed that selfhood was manhood," resulting in a dominant male literary voice that "gave little encouragement to women writers... to articulate revolutionary politics in a distinctly female voice" ("Women and the Left," 153, 154). Rabinowitz has shown that many female proletarian writers developed a combination of the domestic and revolutionary novels in order to address both gender and class concerns. With the publication of *To Make My Bread*, Lumpkin was one of the few female revolutionary novelists who received recognition for achieving proletarian realism. By adopting a working-class subject position and by uniting all workers through feeling, Lumpkin draws intersecting affective bonds between domestic and industrial spaces, refuting the separation between them that domestic novels generally highlight. Thus, Lumpkin is able to portray a nuanced perspective of the working class—one that examines the effects of capitalism on both men and women—and avoid the criticism generally levied at women proletarian authors for dividing men and women from each other.

In writing a sentimental proletarian novel, Lumpkin maintains a connection to nineteenth-century women's writing and expresses revolutionary politics in, to use Foley's words, "a distinctly female voice." However, while Lumpkin finds feminine expression, the voice she uses is not her own. Largely because of the masculinized construction of the proletariat—both the worker and the intellectual—women writers often expressed difficulty finding their voice. Tillie Lerner Olsen, the author of numerous short stories and the unfinished novel *Yonnondio* (1930s), writes in the afterword to the second edition of Rebecca Harding Davis's nineteenth-century novel *Life in the Iron Mills; or, The Korl Woman* (1861) that it was the first piece of fiction written "in absolute identification" with the working class ("Biographical Interpretation," 69). Rabinowitz expands Olsen's reading, arguing that Davis's novel illustrates that the "body of the working-class woman cannot produce a conventional narrative, and the female intellectual finds (a voice for) herself in the expressions of the male worker. These positions suggest that the narratives constructed by female literary radicals retained many cultural assumptions inherited from mid-nineteenth-century ideology" (*Labor and Desire*, 177). Lumpkin, indeed, is constrained by criticisms that middle-class women can have nothing helpful to say on their own. As Hall points out, her later short stories and novels focus on middle-class women "who could not reconcile their romantic desires, family loyalties, and feminist ambitions or, more negatively, transcend the catty, self-involved shrillness to which their race and class supposedly condemned them" ("Women Writers," 31–32). Thus, Lumpkin appears to have embraced criticism that only members of the working class—and "certainly not women like Lumpkin herself—were allowed to be the 'heroes of their own lives'" (32).

And yet, members of the working class were not "their own heroes," because Lumpkin speaks for them, as them, in her text. Lumpkin's sentimental proletarianism achieves a complex sympathetic identification that creates room for middle-class female subjectivity by creatively inhabiting that which is deemed to have a voice by the proletarian realist movement: the masculine worker and the working-class Other. Lumpkin's sentimentalism allows her to move from creating sympathy for the Other to creating space for the middle-class female voice.

The *New York Times* reviewer notes that *To Make My Bread* represents "one more milestone on the road to the return of 'social consciousness' in American fiction" ("A Novel of the Southern Mills," BR7). While Lumpkin's ideologies reflect the 1930s tenets of social revolution promoted by the CPUSA and other leftist organizations of the period, her work participates in a much longer, larger tradition of women's social activist writing. The social consciousness that is built into the characters and community of *To Make My Bread* utilizes rhetorical structures, ideological tropes, and extensions of sympathy found in nineteenth-century sentimental novels. Adopting a narrative method that educates through sympathy, Lumpkin creates a bildungsroman for her characters so that they gradually come to embrace leftist, radical ideologies as a result of their experiences with poverty and their commitments to family and community. Embracing middle-class values that idealize a separation of public and private spaces while also upholding sentimentalized gender roles usually obstructs identification with the working class. However, *To Make My Bread* encourages presumed middle-class readers to sympathize with working-class children, mothers, and families, educating the reader in both communal fellowship and revolutionary ideology through unflinching but compassionate portrayals of their struggles to survive.

To Make My Bread both upholds and deconstructs sentimental ideals, critiquing working-class men's and women's inability to attain human ideals because of their fight for survival. In proletarian sentimentalism, men and women fail to be "good men" and "good women" because they cannot inhabit their "proper," sentimentalized gender roles of good providers, protectors, mothers, and caretakers. The novels instead promote collective action: readers support the proletarians' rebellious acts against larger social forces. The sympathy developed for the characters as they struggle with class issues also crosses gender and race boundaries, showing the ways that the capitalist system denies these characters the ability to fulfill particular roles and, therefore, be defined as men and women in traditional ways. Thus, when contemporary reviewers observed that *To Make My Bread* both "provides horrible but salutary instruction" and that no reader could fail to "be moved by it," they were emphasizing the two key rhetorical aims of sentimental writing embedded in Lumpkin's text—to move and to instruct.

Lumpkin's adaptation of sentimentalism for proletarian literature is an extension of the gendered social consciousness found in leftist women's writings. As Rabinowitz has shown, radical women writers adapted realist proletarian forms that had become entrenched in a masculinized ideology. Women's proletarian writing linked the (feminized) domestic novel with the (masculinized) realist proletarian novel. Women writers who focused on female protagonists and on spaces outside of camps, mines, mills, and fields endeavored to make room for working-class women's experiences.

Proletarian women writers wrote about the effects of low wages on families' ability to live. They wrote about cycles of abuse: those perpetuated by work supervisors and within families. They also described the experiences of women who worked in and outside of the home as well as women's sexual vulnerability and exploitation. In so doing, these writers showed that agriculture and manufacturing—the masculinized public sphere—were not and should not be the only sites for Marxist social reform. Leftist women writers revealed that what happened outside the home affected what happened within it. By breaking down perceived barriers between the public and private spheres, women proletarian writers created various domestic microcosms in which the racial, economic, and gender troubles of the outside world were translated into the domestic struggles of the home and family. Lumpkin's combination of the domestic novel and proletarian realist fiction, however, capitalizes on more than the contours and structure of the domestic novel. By focusing on family life, the mother's plight, and the emotional education that brings her characters to revolutionary consciousness, Lumpkin not only combines domestic and proletarian realist forms but also incorporates the sentimental rhetoric of nineteenth-century novels.

While Rabinowitz has convincingly shown that proletarian women's writing can be categorized as "a genre within a genre," not all women's writing here can be classified as sentimental in mode of rhetoric or operation (*Labor and Desire*, 64). One of the stated dangers women proletariat writers faced in combining the domestic novel with realist fiction was swinging the pendulum too far and presenting what Marxist readers and literary critics considered an over-feminized portrait. To write about female spaces or gendered concerns risked disqualifying their work from the (assumed ungendered) ranks of proletarian realism for not focusing critical attention on (masculinized) industrial or agricultural workspaces and the (male) worker's struggle. Leftist women wrote about the home to expand the realm of the working class and included the home and the domestic as important components of revolutionary ideology, a place where reform was also needed. However, domestic fiction is based upon—and is in fact credited with creating—an ideology that separates a public, masculinized workspace from a private, feminized home space. Writers who participated in revising a domestic fiction for proletarian aims struggled with the separation of these spaces, as the elision of the home was a necessary foundation for a mythology of working-class solidarity. If workers are to be united by their class status—as Marxism proposes—they must ignore gender and race nuances within the group, which meant that the Marxist "Worker" was assumed to be white and male. However, the "separate spheres" ideology and the ideology of working-class solidarity ignored the reality of working-class experience. The "separate spheres" ideology is a white middle-class construction that helps differentiate the middle class, as only it had the economic resources to support a family with just one (father/husband) provider. Leftist women writers also wanted to show that working-class women had different—and potentially opposing—needs from working-class men, particularly in relation to sexuality and the simultaneous burdens of caring for a family while also working outside the home. Women proletarian writers were also far more likely to address racial conflict, touching not only on the complex ways race affected social interactions within the working class but also on the ways race became an instrument for division by capitalist supporters and, accordingly, how working-class racism engendered further oppression within the ranks of this "unified" group.

Extending the Sentimental Community to Promote Radical Reform

To overcome the ideology that separates women from men and creates two distinct social and work spheres, Lumpkin turned to sentimentalism. Incorporating a literary form that promotes a middle-class ideology based upon particular gender, racial, and social roles—the domestic novel's "separate spheres" ideology—for working-class women presents challenges for women writers who seek recognition within the (white, male, public) proletarian tradition. Texts that focus on female protagonists as well as on the home and family not only risk criticism for being overly feminized; they also reveal the potential ways in which working-class women do not meet society's definition of "proper" women, mothers, and wives. By showing women at work in the home and then extending that work into the "male" space of industry and by equating in various ways the work of the factory and home, Lumpkin doesn't just lend sentimental power to the workers' plight; she makes the industrial workspace itself a sentimental zone. The workers of the factory are cogs in a machine and organs in a body: men and women work together in both domestic spaces and industrial spaces, and both places oppress them.

Following in the tradition of sentimental texts, *To Make My Bread* prioritizes affectional bonds throughout the novel. The primary tragedy of the text is the separation of families and loss of community. Lumpkin's text uses familiar sentimental tropes of vulnerable women (who experience the loss of male protector/providership), domesticity, death, and motherhood to attribute the loss of family and community directly to working-class hardships caused by the capitalist system. Linking home and workplace, Lumpkin reveals the ways in which members of the working-class community are bonded by their experiences but threatened with separation by social institutions—such as the mill and the church—which oppress and shame working-class men and women. Thus, the text extends the sentimental community from the hearth into the factory and the strike zone, so that both the men and the women of *To Make My Bread* (and their sympathetic readers) come to a radical awareness.

Modeled on the real-life events of the Gastonia textile mill strikes, *To Make My Bread* follows the trials of the McClure family in the late

1920s. The first twenty-one chapters focus on their lives within an Appalachian community, while the subsequent thirty-eight chapters describe their experiences working for a textile mill. Emma McClure struggles to raise a daughter and three sons with the help of her ageing father, Granpap Kirkland, because her husband has died. The McClures struggle through several difficult Appalachian winters and come close to starvation. They are eventually persuaded to sell the house and land but then cannot afford to pay rent. Subsequently, Emma moves her family to a town where she can find work in a textile mill. At first the family is grateful to have a home and steady work, but the debilitating effects of working in the mills become clear: Emma and her family are frequently ill and grow feeble but cannot afford to stop working long hours. When of age, Bonnie McClure and her brother John both go to work in the mill, and John befriends a worker who introduces him to left-leaning ideas. Bonnie and John become vocal critics of mill practices, call for reforms, and help organize a strike. Bonnie—modeled after real-life mill worker, strike leader, and balladeer Ella May Wiggins—writes popular protest songs and coordinates women's and African Americans' participation. The mills evict people from their homes and raid strike headquarters; conflicts increase between strikers and deputies hired by the mills. At the novel's close, Bonnie is murdered during the strike. Bonnie's funeral draws crowds of mill workers, and John speaks at her grave about the injustice of her death and the tyranny of the mill owners. As a final injustice, mill sympathizers take Bonnie's children, forcing them into state care.

Although Lumpkin wrote movingly and insightfully about the experiences of working-class Appalachian farmers and mill workers, she herself was not working-class, a laborer, or from the Appalachian Mountains. Lumpkin was born in Milledgeville, Georgia, a town approximately ninety-eight miles southeast of Atlanta, in 1891, to a well-respected upper-class family that had lost much of its wealth during the Civil War. Her sister, Katharine, chronicled the family's plantation history as well as their formative years in her memoir *The Making of a Southerner* (1947). No longer able to sustain the family as a gentleman farmer, Lumpkin's father found employment with the railroad, which eventually brought them to Columbia, South Carolina, where neighbors considered them to be from a "good family" and they joined the socially elite Trinity Church (Sowinska, Introduction, ix). Around 1910, Lumpkin's father purchased a farm in the Sand Hills region, hoping to recapture the family's lost plantation heritage. On this farm, Grace and her sister interacted with black and white sharecroppers and attended school with white children from "the poorest classes," even though, as Katharine describes, "[t]here was everything, it seemed, to keep us separate and hardly anything to bridge the gap save our common childhood.... My clothing was different.... My lunches were different.... Even our language tended to separate us" (Lumpkin, *Making*, 158–59).

After Lumpkin's father died, the family experienced further financial difficulties and struggled to make a living from the farm, eventually moving back to the Columbia area. After Lumpkin completed a teacher's training program at Brenau College in Gainesville, Georgia, she "worked at a variety of jobs that provided her with background material for her novels and helped shape her early political consciousness" (Sowinska, Introduction, x). She taught school in Tennessee and South Carolina, organized a night school for farmers and their wives, and worked for the government as a home demonstration agent. She spent summers living in the North Carolina mountains and, at times, stayed with people who worked in the cotton mills. Lumpkin spent a year in France working as a recreation director for the French Girls in Industry organization and as a YWCA director before returning to South Carolina to spend two years working as an industrial secretary for the YWCA.

In 1924, Lumpkin moved to New York to become a writer, working for the *World Tomorrow* magazine and studying writing at Columbia University. She published an article in 1926 on the convergence of the New Negro literary movement and proletarian literature, and her first short stories were published in the *New Masses* the following year. Although she never officially joined the Communist Party, in 1928 she joined the staff of the *New Masses* and was sent south the next year to organize among black sharecroppers and observe the 1929 Gastonia strikes. Her time in Gastonia, combined with her previous experiences in South Carolina and the North Carolina mountains, provided her with the material to write *To Make My Bread*. Lumpkin returned to New York to write, publishing *To Make My Bread* in 1932, and producing articles and an additional proletarian novel, *A Sign for Cain* (1935). However, Lumpkin eventually moved away from the Communist Party, and her third novel, *The Wedding* (1939), avoided communist politics and focused instead on domestic drama. Eventually, Lumpkin became actively anticommunist, joining the Moral Re-Armament Movement, informing on her former communist friends to the Federal Bureau of Investigation, and devoting her writing to exposing the evils of communism. She published *Full Circle* in 1962, about her changing ideas about communism. Lumpkin continued writing, lecturing, and attending church functions until her death in 1980.

Vulnerable Working-Class Women

Although *To Make My Bread* is a fictional account of the real-life events of the 1929 Gastonia textile mill strikes, Lumpkin chose not to focus the narrative entirely on workers in the mills, set the story only in the labor camps, or narrate from the perspective of a male mill worker. Instead, she began the narrative prior to the trouble with the mills, telling the story of an Appalachian community representing where many of the mill workers originated. Although the third-person narration follows various members of the McClure family and the Swain's Crossing community, the novel centers upon the experiences of Emma McClure and her children, Bonnie and John. While all three characters are significant to the text and its revolutionary message, this character triptych has the effect of magnifying Bonnie's importance because she serves as a balance and foil to both Emma, her mother, and John, her brother. To Emma, she is witness to the suffering and hardships of motherhood and inheritor of her condition. To John, she is a matched set, the female embodiment of the workingman's efforts to provide for the family and organize against the mill owners, who represent capitalism's abuses. Through it all, Bonnie is a sentimental exemplar—at once the abandoned child, the vulnerable woman, the caring mother, the domestic economist, and the heroine who experiences emotional attachment and moral growth. She is the child, mother, and metaphoric slave in one body upon which a reader may confer sympathy for her plight and her actions.

To Make My Bread is not just the story of the Gaston County strikes, nor is it the story of an Appalachian family who cannot survive in the mountains, turning hopefully to textile mills but finding instead disillusionment and suffering. *To Make My Bread* is essentially a story of mothers and children. The novel is focused primarily on Emma and Bonnie, with significant attention to Emma's sister-in-law Ora as well as to an extension of the primary family. The novel narrates the experiences of two generations of women. In so doing, Lumpkin captures two crucial elements of the sentimental mode: (1) vulnerable women who must survive the hardships of their gendered, social circumstance and (2) the development and prioritization of a kinship network, which redefines the family according to affection. Not only do Emma's, Ora's, and Bonnie's anguished attempts to protect and provide for their children develop reader sympathy for mothers who care so much and work so hard only to accomplish so little, but they undergird Lumpkin's argument about the injustices of a social system that would make supporting children impossible while judging these women for their failures. Women who are unable to provide for their children are considered to be bad mothers who have made poor emotional, moral, and economic choices. Lumpkin shifts the sentimental critical lens to the economic system to reveal that working-class women are vulnerable in ways similar to middle-class women and to show that they, too, embrace the ideals of loving and caring for their children. However, *To Make My Bread* illustrates the ways that working-class women are prevented from achieving those ideals by the very social system that promotes them.

In Bonnie, Lumpkin draws a child who witnesses her mother's suffering but, when she grows up, believes that she can somehow do better for her own children and find a way out of the cycle. This is the narrative of capitalism and of the middle class. Bonnie, however, is caught by a system of oppression that forces her to repeat the same suffering her mother had experienced.

Not So Sweet Home: Danger in the Domestic Sphere

To Make My Bread's opening blizzard scene at the McClure's isolated Appalachian cabin immediately undercuts the ideology of the domestic haven that is frequently linked to sentimentalism and middle-class beliefs about familial relationships. Emma is later reminded of the home's vulnerability when Minnie, the wife of her son Kirk, carries on an affair with a neighbor whenever Kirk is away. Emma had suspected Minnie's unfaithfulness during her son's long absences, but she is shocked when Sam McEachern begins to call. One day, Sam and Minnie get up and leave the cabin: "Those two were over in the other room under Kirk's roof. And she knew. She was Kirk's kin, and it was a McClure roof" (104). The sanctity of the home is not enough to prevent Sam from seducing Minnie, nor is Emma's presence enough to shame them from having sex in the family home. Emma, having kept the knowledge of Sam's visits from her son, determines to put an end to this behavior, so she picks up Granpap's gun and waits for them to return to the main part of the cabin. Emma tells Minnie, "I don't aim to hurt ye," because her goal is protection, not harm; she wants to protect her son's reputation, the relationship, and the McClure home (104). In response, Sam pulls out a revolver, insisting, "I ain't done nothing," but he eventually walks off, declaring that "[a] man can't fight a woman" (105). However, Sam has violated the home—both literally and morally—and he presents a serious threat to Emma because he is willing to harm her for personal benefit; he later follows through on his threat of violence when he ambushes and murders Kirk.

In *To Make My Bread*, men outside of the family are not the only threats to women or to the safety of the home. Often, men's despair and frustration over their failure to provide ends in emotional or literal abandonment of the family. The novel links the relationship between men's anger outside the home with violence within it, while also showing that abandonment can result from an inability to cope with feelings. John, Bonnie's brother, is ashamed by the visible physical toll the millwork takes on the women: "He looked into her eyes and saw on her face that had been so full of grace and fineness, a sickliness, a beginning of wearing out—the lines that in another ten years would make her like an old woman.... He touched Emma's hand and turned away, strained and impotent. There was an impulse in him to pick up the gun, kill them all, and then himself. The impulse passed, but he was trembling when Bonnie came and stood before him at the door leading on to the porch" (297). John considers violence against the very family he wishes to protect, projecting his frustrations and desperation onto the people he loves. After Bonnie's husband loses his hand and is unable to find work, he becomes abusive toward the children before eventually leaving entirely. Bonnie "was almost glad something had made him leave her. It was not his fault that he had become worthless.... [S]he gradually came to hope that he would find a life away from her" (322). The men's inability to provide becomes a threat to their masculinity, which they can only reassert through violence or recover by escaping the women and children who serve as constant reminders of their failures.

The novel acknowledges that while there are good men, women are always at risk of danger because men are the ones who decide their treatment. Ora tells Emma: "A man is a danger to every good woman and she's got to know it.... A danger to every woman good or bad. I tell my Sally to look on men that they're deadly as rattlesnakes" (94). Although Ora refers to men's sexual desire and the risks of extramarital sex, her use of the words "danger" and "deadly" implies a risk of violence.[3] When Emma defends the "good men" she knows, who Ora points out are husbands, Emma observes that she might have been willing "if Jim had a'wanted to take advantage" before they were married but that once they were "he was kind *for a man*." She continues: I would a'done anything he said. If he'd a'told me to put my hand in the fire and hold it there I think I would a'done it. But he never did" (94; emphasis mine). Jim's kindness is notable, but it is marked by his lack of violence rather than emotional connection. Significantly, too, Emma acknowledges that Jim had the power to command her to do acts of violence to herself; although Emma attributes this power to love, it also signifies the type of mastery a man can maintain over a wife in a marriage and home, making decisions for her benefit or harm depending on his will.

Men, however, are not the only ones who become a threat to the home as a result of frustration and despair. *To Make My Bread* also reveals the depths of despair working-class women feel as failed mothers and how the extreme deprivations of poverty can lead to the loss of emotional connection with their children, making them numb to anything but survival. Although the women love their children, in the face of extreme hardship, they can—like men—direct their anger toward those who are the victims rather than those who cause the suffering. For some mothers, the stress of caring for their homes and children, while providing income and food, places them in danger of losing the emotional connection that sentimental ideals assume all mothers must feel for their children. Emma's helplessness leads to anger, and like the men's, it is misdirected at those she fails to care for. However, because she is a woman and a mother, whose role more heavily emphasizes caretaking and de-emphasizes power over others, *To Make My Bread* reveals how this anger paralyzes working-class women and results in emotional disconnection. When her oldest sons begin feuding with each other, Emma is frustrated by their poor decisions and saddened by their selfishness. She still loves them, but she is hurt by Basil's indifference and Kirk's sexuality. It is unusual for a text that relies so much on sympathy through motherhood to reveal that a mother "almost hated" her children or that she felt paralyzed by them. Emma, however, does not act on her impulses and abuse her children; instead, she holds her anger inside, feeling torn between her love and her frustration, suffering over her inability to care for her family. Her anger is directed inward instead of outward.

By showing the flaws and failures of these mothers, Lumpkin criticizes a system that holds women accountable for maintaining economic and emotional stability while placing that stability out of their reach. At one point, Emma and Ora walk through an upper-class section of town and see the mansions in which the mill owners live. A liveried servant pushes a carriage into the garden, and the two women wonder if the silver goblet and spoon—for which a collection had been taken among the workers—is in the carriage with the baby. The workers were obliged to sacrifice necessities to provide a gift to the already wealthy:

> "I gave ten cents, and had to tell Bonnie to wait for a tablet till the next week."
> "Frank gave a quarter for both of us." (222)

Reflecting on the encounter, Ora tells Emma: "Hit's funny . . . how some have such fine, pretty things and others not . . . right after we left hit, I started feeling s' mad. Mad at everything and at nothing, because my babies couldn't have a thing" (227). Anger is not a traditionally acceptable female emotion; Lumpkin develops maternal anger as a natural result of the frustrations of the women's poverty.

Over the course of the novel, Lumpkin develops a sentimental bildungsroman so that these failures eventually lead to an anger that is properly projected by the characters—and by the reader—toward the mills and the capitalist system that empowers them. Emma and Ora are drawn as women who are the natural products of a system that destroys maternal and familial connection, but Bonnie is the sentimental hero who will carry the proletarian message from maternal suffering to revolutionary action, teaching others to embrace her views.[4] Bonnie witnesses Emma's suffering and suffers as a mother herself. However, instead of experiencing emotional disconnection from her children, the death of her baby fully awakens Bonnie to the injustices of her life. Speaking at a union rally, Bonnie directly connects her motherhood to her activism: "I am the mother of five children. One of them died because I had t' work in the mill and leave the baby only with my oldest child who was five and didn't know how to tend it very well. And with four left I have found it hard t' raise them on the pay I get. I couldn't do for my children any more than you women on the money we get. That's why I have come out for the union, and why we've all got t' stand for it" (345). Bonnie explains that her child died not from her failing as a mother but from the mill's failure to provide; every mother in the audience is in the same impossible position and can sympathize with her loss and her fears. However, sympathy must be paired with action in order to prevent future deaths, so Bonnie argues that all mothers must join the union to force the mill to pay mothers enough to raise their children in safety.

One of the enticements the mill company provides to its workers is "free housing," but the cost of this housing is, in effect, the mill's ownership of the people who live there. The company promises improved housing over the mountain cabins: "[Y]ou get a house with windows and cook on a real stove,—no more bending over a chimney." But, Granpap counters, "[T]he house ain't your own. . . . Nor the land," land that under a capitalist system symbolizes freedom and independence (39). Workers' homes are often overcrowded because in lieu of rent (or in exchange for low rent), the mills require a minimum number of full-time workers to live in each house, coercing families to live together so that enough working adults meet the minimum requirement to obtain a house. Family arrangements frequently shift as death or other changes in family structure threaten their ability to stay in a house.[5]

Mill owners also use the threat of eviction, but once workers begin to organize and strike in favor of labor unions, they make this threat a reality. As tensions escalate, supervisors begin to eject strikers and their families: "[T]hey felt the power . . . men went to the houses of those who had not gone back into the mill, emptied them of furniture, and locked the doors of their own homes against them" (353). The safety of the home is shown to be an illusion. After being forced to sell the homes and the land they had previously owned to pay for food, workers realize that company housing is not so much a form of labor compensation as it is a tool of capitalist control.

The cycle of labor in the factory and work in the home takes a toll. In sentimental literature, housework is presented, as Elizabeth Maddock Dillon argues, as a "moral and aesthetic endeavor," one that is guided by "free will, love, and desire rather than by material need or compulsion" ("Sentimental Aesthetics," 510, 509). However, *To Make My Bread* emphasizes that housework not only is based in material need but—when combined in a cycle of unrelenting work outside of the home—is downright exhausting. Under these circumstances, the home cannot serve as a private space of moral uplift, nor can it buffer workers against outside demands. In Swain's Crossing, families engaged frequently in public/private interactions, gathering at the store to gossip, helping families build sheds and cabins, and visiting each others' homes for dances, quilting circles, and tending the ill. Although material needs are present in these events, the established emotional connection becomes the focus.

This sense of family linkage and communal relationship, however, is fractured by the move to town. Although working families live in the same neighborhood and share a common Appalachian background, they lose the ability to connect with each other. Prevented as they are from bonding in the weave and the spool rooms, they are too tired and burdened with too much work at home to establish communal connections. Emma and Ora carefully prepare their house for visitors by hanging a picture in the front room "where everyone could look at it while they sat" and putting a family Bible on display (201). However, few visitors ever come. *To Make My Bread* suggests that certain kinds of work can have both a material purpose and an affective result. The sentimental tragedy of the capitalist system, however, is that it fractures these bonds, prevents workers from developing kinship systems that enable community, and pushes men and women beyond their physical and emotional limits.

Tragic Mothers: The Mill Mother's Lament

Although twentieth-century cultural norms continued to embrace a universal, feminine standard of a contained domestic sphere, it reflected largely a middle-class social ideal. In effect, it excluded working-class women. Not only did working-class households usually require the incomes provided by both husbands and wives in order to survive, but this cultural view maintained a racial divide: the United States' history of slavery and discrimination meant that women of color were not included in the domestic sphere ideology. After Emancipation, throughout Reconstruction, the Jim Crow era, and decades of economic practices that advantaged whites economically, nonwhite families could rarely achieve the middle-class prosperity that allowed for single provider families.[6] Because of domestic cultural ideals based on the sentimental Cult of True Womanhood, both working-class and nonwhite women were viewed as less feminine, women who did not achieve their full potential as women, because of moral rather than economic failures.

In writing about working-class women and economic or racial troubles, proletarian women writers such as Lumpkin risked emphasizing this divide and therefore losing the sympathy of their readers. Showing how their lives were laborious, and, at times, tragic, risked adding to unkind stereotypes of the working class. However, Lumpkin often drew upon sentimentalized views of motherhood in order to build common feeling with readers and create opportunities to show how the class system—and not an individual's moral failures—made it impossible for working-class women to meet these standards. These mothers were sentimental precisely because they felt the same as their middle-class counterparts: they loved their children.

To Make My Bread relies on the belief that women who have children would prefer to devote their energies to caring for them—a sentimental ideal—while also challenging the view that women who work outside the home are somehow selfish, choosing a career over caring for their children. It emphasizes repeatedly that working-class women are, in fact, providing for their children by working outside the home. As Emma says, "I wanted so much, Ora, t' give my young ones a chance in life and see them have things that children should have. But I have made only misery and unhappiness for myself and them" (307).

Emma's labor on the farm is treated as part of the same continuum as her labor in the home; the text refuses to divide farmwork from domestic labor. Her work supplements the (small amounts of) meat and cash supplied by her father and older sons. She moves seamlessly between her labor outside and inside the home: "Emma walked about the clearing and the cabin, helping Bonnie and John [pick potatoes], and making supper" (92). Thus, her external labor complements the traditional women's role of cooking, cleaning, and caregiving as part of a holistic endeavor to survive. The loss of the farm prompts her decision to move the family to town, where she can work in the textile mills and the children can attend "a fine city school" (136). Emma hopes not only that the promised high wages and housing will result in a stable supply of food but that her children will have the opportunity to receive an education and be able to achieve more in their own lives.

Emma hopes that she can achieve a balance between working outside the home and caring for her children within it, but she quickly discovers that to be impossible: "It was like a circle.... If she didn't rest, she couldn't work, and if she couldn't work, they couldn't eat, and if she couldn't eat, she couldn't work" (245). She works the night shift, alternating with Ora's days so that someone will always be home. But Emma finds that she does not have the strength to work twelve hours in the spooling room and still care for her children: "At first she had tried to stay awake in the mornings to talk with Bonnie and John. This meant the loss of two good hours of sleep. Now, on coming home she went to the bed, still warm from Bonnie's sleeping there.... During the day she must keep herself awake to look after Ora's youngest. When Bonnie got home about two she could sleep again. Then at five she must have supper, get her lunch, and start out for the long night" (213). Once she becomes an adult, Bonnie too finds it impossible to balance working outside the home with caring for her children. She rises each morning at four to cook breakfast, leaving it on the stove for her children to eat when they wake. Leaving them "regretfully," she worries throughout her workday, afraid that "some accident had happened to one of them" (317).

These working-class women must work to support their families because men alone cannot earn enough. According to Marxist ideology, this is a failure of the capitalist system—a man should be able to sustain a family with his income. According to sentimental gender ideals, this deficiency instead means that a woman's provider has failed her and her family, which is a failure of his morality (and his masculinity). Lumpkin's text, however, critiques the system that causes masculine providership to fail, altering what it means to be a "mother" in the working class. Lumpkin develops a sentimental proletarian argument by emphasizing the suffering of these mothers and building upon the sympathy this suffering creates. While living in the Appalachian mountains, not only does Emma suffer to a degree that only mothers with the responsibility of managing household resources can understand, but the evidence prompting this concern—witnessed through daily domestic activities such as cooking meals—is unseen, unknowable by the male provider of the family: "Granpap could not understand how they needed money for food. A man did not watch the meal get lower in the bag and wonder where money for the next lot would come. He didn't see the slab of fatback get smaller until there was just a greasy end left for boiling with cabbage. And then no more" (23).

Bonnie, too, works to stretch her meager resources, suffering over her inability to economize enough to provide basic necessities for her children: "She made many figures at night on scraps of paper trying to work out a way to make the money go further than it seemed able to do. There were so many items:—rent, kerosene, life insurance.... [L]ike all the rest, she had very little left for food and clothing. And the children, dressed almost in rags, looked pale in spite of all she tried to do" (323–24). According to sentimental standards, Emma and Bonnie fail as mothers: their children are poorly fed and poorly dressed. They lack formal education because—despite the promises of the recruiters and the availability of "free" schooling—books are expensive, and most children must leave school to work in the mills.

Although she had witnessed Emma's struggles to support her family, Bonnie at first believes in the capitalist myth of hard work as the way out of destitution. She begins in the middle-class position of blaming the worker for being unable to work hard enough or manage well enough to escape the deprivations of poverty: "'Our young ones will have things better,' Bonnie often thought to herself, and she did not mean to sit down and expect the good things to come. She must work for them.... Emma had wanted good things, but somehow had not managed right—and neither had Granpap who worked so hard on the farm and got in the end only feebleness and discouragement. She and Jim, young and happy, could do anything" (275). Bonnie doesn't recognize the forces beyond the individual or see the cycle of poverty, replicating a middle-class viewpoint that places blame on personal actions and achievements rather than acknowledging a system that inhibits individual attainment.

The refusal of her manager to let her take unpaid nursing breaks triggers Bonnie's first awareness not only that the capitalist system limits individual achievement but that other women are subject to the same pressures. Rejecting her appeal, the supervisor tells her: "If I let you... I'd have to let every other woman who's got a young baby do the same. And there are plenty of babies in this village" (283). Bonnie replies, "And plenty of them dies."

Despite Bonnie's fears, it is not an accident but illness that kills one of her children. Upon receiving word that her child is ill, she hurries home: "The child was still.... She shook him almost angrily, then held him close.... Then she had to accept what she had really known when she took him up. There was no life in him. She laid him down on the bed and turned to the other young ones" (320). Bonnie was physically parted from the child by her work at the mill before the permanent separation that comes through the child's death. His death is a result of larger, institutional factors such as poor diet, lack of medicine, and a lack of proper supervision. She holds him as a tender gesture of love and shakes him "almost angrily" hoping to wake him up, but the gesture also reveals her frustration that she cannot save him—it is "almost" angry because she would not harm her child, but it is "angry" because she believes the death was preventable. She has to "accept what she had really known when she took him up," yielding to the knowledge that her son is dead but also that working under her conditions results all too often in child deaths.

Bonnie turns to her other children because she has others to care for; however, Lumpkin indicates that this death is the turning point that will become the foundation for Bonnie's revolutionary consciousness. Bonnie's turn to her children is a symbolic recognition that there are other children who can be saved. As Gillian Brown points out, the loss of life is important in sentimental texts because "[d]eath or some form of escape enables homecomings and family reunions. As much as divine love and maternal care, death generates the domestic economy that maintains family unity" (*Domestic Individualism*, 33). The death of Bonnie's child spurs her alignment with proletarian beliefs and her activism on behalf of mothers and children. In her later protest songs and speeches, Bonnie cites the death of her child and the potential losses for all mothers who work. By situating this moment of loss as a site of realization, Lumpkin combines ideals of family unity with Marxist philosophies of social equality.

Bonnie is frustrated at her inability to earn enough money to provide for her family, but she's aware that her experience is not unique. When she writes the pro-union ballad, "Mill Mother's Lament" (voicing the real-life song written by Ella May Wiggins), she expresses the shared frustrations of working-class mothers:

> We leave our homes in the morning.
> We kiss our children good-by.
> While we slave for the bosses
> Our children scream and cry.
>
> How it grieves the heart of a mother
> You every one must know.
> But we can't buy for our children;
> Our wages are too low.
>
> . . . .
> But for us nor them, dear workers,
> The bosses do not care. (345–46)

Bonnie's song speaks to the "heart of a mother" and women's shared grief. Furthermore, the crime of the mill bosses is that they "do not care" about either the women or their vulnerable children. The children's screaming and crying is both a representation of normal children's behavior—they cry when parted from their mothers—and a result of their starvation and neglect; it is also a representation of the abuse the women suffer as the "slave" inside the mills. But, the song continues, the bosses "fear" a union, so the workers should stand together and "have a union here" (346). Thus, Bonnie transforms children's and mothers' suffering into a moment of sympathetic connection, one that inspires action—that of joining a union. The implication is that this union of feeling will become a union of political views and a literal labor union: shared feeling thus becomes an education toward political action.

Crossing from Class to Race

The use of sentimental sympathy in *To Make My Bread* allows Lumpkin to extend radical awareness across race boundaries, incorporating a critique of racism that is frequently omitted from male-authored proletarian texts. Many proletarian novels written by white authors in the 1930s and 1940s avoided a critical treatment of race; they often relegated racism to the words and actions of the bourgeois and their allies or by ignoring race altogether. A few authors did offer a somewhat more complex view of American racial politics by placing a racist antihero at the center of the story. However, women writing proletarian fiction did not see race, gender, and class as discrete subject positions and often wrote about connections among the forms of oppression experienced by individuals who identified with various (and/or multiple) categories.

After first establishing that within the working-class community whites discriminate and hold negative views of African Americans—therefore dividing members of the working-class against themselves—Lumpkin capitalizes on the shared experience of suffering working-class motherhood to cross racial boundaries. She develops a cultural history of racial tension through Granpap's Confederate past, both through his extreme efforts to attend a Confederate memorial parade and in his wartime reminiscence about stealing a piece of cornbread from "a little nigger" while he was scouting (86). Granpap lacks remorse for stealing bread from a starving child because he was also starving, and he doesn't see the child as anything but a "nigger." The anecdote also implies the ways whites in Granpap's position often view themselves in competition for resources with African Americans—one group can survive only by taking from the other. Granpap later expresses exactly this view when looking for work in the mill town. When he can find no work cutting wood or tending gardens, Granpap complains: "If hit wasn't for niggers . . . I could get work; but they want niggers, because the black man charges less than the white" (201).

Although other members of the McClure family are not portrayed as overtly racist—rarely coming in contact with nonwhites in the Appalachian mountains—they learn racist ideologies from Granpap and from other workers in the more diverse mill town. Granpap passes on his views when the family first arrives. Tired from their journey, the family stops to rest on their way to the mill; Bonnie asks if she can drink water from an African American woman's bucket. Although Emma gives permission, Granpap curtly orders the children back saying, "They're niggers, Emma. . . . White and black don't mix" (144). Granpap explains the concept of separation, teaching Emma about racial difference. The effects of Granpap's "teaching" are quickly evident when John inquires what is wrong and Emma tells him that the children are "niggers." John then returns and reports back to Bonnie: "'They're niggers,' he said and looked contemptuously over his shoulder" (144). John shares what he has learned, passing along this newly acquired perspective and demonstrating contempt for this other family because he has heard the derogatory term "nigger" and witnessed Granpap's attitude toward those whom he has labeled.

As a way to overcome mill segregation—white workers and African American workers historically worked in separate mills and lived in different neighborhoods, so the few African Americans who worked in the "white" mill served in low-paying custodial positions—Lumpkin develops a bond of maternal sympathy between Bonnie and an African American woman who sweeps the floors.[7] Maternal suffering, thus, becomes a way not only to develop sympathy among working-class women but to cross racial boundaries. After Bonnie returns to the weave room, "all who worked there were sympathetic and kind. Mary, the colored woman who swept on Bonnie's side of the room, came up and said: 'I heard about your baby, and I'm real sorry'" (320). Prior to this moment, Bonnie and Mary had no personal interactions. Yet Mary offers to send her own daughter, Savannah, to stay with Bonnie's children, "until you get more peaceful in your mind." This moment causes Bonnie to reconsider her own racial biases: "Bonnie looked at Mary Allen, at her plump, good natured black face that was full of sympathy.... For a long time afterward Bonnie remembered with shame the thought that was behind the look she had given Mary. For she was thinking of what people said—that colored people were all shiftless and no account; and had believed what they said in face of the fact that Mary Allen did her work in the mill quietly and as if she was willing to do her best" (321). Mary's motivations are sympathetic; she understands Bonnie's fear and pain, reaching out to her as one mother to another. However, the result of her actions is to create more than an emotional bond; it is a sentimental moment insofar as Bonnie is taught by her feelings that Mary is a person just like herself, a mother who loves her children and fears their loss.

Maternal sympathy transforms to class solidarity when Bonnie and John begin organizing union strikes. The mill hopes to hire African American workers to "scab," and Bonnie willingly travels to Stumptown, the African American neighborhood, to talk about the union and argue for class solidarity. After the strike commences, a handbill criticizing the union for promoting interracial organizing appears, reading: "YOUR UNION DOES NOT BELIEVE IN WHITE SUPREMACY. THINK ABOUT THAT, WHITE PEOPLE" (350). Not all whites are comfortable with interracial organizing. When Zinie admits that she told John he shouldn't support the union, Ora and Bonnie counter her views: Ora focuses on the sentimental humanist argument—that African Americans are people—and Bonnie focuses on the sentimental proletarian argument—that African Americans are also workers. Ora admits, "I've come to see that if people let colored folks tend their babies and cook their food, they really don't think their color makes them dirty.... [T]hey've got souls the same as us.... [I]t's a shameful thing for ye not t' know they're human beings the same as us" (350–51).

Bonnie, as the female leader of the revolutionary position, is branded a "nigger lover." She receives death threats, but she refuses to back down. She continues going to Stumptown, "for she was strong in knowing that Mary Allen and the others there needed the message as much as her people did. She could not be so selfish as to keep it only for herself and hers" (354). Bonnie becomes a sentimentalized, Christlike missionary, sharing the "good news" of the union and the communist message. Thus, her murder, which is promised in retribution for interfering with the mill's efforts to recruit scab workers from African American neighborhoods, implies a martyr's sacrifice on behalf of the poor and oppressed. Although the text largely downplays religious symbolism, Bonnie's role as a Christ figure highlights the ways that the importance of religion in *To Make My Bread* is its community role and its ability to create kinship bonds.

Bonnie's brother John is left to carry on the revolutionary work after Bonnie's death. John undergoes a different form of racial education, so that he is an acceptable inheritor of the legacy. Because John had more exposure to Granpap's Confederate history and racial views, several of his racial encounters occur in tandem with Granpap. As a child, John experiences kindness from Jake, the African American cook at a restaurant Granpap frequents. Later, when Emma moves the family to a farm at the edge of town, John witnesses Granpap learning how to grow cotton from an African American man named Moses.

As an adult, John is courted by the mill bosses to work for their interests, which includes segregation because preventing white and African American workers from finding solidarity helps keep unions out of the mill. John is persuaded to join a "lodge" in the village whose motto is "Keep out the foreigner and the nigger. Neither belongs" (293). However, John finds it difficult to accept the ideology of the lodge and the privilege it represents. Because of his sympathies, John recognizes the hypocrisy of the organization—it is dedicated to upholding privilege, not to helping others.

Resisting Authority: Feeling Wrong to Feel Right

Religious institutions and theological debates were a central force in shaping culture and mores in the nineteenth century, and many sentimental texts founded their moral arguments in Protestant principles. By the twentieth century, religion remained an important cultural force in American society, but other political and social institutions—such as naturalism and modernism as well as science, medicine, and increasing urbanization—had begun to rival it for influence. As a proletarian text, *To Make My Bread* challenges the morally instructive force of religion, as well as the institutional forces that shape moral ideologies. Although it does not explicitly argue a Marxist position against the need for religion itself, it critiques figures who blindly endorse certain beliefs without paying attention to the social realities of those who are meant to be made virtuous by those imposed ideals.

Ministers and doctors in the novel are generally associated with blindness about the working-class characters. They can, at times, work against the bonds that hold the community together. While acknowledging the important function they serve in caring for the community—healing the sick and providing spiritual guidance—Lumpkin points out that both doctors and ministers belong to the middle class, with economic and social interests that separate them from the people they serve. Because doctors and ministers inhabit different class positions and benefit from a system that exploits the working class, the ideologies they impose on workers do not reflect the realities of working-class life. By highlighting the disconnect between these authority groups—those who are meant to offer sympathy but fail to do so—and the people they serve, Lumpkin reveals fundamental misunderstandings by the middle class. As working-class characters feel ashamed for their failures but then grow frustrated and angry at being held accountable by individuals who do not understand their life experiences, their shame transforms to a revolutionary consciousness—"feeling right." Thus, readers, who sympathize with the men and women who long to live up to sentimental ideals, sympathize not just with the workers' suffering but also with their transition from shame to resistance.

Lumpkin acknowledges that religion is an important facet to working-class and Appalachian community life, but she shows that ritual is a communal rite of passage as much as of religion. "Whether a person was religious like Basil, or defiant like Granpap, they all attended Baptizing," Lumpkin writes. "It was an occasion for neighbors and kin who had not seen each other for a year or more to meet" (55). Lumpkin also highlights the inherent economic aspect of religious rituals: although most of these families have starved all winter, the baptism requires special clothing purchased from Hal Swain's store "at a special price" (61).

Rather than serve as a support and spiritual guide for the Appalachian community, the minister Lumpkin draws judges and looks down on them: "To Preacher Warren all the people in the company were pinch-faced and uninteresting.... [H]e felt a load in his heart because as far as he could know he would be doing this very thing summer after summer. He longed with his whole soul to live in town, where his children might grow up in the proper manner, and he might have a congregation of live people" (59). The minister does not view the people around him as human beings, as souls who are in need of guidance or spiritual salvation—the sentimental view of a Christian pastor. Instead, Preacher Warren's perspective is informed by class. His desires are selfish and material but couched in the language of religion: he wanted "a church with stained glass windows, a baptizing pool under the platform and a regular Bible rest where his big Bible would stay from week to week.... He wanted refinement and reserve" (59–60).

Ministers in town are no better. The mill operates every day except Sundays, but Bonnie "stayed away from church, partly because that was the only day on which she could be with the children" (317). Ironically, by further reducing the free time mill workers had, attending church has the potential to separate families instead of bringing them together. However, Bonnie also stays away because she is angry that Mr. Simpkins, the minister of her village, preaches on the "sacredness of the family" and criticizes "those who did not keep their families together" (318). Bonnie points out the hypocrisy of Simpkins's middle-class privilege: "Nothing would have pleased her more than to stay at home and raise her children in the best way she knew how. And there were many other women like her in the village. Mr. Simpkins seemed to think if they wished they could stay at home and have a life of comparative ease. Because his wife could stay at home, he thought that other men's wives could do the same" (318). Mr. Simpkins believes that the working-class failure to meet a cultural ideal he espouses is a moral failure rather than an economic one. Later, Bonnie points out a further hypocrisy in Simpkins's stance when the mill forcibly evicts families during the strike. Simpkins does nothing to stop the evictions, even when babies and sick people are thrown into the dirty streets: "If that isn't breaking up the home, I don't know what is" (364). Her love, her shame, and then her anger thus serve as both rebuke and resistance to traditional authority figures, creating a new form of education through feeling.

Like preachers, physicians often "ministered" to the working-class community, providing needed services while also instructing people how to "live better" from a perspective based upon middle-class ideologies. Doctors and health care providers (as well as social workers) appear frequently in proletarian texts as individuals possessing the knowledge to save lives, but they also have the power to deeply shame. Emma grows sick with pellagra, and when the doctor is called, he is angry that she, like so many other poor women, is terminally ill with a preventable disease. He prescribes "plenty of lean meat, milk, and other nourishing food" (253). Emma clearly would have better food if the McClures could afford it. When Granpap admits he doesn't know how to provide it and asks for help, the doctor becomes "angry enough to frighten Bonnie": "Don't ask me how.... A doctor can't produce decent food for the many that need it. What can I do? Don't ask me." Echoing a scene that occurs in many proletarian women's texts, the doctor offers an answer for Emma's illness—she needs more food and rest—beyond the reach of those he is addressing. He has no answer as to how to obtain those things when they are economically out of reach. Thus, Lumpkin pits her working-class family against a doctor who represents the indifference and ignorance of a middle class that assumes that a lack of education and laziness, not lack of resources, is the problem.

When Bonnie loses her child, she is herself subject to the condescension of a doctor who judges her for perceived moral failure. When the doctor arrives, he is "angry with her for not calling him before. The baby, he said, must have had pneumonia for two days at least. Bonnie was silent before him" (320). Bonnie feels ashamed: "If she had not thought of expense and called the doctor earlier. It was thinking of the money involved that had held her back." The loss of her child not only shows Bonnie's suffering, but it also emphasizes the tragedy of poverty whereby a mother—despite her hard work—cannot afford to call a doctor. Bonnie is silenced by the doctor's anger and by the shame his criticism induces, but the loss of her child and her grief is powerful, speaking against the implication that her indifference caused the child's death.[8]

As a social worker, the character of Miss Gordon serves as an extension of the medical community. Working for the mill, she sponsors clubs whose purpose is to educate working-class women about proper domestic behavior, echoing the conduct books and advice manuals of nineteenth-century domestic literature. When the women workers ignore her, "their indifference hurt her badly," and she fails to understand why they aren't interested (301). Miss Gordon represents a middle class that pities the working class but does not comprehend their struggles, instead believing the solution is to reinforce more strongly middle-class values. By pointing out the problems in Miss Gordon's thinking, Lumpkin's characters resist the middle class that criticizes them without clearly understanding their experience of poverty. Bonnie provides a critical commentary on why simple sympathy is not enough:

> "She tells us, 'You must feed your children milk every day and plenty of eggs, for otherwise young ones will get pellagra.'"
> ... John knew his sister was crying.
> "I'd like the best food," she said. "And everything for my young one ... but how to get them ... I don't know." (302)

Although Bonnie feels sadness and shame for her inability to live up to the ideals Miss Gordon represents, she resists this criticism because the gap between the ideal and the reality is so great.

Despite their ability to criticize the hypocrisy of figures who represent middle-class criticism, women in the working-class community also internalize shame. While it is possible to point out the flaws in ideology promoted by outsiders, *To Make My Bread* illustrates a real danger from criticism within the working class itself. Not only do Emma and Bonnie suffer over their inability to provide fundamental necessities, but they also worry over how to manage in the face of peer disapproval. Even among the working class, views on how to maintain a home—such as keeping it clean and not doing housework on Sundays—reflect domestic ideologies. However, their material circumstances require these mothers to work in the mills, leaving them with few options regarding the time they have available to complete housework. Aware of the women's stress over their inability to work full-time shifts in the textile mill while also completing domestic duties, Bonnie's brother John transgresses traditional gender roles and tries to help with the housework: "When no one was looking John made up for Bonnie's worry by helping with the dishwashing and cooking. He even scrubbed the floors when Ora and Emma had no time to do so. Ora and Emma, having to do washing on Saturdays and ironing Monday nights, had little time for scrubbing. It would have been against the feelings of the whole community for them to do scrubbing and ironing on Sunday. Yet in secret they sometimes did this, and probably the other women did this, too, and never told outside"

(204). The women are caught between the demands of caring for their homes and families and the criticisms of their neighbors (and, by extension, their readers). While other women in their community presumably struggle with the same burdens, the social ideal is so strong they attempt to accomplish their work in secret so as not to appear to violate these norms. These circumstances lead to a silence about the actual experience of the working class, a fracture within that community, and an inability to challenge unfair labor standards both outside and inside the home, maintained by a capitalist economy and its companion, cultural ideals.

Despite clear moral justification for breaking social convention in her own life, Ora still directs criticism against another woman who works outside the home, questioning her motivations:

> "What business would keep a mother away from her young ones?" Ora asked.
>
> "I reckon the same kind that keeps us from ours, making money to live on."
>
> This quieted Ora. Only she thought to herself, "If I had a house like that I'd think myself rich enough to stay at home." (248)

Emma serves as a foil to Ora and other women in the community, showing the ways that they can resist the social fracturing created by judging each other against impossible middle-class ideals. Bonnie shares Emma's perspective, which she eventually develops into an activist role. Prior to becoming a union organizer, however, she resists criticism for perceived gendered failures from friends and members of her community who see her work outside the home as a failure to be a proper wife and mother: "She knew they might think it queer for her to work, when she had a husband. They did not realize the money it took to pay for a doctor for Emma.... The others would soon learn for themselves how hard it was to get on" (285). Like her mother, Bonnie resists division within the working-class community by building upon common experience to show that their lives do not meet sentimental, gendered ideals, which should not subject them to judgment and shame. They see this as a source of common feeling, which should create sympathy for others and thus strengthen community instead of weaken it. However, the desire to be good mothers and the realities that prevent them from meeting these ideals still serve to extend sympathy between the working class and the middle class because they acknowledge the similarities between them: although both embrace the ideal of women who can stay home to care for their families, only middle-class women are able to achieve it.

Working-class women fail in this regard through circumstance rather than character and are, therefore, deserving of sympathy.

Feeling Right to Strike

Although *To Make My Bread* dismantles sentimental ideologies about the home as a place of refuge and feminized emotional connection, Lumpkin also uses the sentimental mode to show a parallel between the home and the factory. The novel reveals the ways that shared labor and shared experience create community, arguing for the factory as a pseudo-domestic space that mimics the sympathies and affectional bonds that are developed in the home. In *To Make My Bread*, individuals who are brought together in the public workspace relate to one another and develop common feeling; they are, therefore, taught by sympathetic connection to develop a moral awareness about the capitalist labor system that oppresses them all. Such realizations, in proletarian sentimentalism, educate subjects toward a revolutionary consciousness.

Beyond critiquing the home as a space of refuge and respite, Lumpkin also establishes the domestic space of the home as a space of labor. In addition to a place where the labor of birth occurs—as it does in the opening pages—women work in the home to cook and clean, endlessly. The presentation of women's labor—making women's work in the home visible—is a common theme in women's proletarian fiction, but Lumpkin also connects this labor to the development of community. In Appalachia, the men and women "swap forces" on a day when the McClure men go to Possum Hollow to help Frank put up a shed, while Ora McClure and Jennie Martin come to Swain's Crossing to help with quilting. The women's sewing is placed in parallel to the men's building. As they stitch, the women reminisce, talking about the quilting parties of their youth, religion and drinking, and even telling ghost stories, imparting some of their background to Jennie Martin (who is new to the area) and initiating Bonnie into the narrative history of her community.

Another form of women's domestic labor that extends beyond the daily work of cooking, cleaning, and caretaking is weaving. Women convert wool into thread and cloth, producing fabric and clothing while working in the home. In Swain's Crossing, Granma Wesley's loom becomes an important tie between the workspace of the home and the workspace of the factory when Emma begins to consider moving her family to town and working in the textile mill.[9] During a visit to the Wesley's home, Emma wants to try it. As she works the heddles of the loom, she thinks "of herself sitting in a factory beside a quiet machine working it easily, talking to the other women who would be working at the machines beside her. It would be a very neighborly arrangement, as if neighbors had gathered to sit around and talk at a quilting" (140). Emma connects the labor of weaving in the factory with the experiences of quilting bees in domestic settings, transforming the factory into a domestic space. Although her later experiences in the factory will belie this dream of domestic connection, *To Make My Bread* draws a link between the labor of home and factory, showing that the people who labor together in both places are part of a community that extends past the mill gates.

Once they are working inside the mills, the McClures and others discover that the noise, dangerous machinery, sharp-eyed managers, and exhausting conditions actively work against the "neighborly arrangement" found in quilting circles and pit employees against each other. Although Emma imagines neighbors chatting as they work, the noise in the mill is deafening: the sound of machines "fills the whole room," and people "shouted trying to make their voices heard above the grinding" (326, 258). Over time, the sound of the mill becomes emotionally significant, symbolizing the way in which workers are worn down over time by their exhausting and endless labor: "At first the throb of the mill had been like the throb of a big heart beating for the good of those who worked under the roof, for it gave hope of desires to be fulfilled. A woman, one of the weavers, said . . . 'The weave room has a sound different from the other rooms. It's like the sound of sinners' teeth grinding in hell.' Now to Emma the throb of a heart had changed. She was feeling the grind of teeth. The mill crunched up and down—'I'll grind your bones to make my bread'" (219). The mill beats like a heart, suggesting that the emotional center of worker's lives is not limited to the home but is also shared in the workplace. But the sounds of the heart change from hopeful to hellish. The sinners' grinding teeth references Matthew 13:41–42, which states that the "Son of Man will send out his angels, and they will weed out of his kingdom everything that causes sin and all who do evil. They will throw them into the blazing furnace, where there will be weeping and gnashing of teeth" (King James Version). Although the anonymous worker likely draws her vivid simile from a recollection of the "fire and brimstone"–style sermons common to evangelical churches, it also suggests that the workers feel cast off, weeded out of common society, that they feel trapped in a hell of ceaseless labor with no hope of salvation. Emma, however, connects the grinding teeth to a children's tale about an ogre who grinds human bones, a deadly and domestic metaphor that portrays the big literally consuming the little, shifting the metaphor to a critique of capitalism and its abuses of the laborer.

Workers are expected to focus on the individual in order to survive, to get ahead. Basil, Emma McClure's estranged son, espouses this ideology, pursuing his studies and distancing himself from the family as he tries to enter the middle class. He tells John, "If you want to get along ... you can't think too much about other people. If you rise in this world you've got to rise by yourself" (233). Basil promotes exactly the kind of every-man-for-himself ideology at the center of capitalism and American individualism. It's the view that the mill owners expect John to embrace when they make him a section boss. However, *To Make My Bread* shows that this individualism is at odds with a strong, healthy community; a capitalist system pits workers against each other so that they must sacrifice community for success or sacrifice success for community: "[T]here were plenty of hard workers who hadn't risen. The higher-ups had to short the regular hands in weighing and making out the pay checks in order to make as much money for the mill as possible. It was a known fact that the high-ups had to do this as part of their job. But the best ones hated to do this against a neighbor, so it kept them from rising" (221).

John, like Bonnie, at first naively believes that he can achieve success as a faithful worker who serves the priorities of the mill while still valuing his bonds with the community: "John was beginning to rise in the world.... Would he go on the side of those above or stand up for his kin and friends? ... He would show them that he could be fair, and yet climb higher than others had done" (298). However, when John suggests raising worker wages because if people "did not have enough food, and enough sleep, and were worn down, they could not do the best work for the mill," his bosses are affronted, saying, "[We] didn't think ... when we made you section boss that you would turn on us like this" (299). Attempting to explain that taking care of people has economic benefits, John argues that "it's just as important t' keep a man or woman that's working at the machines in good order" (300). However, the mill boss explains that "a machine costs the management lots of money to replace," implying that people are easily and cheaply replaceable. Mr. Burnett threatens to fire John, saying that if he keeps expressing such ideas, he "can't be of use" to them. Like a machine, John is expected to be "of use," and he comes to the realization that he cannot simultaneously be of use to the factory, serving the priorities of material production, and to the community, serving the priorities of human need.

People are not machines, and the unforgivable flaw of the capitalist system *To Make My Bread* critiques is that people are treated like easily replaceable parts in a machine. What distinguishes the human from the machine is his or her ability to feel and to suffer. As John argues with his supervisor he reasons that "it's even more important, for they are people, and the machines, they aren't human, and can't feel misery" (300). Indeed, as Bonnie observes, "They pay themselves for wear and tear on the machines.... I don't get paid for wear and tear on myself" (319). Such is the heart of Lumpkin's sentimental proletarian argument: human feeling leads to a moral imperative. If by definition, as Dillon argues, "sentimentalism involves both emotion and a subsequent reflection upon that emotion—a putting to use of emotion, as for instance, when it opens a subjective path toward autonomy or moral sense," then this realization—people are not just machines, but they are more important than machines—is a sentimental call to a Marxist awakening ("Sentimental Aesthetics," 515).

Lumpkin's proletarian sentimentalism counters critiques of nineteenth-century sentimentalism that the project of sympathy is to indulge in emotional identification but ultimately requires no action to alleviate suffering. For Philip Fisher, tears in sentimentalism are a sign of "powerlessness ... a witness who cannot effect action will experience suffering as deeply as the victim," and the common trope of death emphasizes passivity and the inevitability of suffering (*Facts*, 108). Lauren Berlant argues that the emphasis on universal pain creates "a passive and vaguely civic-minded ideal of compassion" so that the "political as a place of acts oriented toward publicness becomes replaced by a world of private thoughts, leanings, and gestures projected out as an intimate public of private individuals inhabiting their own affective changes" (*Female Complaint*, 41–42). However, Lumpkin demonstrates that the moral awareness created by the sentimental inevitably leads to action; the force of feeling, in fact, requires it. The more John comes to feel the workers' misery in the face of indifferent bosses and wealthy overseers, the more of an advocate for change he becomes. John works to share "the sound of the sorrow of those that work" (326). Sentimentalism extends emotional identification across social boundaries to those who have been excluded, but rather than being brought into the fold (so to speak) by an insider who extends sympathy to outsiders, this group of victims extends sympathy to each other in order to feel recognized and validated by their suffering, which unites them into an affectional community. Thus, they bond into a group that can act in their own interests. Once John unifies sympathy with a desire to act, his feelings affirm this emotional and radical evolution in the symbolic space of the factory: he returns to work, where he arrives late and has his pay docked a full day's wages, but he ignores the overseer's criticisms, for "there was something else in him greater than the overseer's words. He stood before his machines with a joyous feeling swelling in him" (328). John has begun "feeling right," which has resulted in joy and a readiness to act.

The mill itself is figuratively given the ability to feel because the workers who inhabit the space share the same emotional responses. After conditions worsen and the management insists that workers must accept longer hours with less pay, "a feeling of misery came over the mill. Before there had been a feeling of deadness, which nothing perhaps could arouse, a feeling of stolid endurance. Now the feeling was different. It was one of acute, active misery" (330). In the midst of the misery and fear, as well as company intimidation, John and Bonnie encourage workers to attend secret union meetings. When John is fired, other workers witness the exchange and refuse to continue working, starting a moment of resistance that is marked by their awareness of sympathetic feeling and emotional solidarity: "In the short time that they had stood together they had felt something. They had felt a sense of standing up for each other. For so long each had been alone with his family striving after enough food to keep from starving, and enough clothes to keep from going naked. And they had been alone in that fight. Now they were going to stand together, side by side, and there came to them the feeling of strength" (333). Sympathy leads to solidarity and strength, an affectional bond that moves them toward collective action. From this moment forward, families no longer suffer individually but are joined in a group that shares food, shelter, resources, and emotional support in the fight for fair treatment and the ability to earn a decent living.

Shortly after he is fired, John and several union organizers call a meeting: "There was a feeling like that of an outdoor church meeting in the mountains, for people were talking as neighbors do who have not seen each other in a long time" (338). Although they are meeting on the road next to the mill, it is "as if the open road was a house full of hospitable people." Lumpkin's description connects the union meeting to both the community gatherings of Appalachian church services and socializing in neighbors' homes, emphasizing the ways that workers have been drawn together by sympathy, which in turn reignites the sense of community that had previously connected them. Both the church and the home are sentimental spaces in which people develop emotional, community-building connection; Lumpkin's description equates the union meeting to these forms of sentimental space.

As the company cracks down, Lumpkin underscores the importance of affectional bonds in keeping the workers united. Strike organizers rent a building to distribute donated food, knowing that families already have too little. Those that send the food also send a message: "What we send is not charity. Because your fight is ours, in sharing what we have with you we are only helping our own" (349). Thus, the family group is extended outward, to include other union supporters and working families in other mill towns who are in need of the same reforms. The members of the town are so moved by this gesture that many come to touch the truck that carried the supplies, even after it has been emptied. After the mill evicts families of strikers, they move into tent cities, sharing a home space that had once been divided by walls. They "put up a rough shelter for a kitchen, and ate in the open," taking their food in the tents only if it is raining (358). The women share domestic duties, with some of them taking charge of the children each day, leaving others free to participate in strike activities such as picketing. Thus, the women share child care, housework, and organizing responsibilities as an extended family, achieving the proletarian ideal of a collective group.

Sentimental sympathy is the key element not only to Bonnie's and John's—and their coworkers'—radical awakening but also to their ability to organize effectively and bring additional workers into the strike. When Bonnie writes her "Mill Mother's Lament," Ora advises her to keep composing and let others take care of the meal that evening: "You write that ballad. We've got t' reach people's hearts as well as their stomachs" (343). Bonnie's song works in conjunction with the speeches to capture the crowd. They demand that she sing it again, so she invites them to "join in" when they can: "You all know the tune. . . . So just listen to the words" (346). Bonnie's ballad operates by engaging the listeners on an emotional level and then inviting them to participate. Just as Ella May Wiggins did in real life, Bonnie takes a familiar Appalachian ballad and changes the lyrics to capture the audience's enjoyment of the music and emphasize her political message. Sentimental tropes, Dobson argues, operate by incorporating the conventional and familiar to create "evocative metaphors" and serve as "vehicles for depictions of all-too-common social tragedies and political outrages stemming from the failure of society to care for the disconnected" ("Reclaiming Sentimental Literature," 272). Not only does Bonnie's song operate in just this manner by focusing on a sentimentalized version of motherhood, but it also takes a ballad familiar to its Appalachian audience and, altering the words, becomes a song of protest as well as a remembrance of their shared mountain heritage. Further, by singing the song along with Bonnie, the audience members become active participants in developing the sentimental metaphor of the protest song.

Bonnie feels that her activism is "a loving care toward all the people" (344). The process of moving everyone toward revolutionary consciousness occurs on an emotional level, so that those who do not convert—those who give in to the pressures of the mill or the need for work and scabbing—deserve pity rather than anger. When Ora recognizes her son, Young Frank, among the militia called out to subdue the strikers, she asks him if he will "fight against [his] own" and addresses the line of soldiers asking, "Air we not your people?" (351). Similarly, Bonnie "felt sympathy for [the scabs], since, like her, they were poor and only wanted to make their bread, but she knew they must learn that if they scabbed then they were really cheating themselves in the end, and were also being traitors to their own people" (359). While the strikers feel anger at workers who undermine their cause, the true tragedy is separation: those who cross that line betray their own people and are separated from them.

The revolutionary education that occurs throughout the novel is rooted in feeling and sympathy. Thus, the novel closes with Bonnie's murder and funeral, focusing upon the emotional impact of her death. *To Make My Bread* leaves readers and characters in the midst of the struggle, but—while the outcome of the actual Gastonia strikes doesn't change—a reader's response to these events may carry a revolutionary consciousness forward. Like Ella May Wiggins, Bonnie is murdered during the strike. Although Bonnie's death is not the voluntary, Christlike sacrifice depicted in nineteenth-century sentimental novels, her death is a tragic separation that represents the sacrifice of a martyr.

Bonnie's death sets more events in motion: during a clash with deputies, one of the sheriffs is killed. The tent city is destroyed, and many of the strikers and relief workers are put in jail. Families are separated, and when the women are released from jail they must search for children "who had been driven from the tents that night" (379). Despite the chaos, John holds Bonnie's funeral. The procession that carries her body to the cemetery passes the mill, and "those who were working there left their looms and frames and crowded to the windows." As the rain falls, people "gathered around the grave—faces drawn down with grief and thin with lack of food" (380). John addresses the crowd, exhorting them to place blame on those responsible for her death: "A preacher would tell us that the people who killed Bonnie are fine, honest men. Maybe they are, but they killed Bonnie. I don't mean those misguided ones that fired the shot, but the ones who are behind the killing. The ones with Power, they killed her" (381). John connects Bonnie's death to the larger, systemic forces of oppression, transforming grief and feeling into a call to action.

In the novel's final scene, John visits his friend Stevens, who tells him, "I cried when I heard about Bonnie . . . cried from anger and shame" (383). Stevens's tears result from his grief at her loss, but rather than represent passivity, Lumpkin suggests that these tears will be transformed into greater political action. Stevens and John will direct their grief toward the proper target; thus, the novel's sentimental message is to direct suffering into a critique of those who cause it. The tears signal Bonnie's death as a sentimental event, one that draws out the sympathies of the entire community. Her funeral captures the attention of strikers as well as mill workers, and the tragedy of her loss is compounded by the additional loss of her children, who are taken into state custody and permanently separated from their family. These tragedies are laid squarely at the feet of those with "Power"—the power to cause these events and the power to change them—encouraging readers who sympathize with Bonnie, John, and their working-class family to carry forward the revolutionary consciousness. Thus, while John's grief causes him to feel "as if everything was finished," Stevens closes the novel by assuring him of the revolutionary message, "No. . . . This is just the beginning" (384).

Lumpkin's use of sentimental proletarianism not only argued for the development of a revolutionary consciousness based on affectional bonds, but it created room for a female proletarian voice in the masculine Marxist realm. She did so despite a problematic appropriation of the working-class voice and its assumption of Othered narratives. *To Make My Bread* opened up the proletarian landscape to further sentimental appropriation—although female proletarian writers would continue to argue that homes and the domestic sphere were valid working-class spaces on par with agriculture and industrial factories, writers such as Josephine Johnson would extend Lumpkin's feminized critique to masculinized spaces, writing about factories and farms within the compass of the domestic realm, demonstrating the sentimental tragedy at the heart of capitalist failures.

3 / Josephine Johnson's *Now in November*: Not Plough-Shares but People

Josephine Johnson was just twenty-four years old when she submitted the manuscript of *Now in November* to her editor, Clifton Fadiman at Simon and Schuster, in the summer of 1934. It was her first novel, and Johnson was still a student at Washington University in St. Louis. She had been an aspiring writer since her childhood in Kirkwood, Missouri. From the early 1930s, her stories and poems began appearing in national magazines, and based on the strength of her early writing, multiple publishers courted Johnson for her first book-length project. *Now in November* appeared in September 1934 to a great deal of enthusiasm and praise. In an atmosphere in which mainstream publishers were reluctant to publish radical novels, *Now in November* was hailed as a success for "its ripe understanding of things, places, and people, its unaffected sensitivity to the minutiae as well as to the major issues of life" (Rattray, "Johnson and Fadiman," 224). The novel "was deemed both timely and timeless, politically astute without resorting to polemics and the prose style inspired rapturous praise," and reviewers praised the novel as "'exquisite,' 'extraordinary,' 'almost unbelievably good,' 'like profoundly moving music'... and 'nearly perfect'" (Rattray, "Editing," 190). Edith Walton, of the *New York Times Book Review*, compared the discovery of Johnson to that of Emily Dickinson and Emily Brontë and "concluded that it lay 'within her power to go, like them, very far'" (Rattray, "Editing," 190). *Now in November* went on to win the Pulitzer Prize in May 1935, beating contenders such as F. Scott Fitzgerald's *Tender Is the Night*.

The flurry of praise showered upon Johnson's first novel points to reviewer interest in the book's aesthetic and literary qualities over its critique of capitalism. However, the timeless life issues for which Johnson was commended were actually fundamental class critiques in which she addresses a breakdown of capitalist faith and domestic harmony. Johnson, though, frames her criticism in the form of a tragically reflective bildungsroman, avoiding the didactic Marxist tenor of conventional proletarian literary forms. Indeed, the humanist critique found in *Now in November* is complex and more subtle than is found in contemporary proletarian novels such as Jack Conroy's *The Disinherited* (1933), Robert Cantwell's *The Land of Plenty* (1934), James T. Farrell's *The Young Manhood of Studs Lonigan* (1934), Albert Halper's *The Foundry* (1934), or Clara Weatherwax's *Marching! Marching!* (1935). Although proponents of proletarian realism often cast the genre in masculinized terms, Johnson achieved her critique and "unaffected sensitivity" by adopting the sentimental mode.

Now in November has been described within the tradition of the pastoral novel, as feminist scholars have paid attention to the intertwining of "women/nature/culture" within its pages (Hoffman, Afterword, 238). However, the sisters in *Now in November* also draw comparisons to novels of sensibility such as Jane Austen's *Pride and Prejudice* and George Eliot's *Middlemarch* in which

> [u]nspoken rules and social mores shape these young female lives: these young women long for freedom to leave home, but they are forbidden to venture into the world alone; they long for sexual experience, for intimacy, but they can do nothing but *be* attractive, useful, and available; they are on the verge of intellectual maturity, but have only books and abstractions, not the dilemmas of the public world with which to grapple . . . they know that decisions about religion and personal philosophy belong to the men of the family, and no matter what independent ideas they develop, these will be tempered in marriage. (Hoffman, Afterword, 243)

While these parallels are true in many significant ways, the sisters Johnson creates in *Now in November* are not the drawing-room decorations of the nineteenth century, women whose entire fate is determined by their success or failure on the marriage market. Kerrin, Marget, and Merle are limited by their femaleness in similar ways: they do not feel free to venture into the world alone, they lack sexual experience and are expected to be available for marriage, and they have only books for access to the outside world. But the fates of these women are determined not by the marriage market so much as by the capitalist market. Johnson takes Elizabeth Bennett out of the drawing room and puts her on the working-class American farm.

Sentimentalism, as I have previously argued, operates by using familiar conventions in order to convey meaning to its readers. By incorporating the mode of novels of sensibility, even the gothic romance with Kerrin's increasing and fitful madness, with her proletarian critique of capitalist failures, Johnson finds a way not only to access the emotional struggles of the working class for herself but also to convey sympathy upon the working class for her readers, avoiding the didactic preaching of so many proletarian texts.

Other critics of the novel emphasize its agricultural setting as well as its unique emphasis on female experience. Nancy Hoffman places *Now in November* within the nexus of "three usually distinct literary traditions: the autobiographical narrative of coming of age, the meditation on nature, and the novel of social protest" (Afterword, 267). Citing both the novel's rural setting and Johnson's lifelong interest in the natural world, a number of critics have contended that the novel is part of the progressive American agrarian tradition. Janet Galligani Casey argues that *Now in November* critiques American agrarianism and is part of a reactionary agrarian-related social movement, challenging masculine clichés and using images of the female form to resist sentimental parallels between the maternal body and the natural world ("Agrarian Landscapes"). Casey also argues that Johnson's agricultural setting is a radically subversive move "as a platform for socially revisionist criticism," inviting "rich commentary on the roles of nature versus nurture as it pertained to the roles of women" ("Radical Ruralities," 124). She observes that the intense pressure on farm families "to sustain themselves despite massive social and economic shifts" creates "a psychological climate that amplifies keenly the significance of every natural event, every seasonal variation, every family tension" (150).

However, *Now in November* not only capitalizes on the agrarian setting to disrupt Jeffersonian agricultural ideals and gendered mythologies, but also appropriates the sentimental mode to create sympathy for the working class as it struggles to live up to those mythologies. In so doing, Johnson reconfigures the working-class farm as part of the domestic landscape and argues that the central, sentimental tragedy at the heart of agrarian and capitalist failures is its destructiveness toward the American family. Through sentimentalized depictions of suffering, Johnson argues for the sympathetic inclusion of the Haldmarnes—and the families they represent—in the national consciousness. In this way, she demonstrates that the deterioration of their family is, in fact, a tragic cultural loss, representing the death of the American capitalist ideal. Although she doesn't directly argue that sympathy inherently leads to action in the same manner as Grace Lumpkin, Johnson's social critique—in which families that at first seem secure lose everything unless helped by their neighbors—suggests that American families require both sympathy and support in the form of systemic change to prevent the tragic failures from continuing to grow.

Like Lumpkin, Johnson was able to write about both class and gender concerns in ways that challenged the conventional proletarian genre. Instead of didactically focusing on the male factory worker or on the consequences of organized labor strikes, *Now in November* depicts the particularly devastating consequences of capitalist failure and class inequality on those who are most vulnerable to it: women and children. Much like the plots of nineteenth-century sentimental novels, Johnson places women at the center of the family and, by revealing the ways in which public social issues affect the family and the women in it, suggests that reform is urgently needed. The Haldmarne family is composed of a father, a mother, and three daughters, one of whom narrates the novel, so that the family's struggle for survival on a Depression-era midwestern farm is mediated through a feminine, familial lens. The mother serves as the spiritual and religious guide for her family, and her death prompts a crisis of faith for those who are left behind. The father fails as provider for his family, leaving them vulnerable to starvation, but *Now in November* makes it repeatedly clear that these failures are a result of the capitalist market system and not because of a lack of hard work. Much like the mill workers in *To Make My Bread*, the narrator of *Now in November* develops a proletarian sensibility because of her suffering and her awareness that other families suffer as hers does. Thus, Johnson's novel not only argues for sympathy for the working class but also develops a critique of fundamental capitalist mythologies that require reform based on a sentimental, humanist ideology.

After the publication of her first novel, Johnson became increasingly involved in the fight for social justice. She not only worked with unions and reform groups but also published reportage about those activities. Her second novel, *Jordanstown* (1937), revealed that "an overt political voice had found its way into the work," and received mixed, if not "bruising," reviews (Rattray, "Editing," 192, 194). While the publication of *Now in November* indicates a young writer's budding interest in social justice, the subtlety of her critique in the novel reveals not only her commitment to proletarian realism but also the influence of nineteenth-century novels of sensibility and sentimentalism. Combining the two genres enables Johnson to portray realistically the struggles of the working class while garnering sympathy for a group from which she herself, as a member of the dominant middle class, was an outsider.

Johnson's father was a wealthy businessman; Josephine was the second of four daughters. She grew up on a farm surrounded by relatives and close family friends. The autobiographical *Seven Houses* (1973) indicates a childhood full of gardens, baseball games, pony rides, fireworks, private school, and a large family house. Johnson "portrays herself as a slow, shy child, tolerant of her own dark side, accepting even of an unemotional and distant father whom she and her sisters feared" (Hoffman, Afterword, 269). In college, Johnson specialized in English and took classes in art. After several trips throughout the United States and Europe, she left college without taking a degree and returned home to write, joining her widowed mother and three sisters on a two-hundred-acre farm called Webster Groves. Johnson had a privileged upbringing and elite education, but she developed an interest in social justice issues. Hoffman suggests that her mother, who was a Quaker, a pacifist during World War I, and an active member of the Fellowship of Reconciliation, may have been a strong influence.

Whether it was her mother's political influence or the crash of 1929 that caused Johnson to pay attention to the plight of the working class, she made them the subject of her first and most highly acclaimed novel. While authors such as Lumpkin found that sentimental proletarianism allowed her to express "a distinctly female voice" within the male-dominated Marxist literary movement, Johnson appears to have had a less overtly Marxist agenda. In many ways, however, this appearance is misleading. As a member of the middle class, Johnson straddles two worlds and seeks to garner sympathy for the working class, critiquing the system from which she herself derived great privilege. As a college-educated writer who would have studied the classics of British literature and someone with little actual experience outside of her class, Johnson combines proletarian critique with British and American traditions of sensibility and sentimentalism. Such classics usually examine the social problems of the upper class as well as the struggle for upward mobility. Working with post-1929 disillusionment and the failure of the American Dream as well as increasing criticisms of rigid gender roles, Johnson transposes familiar literary plot conventions to a working-class setting.

Thus, Johnson appropriates the voices and experiences of farm laborers and convincingly melds them into a sentimental novel.

Capitalist Myth and Sentimental Ideology

Now in November is cast as retrospection on a mature young woman's journey to consciousness. At age twenty-five, Marget narrates the novel, looking back in November of the eleventh year of her family's tenure on the mortgaged Haldmarne farm. Although she immediately gestures toward the novel's status as a bildungsroman, she undercuts the conventional growth pattern of that form: "It has been a long year, longer and more full of meaning than all those ten years that went before it. There were nights when I felt that we were moving toward some awful and hopeless hour, but when that hour came it was broken up and confused because we were too near, and I did not even quite realize that it had come" (3). Marget's reflective journey is a reeducation of the self, tracing the evolution of her consciousness through events that appear "strange and unrelated and made no pattern that a person could trace easily" (4). It does not follow a linear progression. Instead, the novel is punctuated with flashbacks and reminiscences that reveal a collective learning process rather than straightforward sequences of individual development.

Marget is the primary revolutionary consciousness in the novel, but she comes to her awareness through a combination of her family's collective experience and her own introspection. She does not lead her family toward understanding but instead acts as a quiet observer, a recorder of circumstances that drive her family further from security. Her narrative position as an adult who reflects on the past allows her to occupy both childlike and adult perspectives, embellishing a child's evenhanded storytelling with adult perceptions and insight. Johnson's technique allows Marget to overlay the story with observations that imaginatively and sympathetically reach into her parents' and sisters' psyches and, in turn, reflect her own. Marget observes her father's struggle to accept his economic downturn: "It's a queer experience for a man to go through, to work years for security and peace, and then in a few months' time have it all dissolve into nothing; to feel the strange blankness and dark of being neither wanted nor necessary any more" (6). She also describes, and takes solace in, her mother's quiet faith: "[S]he took life slowly, and trusted in something a person could neither feel nor see, but knew" (82). While Marget relies on, and loses, her mother's faith, these insights into her parents' consciousness reveal the way in which she seeks to comprehend the interconnectedness of their emotional lives.

Marget's development is not entirely through observation and vicarious emotional connection with her family; her journey toward revolutionary awareness also follows firsthand experiences. Published in 1934 and chronicled as a yearlong reflection with flashbacks over the course of the previous decade, the story is set in the early 1930s and reaches back into the early 1920s. The Haldmarne family is caught in the Depression-era economic downturn and retreats to an isolated midwestern farm community before Marxist ideas have become widespread, so they have not been exposed to common 1930s radical thought. The family's closest exposure to contemporary ideology is a brief period during which Grant, a hired hand, attends "meetings at night up in the school" and forces Arnold Haldmarne to participate in a milk strike that raises prices but not profits (128). By isolating the family and limiting their exposure to local strike activities, Johnson focuses on the circumstances that force Marget and her family into a recognition of the devastating effects of the socioeconomic system in which they are caught. Marget repeatedly meditates on her desire for a sense of security that is always just out of reach: "It would have taken so little to make us happy. A little more rest, a little more money—it was the nearness that tormented" (37).

At the heart of Marget's revolutionary development is the critique of the capitalist myth in the security and salvation of the land. Unlike the McClures who feel that ownership of land provides them economic security but do not establish an emotional connection with it, Marget and the other Haldmarne daughters feel a spiritual connection to the land that is disrupted by their economic and material hardships. In establishing an emotional bond with the land, *Now in November* suggests that capitalist myths are based upon a sentimental ideology that assumes that people can establish an affectional bond with the natural world—that nature can be included in the human family, that it not only provides spiritual renewal but participates in a cycle of caretaking in which human beings receive sustenance if they, in turn, cultivate the land.

Marget feels particularly betrayed by the cycle of labor and debt that undercuts any renewal or sustenance offered by nature: "[I]t came to me as it did at times when the woods seemed all answer and healing and more than enough to live for, that maybe they wouldn't be always ours— that a drouth or a too-wet year or even a year over-good when everyone else had too much to sell—could snatch them away from us, and a scratch on a piece of paper could cancel a hundred acres and all our lives" (68).

Because she lives in an agricultural environment, Marget is surrounded by the natural world and feels a connection to it. The unpredictability of nature and attempts to cultivate the land for food production, however, create an untenable living situation. Nature's erratic bounty and parsimony, as well as market factors, prevent farmers from profiting on either a good or a bad crop and undermine any sense of stability that could be located in the land. Nature is not a sentimental entity, nor can it support the "bargain" the capitalist myth implies. Marget cannot depend on the land for security because crop value is determined by the capitalist market, reducing crops to "a scratch on a piece of paper" that diminishes the worth of their physical reality and highlights land's ephemeral nature.

Marget is angered by the sense of impermanence, the lack of ownership over the labor invested in the land, and the cyclical nature of production. Although capitalism mythologizes land's restorative properties and overemphasizes agriculture's food production, Marget undercuts that myth by emphasizing that the farmer is merely a laborer whose true labor product is the work itself: "There was a bitterness in sowing and reaping, no matter how good the crop might be . . . when all that it meant was the privilege of doing this over again and nothing to show but a little mark on paper. And there was the need, the awful longing, for some sort of permanence and surety; to feel that the land you ploughed and sowed and lurched over was your own and not gone out from under your feet by a cipher scratch" (76). Marget seeks connection and security, finding disappointment in the cycle of production, loss, and renewal in the work of agricultural production. She is frustrated by the ironic fruitlessness of their labor, describing the debt as "a bottomless swamp unfilled," in which they throw hours of work and sweat "only to see them swallowed up and then to creep back and begin again" (35).

Suffering Fatherhood

One of the ways that Johnson dismantles fundamental capitalist mythologies is her presentation of Arnold Haldmarne as a failed breadwinner who suffers because of his inability to provide for and protect his family. Whereas sentimental literature rarely considers the emotional responses of its failed and absent providers, women's proletarian literature has often critiqued the ways that social inequality is harmful to both men and women. However, proletarian writing frequently focuses on how men's anger translates into violence and abuse at home. These texts portray women sympathetically, but because men are the perpetrators of violence and abuse against their wives and children, it is difficult to cast them as sympathetic. Such characterizations often do not explore men's emotional responses to suffering. Arnold, however, is not presented as a violent man. His anger and frustration are turned inward, and the novel offers a sympathetic portrait of this working-class man's emotional life.

Throughout *Now in November*, Arnold is frustrated and angry that his incessant labor does not result in security or stability. Although he constantly works to produce a crop, his efforts are often thwarted by poor weather. Or, if he successfully manages a large harvest, market forces inhibit his ability to profit from it: "If it's good ... so'll everyone else's be. Land'll be drowned in corn.... You ought to be able to sell all the stuff you raise!" (50). He finds similar problems with his dairy enterprise; even though the principles of supply and demand dictate that suppliers should make higher profits when resources are scarce, he doesn't make more money when milk supplies are low. Dairies and stores may increase selling prices, but they don't raise what they pay the suppliers: "Last year there had been too much, and all farmers had it.... This year nobody had very much, but the price didn't seem to change—not at the *back* door of the dairy anyway" (101–2). Arnold is forced into competition with his neighbors because they are all trying to sell the same products: "Prices went up, we heard again, but Dad got no more for his milk and got less for the cows he sold, since nearly all other farmers were selling off" (143). Their participation in the agricultural market contributes to price fluctuations, but they are all vulnerable to those changes.

Traditionally, property ownership has been believed to be a marker of middle-class wealth because of the land's value. Farmers are thought to have more security because they own the land on which they work and they receive the majority of the profits from their labor. Furthermore, agricultural production provides farmers and their families with direct access to food, unlike, it is presumed, laborers who work in urban industrialized settings and must purchase food from stores. Johnson deliberately undermines Arnold's ability to provide in this manner, revealing that property ownership and agricultural labor are not the protections that capitalist mythology purports them to be. The farm, though "owned by Haldmarnes since the Civil War" (4), is mortgaged, and the crop's profit needs to cover not only the family's cost of living and the working costs of the farm but also the mortgage. The land represents promise, but the mortgage contract shifts ownership of the land to a bank, so that the cycle of labor benefits a company rather than the farmer.

In addition to the mortgage, the Haldmarnes are responsible for annual property taxes. Marget observes the tax assessor's visit, facing a clear discrepancy between his understanding of the property and the actual wealth of the Haldmarne farm. Mr. Braille is aptly named because he reads the list of assets—"plows and tractor ... a hundred sheep ... nine hogs ... a hundred chickens" (219)—and notes buildings and property, but he lacks the ability to see that the livestock are not profitable and the buildings store no harvest. Braille observes, "You folks are pretty well off," but Arnold counters, "Them barns are empty. That silo's only three-quarter full. I have to buy feed this winter." Frustrated, Arnold asks, "If a man's no income, how's he going to pay property taxes?" (221). He cannot protect his family just by owning land, because capitalist forces impose financial requirements that must be met, and this debt can only be satisfied by a profit margin that is produced by a market favorable to farmers. In fact, by mortgaging the property, Arnold passes the instability and risk onto future generations who must continue to pay the debt after he is no longer able to labor at his full physical capacity: "I saw how the debt would be Merle's and mine to carry by ourselves—how many years I do not know, but for a long and uncounted time" (230).

Although *Now in November* is a proletarian novel, Arnold doesn't find easy solutions to his problems in Marxist organizing. Forced to participate in a dairy strike in which farmers must hold back or dump hundreds of gallons of milk, he is angry about the waste as well as the lack of change to his precarious situation: "Whether the strike was won or lost nobody ever was sure. Prices went up a cent and we started selling again, but there was another tax to pay and a change in the graded value which canceled the feeble rise.... Father couldn't quite realize what had happened until he balanced his books at the month's end, and there was this three-day strike leaving an empty hole on the page" (132). Since labor reform is less of an issue for farmers who work for themselves, Marxist organizers focus on raising prices. However, the proletarian message of Johnson's novel suggests that just striking for better market shares cannot solve working-class problems in a farming community. After all, Willa Haldmarne asks, "'What if it does shove the prices up? ... We get more and somebody else pays more. Where's the sense in that?" (129). Raising prices shifts costs, but it doesn't address the systemic problems that have undermined the value of owning property and trapped the Haldmarnes, and families like them, in a system of ceaseless labor and debt where neighbor is pitted against neighbor and food is thrown away.

In many nineteenth-century sentimental novels men are portrayed as failed providers who are self-serving and callously abandon their responsibilities toward dependent women and children. Johnson, however, provides a version of the sentimental father as one who fails as a provider not because he abandons his responsibilities, but because he is prevented by outside forces from meeting his obligations. As such, he suffers over his failures and this suffering inhibits his ability to connect emotionally with his family. Thus, like Lumpkin, Johnson reveals that the economic and social forces that destroy working-class families also have an impact on their emotional bonds.

Arnold's experiences have made him hard and bitter. After growing up on the farm, he left to work in lumber factories and found moderate success: he'd "saved and come up hard and slow" (6). But after losing everything in the Depression, "[t]hings had come slow to him and gone fast, and it made him suspicious even of the land." Arnold moved his family back to the farm in a desperate attempt to survive, to provide for them, and to recapture the elusive American Dream promising that hard work will produce security. But he finds only ceaseless labor, as Marget describes: "My father's life had been a sort of fierce crawling to rid us of debt.... He wanted some safety for us, freedom from that fear and doubt he had always known himself" (35).

Because of his fear and doubt and because he is barely able to provide a subsistence living for his family—let alone pull them out of debt—all of Arnold's energies are devoted to his work. He shows care for his family through his work: "This heavy, complaining labor with doubtful profit was almost the only visible sign of love he had ever showed us. But it was one that I'd never doubted" (36). The hardship of that work, however, costs Arnold his emotional ties with his family; he is brusque and distant toward his daughters, directing them to complete chores and unable to connect to them emotionally. Marget suspects that Arnold feels isolated because he is surrounded by women. But, more likely, the lack of sons adds to his fear because of gendered divisions of labor: without sons to help him in manual tasks, Arnold is forced to do all the work on the farm himself or expend scarce resources to hire outside help. However, he also suffers because his failure to provide is a perceived failure of his masculinity: "He felt too that we blamed him because there was nothing left but this land out of everything he had piled together for years; but the truth was that we never thought about this.... But he was so raw in mind himself that he suspected us all" (37). Arnold's sense of self, his masculinity, is tied to the ability to support his family; the farm's failures turn him "raw in mind" because he blames himself and withdraws emotionally—interactions with the women of his household reinforce his feelings of failure.

Thus, Marget and her sisters both love and hate, pity and fear their father, because they witness his suffering and understand the source of his pain. By revealing that Arnold's anger is a result of his own fear and his desperate desire to provide for his family, *Now in November* draws a sympathetic portrait of the sentimental father who loves his family and suffers over his financial inabilities. He, in turn, causes additional suffering because of his inability to hide or release his despair and rage, making the home an uncomfortable, uncertain place. *Now in November* constantly underscores the source of Arnold's suffering, making clear that he lashes out at those closest to him even though they are not the source of his pain. Even as he scorns his wife's attempts to advise him on how to manage after a field hand suddenly quits, Marget observes the fear underneath his anger: "It was awful—the rage he felt; but it wasn't the anger so much as the despair that made us afraid" (50). Although never overtly violent, the constant tension of his anger leaves them insecure and worried in his presence: "He seldom swore aloud, thought it was wrong to do before his girls;—but all the blasphemy was there, bursting and turning sour inside" (65).

Despite their fear and hate, the girls love their father and understand that Arnold's anger comes from impotent rage at the unfair system that traps him as well as his ever-present concern for his family: "[A]ll the time I would feel us there on his shoulders, heavy as stone on his mind—all four of our lives to carry everywhere" (52). Thus, Marget sympathizes with her father's pain, loving him despite his anger and his emotional distance: "I saw the awful unmasking of his face, as if all the underground terror and despair were brought to the surface by his hope, and I felt a jab of pity and love for him stronger than I'd ever known before" (153). By showing Arnold's despair and his daughter's sympathy, Johnson argues that working-class fathers are equally subject to emotional suffering caused by the material conditions of poverty.

Faithful Motherhood

Women serve significant roles as spiritual and moral leaders in nineteenth-century sentimental novels. The spiritual organization of these novels is credited with aiding a cultural, religious shift from the pulpit into the home and establishing women as moral and religious authorities in family and society. Although, as a proletarian text, *Now in November* does not endorse a specific religious or theological viewpoint, it does suggest a humanist philosophy that stems primarily from Marget's mother. While Marget herself struggles to embrace her mother's faith, Johnson presents her uncertainty as a logical result of the pressures of poverty and working-class struggle. Marget's mother, like the women of nineteenth-century novels, is a feminized Christlike figure who embodies a sympathetic, humanist ideal.

Willa Haldmarne, the emotional and moral center of her family, possesses an inherent calmness and quiet faith that enables her to weather hardships more easily than her husband can, passing this ability to endure onto her children through her example: "He had not told her the place was mortgaged. . . . But even in the moment, when she saw that this, too, was uncertain and shifting ground, something she always had—something I didn't know then and may never know—let her take it quietly. A sort of inner well of peace. Faith I guess it was. She stood a great deal and put up with much, but all without doubt or bitterness; and that she was there, believing and not shaken, or not seeming so at least, was all that we needed then to know" (5). By demonstrating a quiet acceptance, Willa calms her daughters, allowing them to "forget for the time this sense of impermanence and doubt." While her husband inwardly rages at the unfairness of their spiraling debt and the ever-present threat of starvation, Willa experiences their poverty differently. Although she worries and suffers hardships, her different beliefs about humanity enable her to endure more peacefully: "She felt things as much as he did, wanted comfort, and yet could more easily do without. A curious warm aliveness under and over some inner core that was not attached to it . . . more wholly alive because less dependent on life" (167).

Marget's mother makes everyone feel welcome and safe at home—despite any fights and tension among the girls or their father—and they confide freely in her: "Mother never talked much herself, but listened to everything that was said, and it made us feel there was a reason in talking because she was there to hear" (17). She encourages her daughters to share their feelings and—as avid readers—develop their minds. She supports them with laughter and affection; although they are often uncertain of their father's reaction to their efforts, they know that she will appreciate any attempt they make to please her. When Marget teaches Merle to recite a long poem, they "hoped that Father would laugh because it was supposed to be funny in some places," but they "knew that Mother would anyway" (21). And when making a birthday present for her father, Marget hopes to please him but wishes the present "was for Mother, knowing that she would like anything" they made (22).

Willa is highly attuned to the feelings of others, not only responding to her daughters' moods and emotional needs but also extending sympathy outside of the immediate family. She frequently intercedes between her high-spirited and different daughters, smoothing over spats and trying to create peace among them. She notices even unspoken anxiety, offering gentle and practical help to ease worries, such as when the girls eagerly await their father's birthday: "Merle did not ask Is this the day? each morning, but Mother could see how she was fearful of not recognizing it, and so taught her how to mark the days on the calendar each night" (25). She is so attuned to others' feelings that Marget characterizes her as living "in the lives of other people as though they were her own" (16). Thus, when Kerrin has yet another confrontation with her father, Willa is hurt by her daughter's pain: "[I]t was like being bruised inside each time." Her sympathy is so strong that her daughter repeats this assessment when describing Willa's concern over a missing field hand. Willa doesn't share Arnold's anger that Max Rathman has quit and left him without help on the corn harvest, instead worrying that his absence may be a result of illness or injury: "She saw him sick, hurt to death, wagon-pitched and already dying. She lived in the lives of others as though she hadn't one of her own" (49).

Willa's sympathy prompts her to advocate charity in spite of the Haldmarne's own poverty. Like Lumpkin's working-class mothers who attempt to stretch scarce resources, Willa knows that her family continuously teeters on the brink of starvation and does as much as possible with the little they have. Her traditional role is to take charge of cooking and managing domestic resources, so she cans produce for the winter and makes supplies last as long as possible. With very little cash, they cannot afford to buy food or other supplies from the store. Thus, she is careful with their resources but willing to share with Grant, the new hired hand, despite Merle's concern about having another mouth to feed: "'We'll have food enough to eat anyway. Food enough if nothing to wear.' . . . She looked worried, though, and I saw her go back and recount the jars, as if by doing it over often enough she could make them more" (75). When, at times, the farm produces more food than the family can eat or sell, Willa advocates sharing with others, regardless of whether it will bring them a profit. After canning cherries with too many left to be sold because "the Union markets were overflooded," Willa instructs her daughters, "Give them away. . . . Better than swelling the jays and worms" (115). When the family is told to dump hundreds of gallons of milk during the strike—or be forced to—she argues that they should "[g]ive it away then.... Give it out on the street. They oughtn't to stop you doing that!" (130).

Willa's sympathetic desire to give to others contrasts her husband's despair over a lack of reciprocal charity; Arnold suggests that this kind of giving doesn't work because they do not live within a communist system of exchange: "A man can't afford to give when nobody gives him back. You can't work without profit when nobody round you does. I'd give for no cost if I could get back for nothing" (116). Indeed, while Willa advocates that the family give away food they cannot use or profit from, such moments of excess occur infrequently and do not stem the tide of poverty that surrounds them because they all exist within a system that requires profit. Willa's suffering comes not just from her own struggle to keep her family alive but from the way that struggle is magnified exponentially by all the other families who suffer just as they do. Willa sees the effects of their poverty as a problem not just of starvation and struggle but also of community.

Willa's belief in the need to help others stems from a personal faith that is vaguely based in the ideological foundation of Christian charity. Johnson, however, is careful to show that these ideas do not require a strict adherence to the church. Regular church attendance is difficult to manage because of the demands of the farm: "The minister used to come once a month to preach, and for a whole year after we'd moved on the land Mother had wanted to go and hear him, but there always seemed something else that had to be done ... the farm like a querulous, sick old man whining for attention every hour" (134). However, once Willa brings her daughters to services (while Arnold stays home), Marget observes that the minister shouts about sin, while her mother was "sitting there, listening quiet, but more as though she were having some inner communion of her own, feeding and watering some faith of which the organ and church and minister were only the symbol and surroundings. She listened only to hear the sound of faith in his voice, and not to the words that meant little or nothing" (139).

As Johnson draws it, the minister and church are only outward symbols of a deeper faith, one that stems from somewhere deep within Willa. She "trusted in something a person could neither feel nor see, but knew" and demonstrated "a sort of faith in the dignity of human spirit" (82, 145). In fact, Willa and her daughters are abruptly asked to leave the church when communion begins. A deacon whispers as the whole congregation stares, "You'll have to get out.... You don't belong to the church. Only church-members take communion" (140). During the service, Willa's face held "a rapt and luminous light," but standing outside, staring at the closed church doors, she "looked as if she had lost some irreplaceable thing and had been jerked back suddenly into life, and empty-handed" (140, 141). While sitting in church, Willa engages with a communal spiritual experience, connecting more to a larger emotional and spiritual bond of gathering than with the theological message expounded by the minister at the front of the room. Thus, not only is the church—the religious institution—not the true source of Willa's illumination, but in casting her out, the church itself becomes another symbol of social power that inhibits instead of encourages faith by drawing lines between people.

As a mother, as the moral and emotional center of her family, Willa models humanist philosophy—the idealized communist spirit. Her faith is desirable, but it does little to enact real change and proves ultimately unsustainable. Willa's life is cut tragically short when she is hurt helping the family fight a wildfire that threatens their acreage and their home; she is burned badly and lingers for a few weeks before eventually dying. Like Stowe's Little Eva, Willa is a model of goodness who inspires others but lives according to a belief system that is difficult—if not impossible—for most to sustain. The fire, which consumes forests, fields, and houses, reveals the family's and the community's helplessness against larger forces that can affect every element of their lives and ignores the artificial, man-made boundaries set between work and home spaces. While desperate workers move "against the fire like furious black ants," Willa falters and is caught by the merciless fire that, like the capitalist system, is indifferent to human kindness (193).

Whereas Little Eva's death inspired near instant conversion among her followers, Willa's life and death prompts her daughter Marget to engage in a more complex reflection on the relationship between her humanist philosophy and their lived reality. Marget is open about her struggles, wishing to feel the same way as her mother but unable to fully accept her faith. She longs to share her mother's beliefs, not so much wishing to share a specific theological viewpoint so much as desiring to possess the same calmness and ability to weather struggles and hardship: "I wanted to believe as she did, quietly, very steadfast, without reasoning or beyond reason, with a faith that seemed as much part of her as her hands or face" (139). As a critical observer who carefully examines the positions and beliefs of both her parents, Marget's doubts offer a moderated perspective on two emotional options facing the working-class family: frustration and rage over the unfairness or quiet faith in human dignity. While Marget prefers her mother's peace, she is unable to ignore the realities of labor and suffering her family experiences. Thus, when she observes her sister Kerrin—prone to fights and lashing out—greedily eating spoonfuls of jelly straight from the jar, Marget considers, "[T]here were hours of sun and hours of picking and hot hours on a stove all gone into those few minutes of Kerrin's swallowing and would become a part of her, giving her energy to hate and use loud words and tears; and I wondered how Mother's faith would answer that, for it seemed to make the pattern of things more distorted than before" (62). How, Marget wonders, does one reconcile the reality of work, labor, and deprivation with a belief in human goodness, when humans still fail and still suffer?

Willa's death is not quick, nor is it painless. Her burns are severe, and the family has few resources to aid her beyond a burn salve and a doctor who offers false hope. Although Willa endures without complaint, Marget sympathizes so deeply with her suffering that she must find a limit in order to bear it: "I used to sit up at night beside her, and at first it was almost too hard. It was awful—the pain she suffered. . . . I thought sometimes I should scream out myself, suffering for her and half-crazy with pity and helplessness. But there is a merciful blind skin that comes over the heart at times. You can endure this much, and after that there come intervals of hardness" (214). Marget both sympathizes deeply with her mother's suffering and must "blind" her heart to the pain to survive; thus, there are limits to sympathy and too much sympathy can become a destructive force if the shared suffering is too great. Despite her pain, Willa remains a sentimental model. She "has no doubt, no fear in her own mind," and continues to think about the welfare of others. Even as her "mind wandered off in a web of pain," in her clear moments she asks about her husband, wanting to know if he rests or eats enough: "He's too wound up. Work brings so little anyway. . . . Tell him to rest" (223).

Willa's death results in a crisis of faith for Marget: "I could not pretend or hope any longer, or believe blindly in any goodness. It was all gone. Faith swept away like a small mound of grass, and nothing to live or wait for any longer. God was only a name, and it was her life that had been the meaning of that name. Now there was nothing left" (224). Instead of inspiring Marget to look to heaven for a reunion, Marget sees only additional loss, more evidence that the world was empty and indifferent to their suffering: "I had believed because she had, and if she lost it and came to the darkness where we were, groping along with no more light than I,—then all of my blind belief in goodness was gone.... But all of this was nothing beside the unbearable feeling of loss" (225).

Marget's loss of faith prompts a new realization about the humanist philosophy undergirding her mother's beliefs. As she reflects on the ways their lives have been emptied of hope, as well as the peace and beauty they used to find in nature, she comes to realize that they "are not trapped any more than all other men. Any more than life itself is a trap" (226–27). Marget not only begins to place herself and her family within the context of humanity's entire struggle for survival, but she considers that the world is indifferent to their collective suffering: "Was there anything that we could have done that we did not do? God—if you choose to say that the drouth is God—against us. The world against us, not deliberately perhaps, more in a selfish than malicious way, coming slowly to recognize that we are not enemies or plough-shares. And we against ourselves. It is not possible to go on utterly alone" (227). Marget, thus, combines both her father's critique of a capitalist market system that profits from the laborer but does not help him—the selfish world—and her mother's faith in human dignity—being impossible to go on alone. Marget, in turn, develops a new faith, a budding revolutionary consciousness that will enable her to endure and possibly to change the world that has caused so much suffering: "Love and the old faith are gone.... But there is the need and the desire left, and out of these hills they may come again. I cannot believe this is the end.... [I]f this is only consolation of a heart in its necessity, or that easy faith born of despair, it does not matter, since it gives us courage somehow to face the morning. Which is as much as the heart can ask at times" (231). Through the heart, through feeling, comes a new faith and a proletarian humanism that offers a new hope to Marget, her family, and to the working class. This sympathetic identification reinforces her ability to draw connections among working-class families, which connects them in a sentimental, humanist understanding of the American family.

Drawing Parallels among Working-Class Families

Now in November consistently draws parallels between the Haldmarnes and other working-class families, showing that the ways these families differentiate themselves—drawing boundaries between who is safe and who is vulnerable—are both fluid and meaningless. All the families in the novel are subject to market pressures, natural disasters, and personal shortfalls. Although families believe their suffering is unique, they are, in fact, alike and equally vulnerable, as Johnson reveals, further demonstrating that capitalist beliefs fail for everyone and that they would all benefit from the same systemic reforms and human charity. Showing that all working-class families suffer also enables Johnson to develop a sentimental argument that crosses race boundaries, demonstrating not only that working-class African American families are subject to the same problems as white families but that racism places them even more at risk. In so doing, Johnson argues for the inclusion of both working-class families and African American families within the national, American family, demonstrating that all families have common desires but are vulnerable to external pressures.

Throughout *Now in November* Johnson deconstructs the capitalist myth of security in the land by showing that it does not guarantee sustenance or survival for the Haldmarne family who farm it. When the family encounters officials who represent this mythology, such as the tax assessor, they logically (if frustratedly) point to the flaws in his valuation of the property. But when a beggar approaches Arnold and his daughters in the fields asking to work in exchange for food, Arnold finds him threatening because he not only espouses that same mythology, but he also represents what the family could easily become. The beggar shows them a few half-rotted sweet potatoes and exclaims, "You farmers have got food anyway.... I got a family. We have to eat" (78). Marget's father swiftly points out that a "farmer's pinched as any man," but the beggar frightens him, representing "what might have happened... if there hadn't been land to save [them], and reminding him, too, of what might happen still" (79). Although the Haldmarnes are "saved" from utter starvation by their access to property, their precarious position reveals that land itself is not total refuge from hunger and destitution. Even though Arnold calls the beggar a "lying loafer," it is clear that the man is willing to work but is out of options and resources; the distance between the beggar's family and the Haldmarnes is not great. While both the girls and their father feel fear, Arnold reacts with anger but the girls feel pity. They secretly go to the house and take food from the cellar, but in spite of their cutting across the field to catch him, he does not hear them calling or crying: "I couldn't for fear or shame have called again" (80).

Although the beggar makes Marget and her family feel fear, the Rathmans, their prosperous German neighbors, cause Marget to feel envious. The Rathmans are not significantly wealthier than the Haldmarnes, but to Marget they appear happier, safer, and more secure: "They seemed so solid and sage, and needed so little.... Their land was their own entirely and had no debt. Whatever grew on it belonged to them and went to pay back no unseen owner" (96–97). Marget pays attention to their crops of strawberries and grapes as well as the wine that "Old Rathman" produces, not recognizing that the Rathmans are also close to the line between security and destitution, that a family tragedy or a market crash could easily destroy their seemingly comfortable working life: "I wondered what it was like to live safe. Out of debt. I could not believe that they had their own rawness, too, something bad under all this white-looking comfort" (98). Marget differentiates families like hers, who work mortgaged properties, from those who seem to be debt free: "Here were all of us then, I thought, crawling along the ruts and shoving our debts ahead like the ball of dung-beetles. . . . All of us but the Rathmans, anyway. They're safe, I thought, padded in from fear. They have only to work for the now, and not pay for the years behind" (100). Marget doesn't recognize the precariousness of both positions, seeing the mortgage as the greater risk.

But after Old Rathman breaks his hip, their entire farm is placed in jeopardy; in spite of being "debt free," Rathman must still feed his family and cover property taxes, electric bills, and the purchase of farm equipment, clothing, or other material goods. Although one of Rathman's sons moves home with his wife, "on account of the rent being free," they refuse to help Mrs. Rathman with the full load of farm- and housework. Picked beans go to waste instead of being sold because Lena Rathman doesn't have time to take them to market and feels that she's "done enough" to help her in-laws, while Max and Lena keep the money for themselves when they do take strawberries in, so there's no money for bills. The farm "looked going-apart, too, sliding to seed" with maintenance neglected because Old Rathman can't get out of bed (172). Marget realizes that the Rathmans are equally vulnerable to disaster, placing them in the same precarious position as anyone else: "Old Rathman's accident had seemed a sudden and awful thing, wrenching away the thickness of their comfort and leaving them now no better off than the rest of us. Even worse off, perhaps" (169). While Arnold blames Old Rathman for his accident, claiming that he "had head spinnings before" and "[w]on't never quit work till he can't lift a hand or foot," Marget sees the parallels between Rathman and her father: "*Like you*, I wanted to say. Father wasn't well and he worked too hard" (167). Marget knows that the desperation to survive causes Rathman and Arnold to make similar choices, perhaps at the expense of their health and the family's future security. The Rathmans are different from the Haldmarnes only by degree, which causes

Marget to wonder "if there was peace and security anywhere on the earth" (172). Although hyperbolic, Marget's statement suggests a shared insecurity among all families: no one is completely invulnerable.

The Ramseys are an African American family who are nearby tenant farmers. Reflecting the powerful but elusive American Dream, they hope to own their farm someday despite the fact that they continue to fall further behind: "For ten years Ramsey had rented land and expected to buy, but all that he ever did was make his rent money and put up half the crop to go over the winter.... But every spring Lucia boomed out that *this* was the year they were going to make it" (121). Tenant farming is even more difficult because farmers must pay rent to the landowner in addition to a portion of their crop, which means they keep less than half of what they grow (which is further reduced if the landowner charges them for seed or supplies). As with a mortgage, they always owe rent to the landowner, regardless of what happens to the crop. Unable to make rent, Ramsey asks neighbors for help, but the "wealthy" Rathmans are unable to provide aid: "I got land and vegetables, but no money!... The old lady give him a jar of pickles but no money" (99). When Christian Ramsey turns to Grant Koven, another neighbor, for help, he first advises him not to pay, protesting the exploitative price as "too big a rent." But Ramsey points out that his family is given no leniency because of his race: "'Let'm try to shove you off and see what'll happen,' he'd said. Christian was scared, though, and not willing to risk it. 'Maybe you could get by all right... you ain't a nigger. You don't have a wife and seven children. A nigger can't wait and see what'll happen. He *knows!*'"

Although it angers Grant to contribute to an exploitative system, paying off "Mistah" Turner, "who didn't need it and who'd dangled the debt over Christian's head until he was raw as a Negro could get," he provides the money because he "couldn't stand by and do nothing just because [he] thought it was wrong for a man to be trapped that way" (99–100). Grant's own family, though, is also in debt—two years behind in their taxes—and won't be able to help the Ramseys again. The difference between the debtors and the creditors is only in degree: although the government isn't dangling the Kovens' debt over them, it does trap everyone in an unfair system and threatens the Kovens with the loss of their farm. When the Ramseys seek assistance a second time, Christian approaches Arnold Haldmarne, but he is unable to help: "I'd help you some if I had it, but... I ain't a cent to spare" (157). Arnold asks if any other family can help, but Ramsey says no one is able or willing: "I been every place before. I been up to the county, but they tol' me so long as I don' need food that I got to manage." Not only are the families in similar circumstances—no one has any money—but the only aid anyone can offer is in the form of food. The irony is that farmers do produce food, enabling them to survive—if barely—but if they cannot sell the food and produce cash, they are unable to stay on the land that produces the food that sustains them. Watching the Ramseys struggle, Marget considers that their situation is a more extreme version of her own: "[I]t occurred to me that we seemed to them as the Rathmans did to us. Safe. Comfortable. Giving the appearance of richness, with our dairy and corn and chickens, our steers and team and orchard—although each thing was barely paying to keep itself" (122).

When the Ramseys are eventually evicted, Grant pleads with Turner but achieves nothing. Turner's racism justifies, in his mind, putting the family out: "Ramseys don't make good tenants.... Niggers make poor tenants.... A white man would have managed" (158–59). Grant points out the flaw in this race-based reasoning, asking if "niggers kept rain off their land" to show the ludicrousness in the idea that a white farmer could have managed a crop-destroying drought any more effectively (159). But by explaining, "nobody'd managed this year," Grant also shows that white families are just as vulnerable to the weather conditions and the unfavorable market (158). African American and white families are equal in their capitalist vulnerability, subject to the pressures of working-class conditions. But African American families are subject to the additional burdens of racism, leaving them with fewer resources and options when things go badly. Merle, Marget's sister, cries when Ramsey leaves and "even Kerrin looked sick," because they sympathize with his family's plight. As Marget watches the Ramseys in their overloaded wagon pull away, she considers the parallels between their families: "That's what will happen to us.... We'll go back crawling the same way we came" (166). Marget's awareness of the similarities between the families doesn't stop with just the Ramseys; she understands that all working-class families struggle in similar ways and are subject to the same pressures: "[S]urely, I thought, we have the right to live as fully as anyone else! Are we and all those around us—the Ramseys and Huttons and Meisters and all the rest—any worse than people who have no fear, no slough to fill, are not pawns to drouth and frost? Why were we chosen to be so stinted?" (142). Marget's use of "chosen" is significant, suggesting that the working class are there by external forces rather than moral failures and implying that those outside of the working class are equally at risk to such an intervention or systemic failure.

Kerrin Haldmarne: The Madwoman on the Farm

Though Marget successfully navigates the progression of collective hardships that deny her security and force her critique of socioeconomic factors that undermine her family's attempts to survive, they destroy her older sister, Kerrin. Although she struggles with her mother's faith, Marget eventually finds hope in family and in the awareness that it is "not possible to go on utterly alone," but her sister reveals the extreme consequences of a failure in family connection and social structure. Selfish and erratic, Kerrin lacks the ability to sympathize with others, which is a violation of traditional feminine sensibilities. It prevents her from emotionally or socially connecting with her family, and she further transgresses sentimental gender roles by protesting her limited ability to make economic decisions that affect the family or participate in traditionally masculine activities. Rather than the locked-away "madwoman in the attic," Kerrin is the "madwoman on the farm," descending into depression, insanity, and eventual suicide. Her presence in the story represents a stunted consciousness and helps create an anti-bildungsroman that contrasts with Marget's emotional and intellectual development: Kerrin willfully fights against the social forces in which she is entrapped, spiraling downward in a cycle of mental and emotional decline from which her family cannot save her.

Described as Marget's opposite physically and temperamentally, Kerrin is "beautiful in a dark, odd way... with brown cold skin... wild colty eyes" and vibrant red hair (55). While Marget is the calm, reflective narrator throughout the novel, Kerrin is frequently compared to an animal, heightening the sense of unpredictability and danger that surrounds her: "She did things sudden and wildly, or not at all, and ate sometimes like a dog starved out and savage, chewing and mumbling, and at other times would only pick at her food and stare out the window while Merle and I ate patiently all that was put in front of us. She'd sleep at odd times and hours, stretched out like a lynx in the sun, and creep out of the house at night to wander around in the marshes" (24). Kerrin is unchecked and uncontrollable, straining against convention and particularly vulnerable to the tightening strictures of the family's economic stresses.

Kerrin frequently lashes out at her family, particularly her sisters, "always making scenes" and is quick to separate herself from them (11). Even though she is fast to take offense at any sense of wrongdoing, Marget suspects that "she wanted to feel accused of dark and secret things" and chooses her words carefully, "embarrassed and half-afraid of what she might do to me" (11, 12). Kerrin's fights with her family make it hard for them to connect with her, and they feel a sense of relief when she chooses to eat her meals alone. Her presence creates constant tension: "Even when she was quiet or reading, I could never find rest where Kerrin was. None of us could.... No matter in what sort of mood she was—and there were times when Kerrin was almost fiercely happy and kind—the tautness was never gone, the fear of what she might say or do" (40–41). Although Marget and Merle are close and loving with each other and would like to connect to their sister, her outbursts push them at times to darker feelings. Kerrin would "slam a door somewhere while we pretended not to hear and would go on with what we did, only sick and drawn inside with hate" (16). Because Kerrin works as a teacher, the family experiences some relief during the school year, but Marget finds herself dreading "the thought of her being home all day" once summer break begins: "It seemed to me even then ... [t]hat there was something more inerasably wrong with her than just a fierce selfishness and discontent" (39).

Although Marget repeatedly hints at madness as she reflects on Kerrin's angry, erratic behavior, there are many indications that Kerrin feels utterly stifled by her life, which could also result in many of the actions that worry her sister. She "carried the root of her unrest with her ... a poisoned thing that wasted its strength in pushing down here and there, and found only a shallow soil or one full of rocks wherever planted" (45–46). Kerrin actively protests against her status as a woman, repeatedly frustrated and angered by her father's refusal to allow her to do masculine work. Arnold scornfully ignores her opinion about which crops they should grow; her contributions to the labor of the daily farmwork are unacknowledged until she neglects those tasks. Further, Kerrin attempts to impress her father on his birthday by giving him a knife and throwing it accurately at a target. However, when she surprises her father by demonstrating her skill, he is so enraged that he knocks the knife from her hand, causing it to fatally wound the family dog. Kerrin continually pushes at the boundaries of acceptable female behavior, and her rage and unpredictability are neither understood by her family nor openly addressed. Kerrin is silenced by her family, in turns ignored or repressed, with disastrous results.

It is not just her family who is grateful that Kerrin is hired to teach at the county school; Kerrin enjoys the work and for a time is content instructing the children: "She made a good teacher, good because she understood all those lumpy children in so far as any but God could understand them, I guess, and held them all to her with a kind of hard leniency and discipline. She succeeded because she really cared about them" (41). But even Kerrin's fondness for her students indicates a dissatisfaction with the gender roles that restrict her own life. Kerrin "liked the boys better because their faces were not so stupid and their minds clicked faster," but the "girls were already vacant wives, she said,—not stolid, their tongues slapping around like wheels, but already bounded tight with convention" (42). Kerrin associates the boys with quick thinking, being free to explore and not limited by the expectation of marriage or conventional roles, unlike the girls, who reflect her own limited options.

But eventually, Kerrin's ability to distract herself with teaching comes to an end. Returning to school no longer soothes her, and she "seemed uncertain of what she wanted, furious and balked that she could not reach or do things of which she had no clear idea herself" (174). Concerned about her increasing restlessness, Marget delivers a message to the school and discovers that Kerrin is no longer teaching well. Kerrin is later dismissed because Willa insists that Marget report to the school board that Kerrin isn't "well or able to teach the children any more," knowing that "[they'd] have to take the blame in the end" (183). Kerrin, thus, loses her position largely because of her family, and they try to endure Kerrin's rage "when she came home confused with anger and humiliation" (184). Kerrin accuses Marget of reporting her and intending to take the job herself and refuses—or is unable to bring herself—to go back to working on the farm: "What we asked her to do we could have done ourselves with less time and worry.... [T]here was so much still to do and we could not trust her even to haul the water. It was hard to see her around because of feeling pity; she looked like a thing scratched down to bone, moved by a kind of sourceless energy, not of her own strength any more" (184–85). With nowhere to direct her energies and with no options, Kerrin becomes increasingly unanchored.

Although Kerrin's frustration and lack of agency cause her to withdraw from her family, widening the silence between them, she ironically appears to attempt to resolve her fears and frustration by falling in love, which would presumably result in the traditional role that she has continued to resist—that of wife and eventually mother. While it is possible Marget misinterprets her sister's behavior by evaluating it through her own traditional perspective, Kerrin appears to hover outside the church doors on a family visit "hoping some fellow would speak to her" (135), and she eventually develops an unrequited obsession with Grant Koven.

Marget speculates that Kerrin's desire is that of possession—Kerrin "wanted him more than anything else she had ever snatched at. Because he was tangible, I suppose" (107). Marget herself has also fallen in love with Grant, but because Grant has fallen in love with Merle—who never returns his affection—no one establishes a complete affectional or marital relationship. Because of her own feelings for Grant, and because she fears and suspects Kerrin, Marget views Kerrin's love as less real than her own, based in the selfish competitiveness she has always shown her sisters.

However, Kerrin's attempts to connect with members of the church and her "snatches" at Grant stem from a desperate need to connect with others. Grant offers Kerrin the possibility of recognition, someone who loves and sees her true self: "[S]he wanted love,—not anything we could give her, frugal and spinsterly, nor Father's (having long ago stopped even hoping for it), but some man's love in which she could see this image she had of herself reflected and thus becoming half-true" (46). When her father ignores her planting advice, Kerrin seeks validation from Grant, although she fails to win it from him. She "waited for Grant to say she was right, but he only answered something about hill country and no rain.... She sat near him in a kind of hungry and yet hesitating way, but he didn't move or turn toward her, only stared off after Dad" (168–69). Kerrin falls for Grant because he has the potential to acknowledge her within her family circle, particularly because he is accepted as an insider and yet is not a blood relative. She fights for his attention and his affection because she is lonely and because Grant provides her with the opportunity to resolve her marginalized position by redefining and validating her as a member of the family to which she cannot connect on her own.

Johnson draws Kerrin's suicide as inevitable. She is unable to win Grant's affection, making a "fool" of herself in front of him and becoming an object of scorn to her sisters. Grant not only doesn't love her, but he shifts from liking Kerrin to politely tolerating her presence. After her mother is fatally burned fighting the wildfire, Kerrin loses the only person in the family who treats her with sympathy and affection. The depth of this loss is foreshadowed when Kerrin, who wanders outdoors at night, alerts the family of the impending danger but "suddenly—and strangely, for her—she snatched at Mother and tried to hold her back," begging her not to go (190). In the aftermath of the fire, Kerrin is unable to escape the forces that have destroyed her sense of self, behaving as though "the fire had got inside her" (196). She attempts to kiss Grant—her only overt gesture of seduction—but is interrupted by Arnold. The reactions of the two men—Grant swiftly pulls away and her father angrily demands to know what is going on—mark Kerrin's violation of her acceptable social role and then abruptly return her to it. Responding with desperate rage, Kerrin later hurls a knife at her father—paralleling the scene of the ruined birthday dinner—misses, and grabs the knife off the ground as she runs away.

In these tumultuous moments, Kerrin not only lashes out but also reaches the end of her tolerance for her restricted life. She recognizes that Grant will never love her and is driven to madness—or further into madness—by the depth of her difference. It is her family's failure to see her and the crushing pressure of their silence that destroys any possibility for her survival; her death becomes a blessing for them all: "There was no place for her. . . . She never belonged with us, and maybe there is no place on earth for people like her" (199–200). Later, Marget and Grant find Kerrin, who has died after cutting her wrists, on the ground behind the sheep barn, one arm resting in the water trough, "staining the shallow water" (200). Though Arnold mourns his daughter, he does not comprehend her death, finding himself shocked by this last act of "raw, unnatural" willfulness, doing "a thing a girl had no right to do" (201). Yet that final image of Kerrin remains, a blood offering that serves as both a symbol of the unforgiving natural cycle against which her family has pitted their entire lives and the embodied personal cost of her individual struggle against overwhelming forces.

Kerrin's death at first seems strikingly anti-sentimental because Marget's presentation seems harsh, lacking sympathy for Kerrin's pain and essentially determining that her death may have been a good thing because it ended her suffering. However, Kerrin's death offers an example of the consequences of failed sympathy. If sentimentalism draws family boundaries by including members through affectional bonds, what happens when sympathy fails and a member of the family is excluded? In *Now in November*, Johnson demonstrates that the magnitude of such a failure is extreme suffering and death. It is possible to read this outcome as a critique of women's restrictive social roles as well as a commentary on the risks of passive or ineffective sentimentalism. Prefiguring Toni Morrison's critique of the failures of sympathy in *Beloved*, Johnson complicates her depiction of proletarian sentimentalism by acknowledging that sometimes sympathy fails. *Now in November* argues that middle-class ideologies and capitalist mythologies have left little room for the realities of working-class lives. As a representative of the working-class consciousness, Marget's two options appear to be radical action or further suffering and death. Furthermore, Kerrin's death symbolically feeds into the natural, capitalist cycle, so Johnson observes that additional failures to acknowledge working-class suffering and sympathetically include them in the American national family will contribute to the destruction of working-class families and a further breakdown of American society.

Ultimately, Johnson's novel argues for the development of a radical awareness through sentimental sympathy, despite her warnings about the potential risks of sympathetic failures. Both Johnson and Lumpkin redraw traditionally masculine spaces as connected to domestic and feminized spaces through sentimental appropriation, showing the ways in which both the spaces and the people are interconnected by affectional bonds. They extend the definition of the family to show that families are linked within a larger working-class family that shares feelings, vulnerability, and desires with one another as well as with the middle class. Steinbeck, as I show in the next chapter, also appropriates sentimentalism to extend the boundaries of the family and to argue for a larger, humanist perspective that includes working-class families in the American national family. Like Lumpkin and Johnson, he connects masculine spaces to the domestic, but rather than argue that women occupy and are affected by male spaces, he argues that men occupy and are affected by traditionally feminized spaces and caretaking roles.

4 / Caretaking, Domesticity, and Gender in John Steinbeck's *The Grapes of Wrath*: "His Home Is Not the Land"

> *In the evening a strange thing happened: the twenty families became one family, the children were the children of all. The loss of home became one loss, and the golden time in the West was one dream.*
> —JOHN STEINBECK, THE GRAPES OF WRATH (193)

John Steinbeck is arguably the best-known proletarian author of the twentieth century. The 1962 Nobel laureate's novels about the Depression era have remained a cultural touchstone for generations of readers, and the current economic downturn has renewed interest in his work among the general public. Television news pundits make frequent references to *The Grapes of Wrath*, his 1939 Pulitzer Prize–winning novel, when they discuss the current housing crisis and the families who suffer foreclosure, while a farm policy group argues that the ongoing Texas drought could herald the next Dust Bowl and headlines its materials with the question: "The Grapes of Wrath . . . Part II?" (The Hand That Feeds U.S., n.d.). In 2009, Chris McGreal, writing for the United Kingdom's *Guardian* newspaper, chronicled his journey across the United States re-creating "John Steinbeck's famous fictional journey to reveal life in the worst economic crisis since the Great Depression" as part of a series titled "*The Grapes of Wrath* Revisited: A Modern-Day Road Trip through John Steinbeck's Fiction to Barack Obama's Reality." In 2011, BBC reporter Paul Mason also chose to re-create the Joads' journey for his article, "In Steinbeck's Footsteps: America's Middle-Class Underclass." Editorialists have frequently used comparisons to and quotations from *The Grapes of Wrath* when assessing corporate greed and labor exploitation, for example, when taking Amazon to task for terrible work conditions in its warehouses (Klein) or covering the Occupy Wall Street protests that have spread across the nation (Osborne). Revivals of the stage adaptation of the novel were scheduled in California, Colorado, Ohio, Michigan,

New Jersey, and New York throughout 2012, and Ellen Gibson reports in *Business Week* that Netflix rentals of the film adaption have been on the rise since 2008.

It is worth noting that in the midst of these correlations between today's economic crisis and the Depression-era struggles that prompted Steinbeck and other authors to write dark, angry, and moving portrayals of a broken social system, the vast majority of comparisons are to *The Grapes of Wrath* and not to Steinbeck's other novels. It isn't the only book he wrote about the Depression. Indeed, while the stage adaption for *Of Mice and Men* (1937) has enjoyed a revival in recent years, Steinbeck also wrote *Tortilla Flat* (1935), *In Dubious Battle* (1936), and *Cannery Row* (1945), about strikes, joblessness, economic struggle, and working-class misery. Yet none of these novels has entered the popular lexicon or captured the American imagination in defining representations of the working class to the degree of *The Grapes of Wrath*. One reason for the dominance of this particular novel, I argue, is its departure from the militant Marxism on display in "typical" proletarian texts like *In Dubious Battle*. Instead, Steinbeck's humanist philosophy emerges as he adapts portrayals of the working class with sentimentalism. Signaling an interest in the domestic with his rendering of male caregiving and domestic longing in *Of Mice and Men*, Steinbeck effectively combines a stark proletarian critique of a wholesale, nationwide socioeconomic system with this domestic yearning in *The Grapes of Wrath*. By transforming the unforgiving American landscape into an intimate and familiar homescape, Steinbeck strikes a chord with his readers, engendering sympathy for the struggles of an Othered working class whose families reflect our own. By drawing the Joads as an "Everyfamily," Steinbeck crosses class boundaries to create sympathy for the working class and promotes a humanist argument for collective caretaking and survival. He is also able to push at the traditional definitions of the spaces—originally defined by sentimentalism—in which caregiving occurs as well as of who is responsible for that care.

Steinbeck grew up in Salinas, California, a beautiful and fertile part of the state. His father was at various times a businessman, accountant, and manager, and his mother was a former teacher. Although his middle-class family was not wealthy, they were prominent in the social circles of their small town. Both of Steinbeck's parents were heavily involved in community activities; his father was a member of the Masons, and his mother was a member of Eastern Star, a spiritually based fraternal organization that promotes charity, truth, and loving kindness. An aspiring writer, Steinbeck began producing stories and poems in high school. He enrolled in Stanford in 1919, signing up for courses in classical and British literature, creative writing, and some sciences. Although writing continued to be an obsession for him, Steinbeck eventually left Stanford without taking a degree and began working various jobs in factories and on company ranches throughout California. He briefly moved to New York City to work in construction and as a newspaper reporter, but he returned to California to find more time for writing and leisure. He married Carol Henning in 1930, and they moved into the Steinbeck family's summer cottage in Pacific Grove. She supported them both while he continued writing and also helped him edit and shape his early work, including the novel that eventually became *The Grapes of Wrath*.

Steinbeck's interest in the plight of migrant workers and the working class developed from his experiences laboring in factories and farms while he supported himself during and after college. He worked closely "with migrants and bindlestiffs.... Those relationships, coupled with an early sympathy for the weak and defenseless, deepened his empathy for workers, the disenfranchised, the lonely and dislocated, an empathy that is characteristic in his work" (Shillinglaw, "Biography"). Steinbeck's interest in migrant life resulted in his first successful novel, *Tortilla Flat*, and he continued to be drawn to working-class struggle as a subject for his work. He was attracted to the growing influence of proletarianism, but, according to Susan Shillinglaw, he was turned off by the zealotry of the local John Reed Clubs he attended. As evidenced by the criticism of both greedy factory owners and ruthless strike organizers in his most radical strike novel, *In Dubious Battle*, Steinbeck sought to offer a more human perspective on the people at the heart of the class struggle.

Steinbeck—like many other proletarian authors with middle-class backgrounds and educations—not only worked in temporary factory and agricultural jobs, either to support a writing career or gain a sense of the actual "on the ground" experiences of the working class, but he also wrote nonfiction reportage about working-class conditions. He was commissioned by the *San Francisco Chronicle* in 1936 to write articles on migrant farmworkers. Steinbeck also accompanied photographer Horace Bristol as he traveled to California labor camps in the winter of 1937 for a proposed picture book for *Life* magazine on dust bowl migrants.

Having already written a powerful strike novel that emphasizes factory labor conditions, the masculine realm of the proletarian worker, and the exploitation and violence of that experience, Steinbeck needed a new way to convey the suffering and struggle he witnessed among migrant families. According to Bristol, it was the photographic journey that gave Steinbeck the idea to write his iconic novel of migrant experience: "Envisioning a photo-essay for *Life*, he contacted Steinbeck who agreed to accompany him to the camps. But *Life* turned down the idea because it was 'too far away' and 'not important enough,' Bristol said. He called *Fortune* and got a positive response, but Steinbeck didn't like the prospect of working for such 'a capitalistic publication.' Steinbeck eventually decided the story was worth much more than a magazine piece; he would write an entire novel" (Muchnic, "Travels"). Unbeknownst to Bristol, however, Steinbeck had been working on *The Grapes of Wrath* prior to visiting the camps. He left their joint project in May 1938 to complete the final drafts. While traveling together, Bristol and Steinbeck took pictures and spoke with men, women, and children. Many of the images are in makeshift camps and capture intimate moments, such as "Rose of Sharon, 1938" (originally titled "Nursing Mother in Camp, near Visalia, Tulare County, California, 1938"), which depicts a young woman breastfeeding her infant. The J. Paul Getty Museum, which hosted an exhibit of Bristol's work in 2002–3, records that Bristol, in describing their reaction to the moment this photograph was taken, stated, "[B]oth Steinbeck and I felt it represented a Madonna figure, with the newborn baby at its mother's swelling breasts, a faint suggestion of proud fatherhood in the background legs and hand" ("The Grapes of Wrath").

Although Bristol's photographs were never published in the book he envisioned, some of his images were published in articles that supported the authenticity of Steinbeck's novel. After *The Grapes of Wrath* and its film version had gained popularity, Bristol's photographs were published in two articles in *Life*. In a June 1939 photo-essay titled "'The Grapes of Wrath': John Steinbeck Writes a Major Novel about Western Migrants," nine Bristol photographs illustrated "truths" described in the book, with excerpts from the novel underneath each image as well as a few captions written specifically for the article. Bristol's images were not only used as reference material while casting and costuming the film adaptation, but in 1940 one of the articles paired movie stills with Bristol's photographs to assert the film's authenticity. As Samantha Baskind observes, both *Life* articles "emphasize that the photographs prove the facts of the book and the movie ... providing the necessary proof that Steinbeck's book was an accurate account of migrant life" ("'True' Story," 42).[1]

While proletarian women writers sought legitimacy in a literary world dominated by male intellectuals and turned to sentimentalism in order to assert a female voice into the expression of revolutionary ideas, Steinbeck was an established author whose voice of authority was assumed and accepted. Steinbeck, however, needed a way to move beyond the circumscribed domains of masculinity that dictated a form of realism and authenticity that drew its source from action, violence, and the public sphere. Raised by parents who embraced a humanist philosophy, whose own sympathies were developed by exposure to working-class struggle, Steinbeck needed a way to speak in a broader emotional tenor for the working class. Likely influenced by the women writers who came before him, Steinbeck not only expanded the boundaries of the domestic novel by including men but also changed the space of the domestic. He also expanded the boundaries of proletarian sentimentalism by offering a new model of the workingman of feeling. By embodying and giving voice to workers who had previously been defined more by their actions than by their feelings, Steinbeck developed sympathy for a new kind of family and a new kind of man. Just as Bristol's photographs captured the intimacy, longing, suffering, and humanity of people who are so often unseen and forgotten, Steinbeck sought to write the family that would suffer in a way recognizable to every family, no matter to what class they belonged.

Beyond Ma Joad: Redefining Caretaking and Its Spaces

Earlier critiques of gender and domesticity in *The Grapes of Wrath* have tended to focus on Steinbeck's incorporation of Robert Briffault's theories of matriarchal family structures or to critique Steinbeck's portrayal of Ma Joad's power as one-dimensional and limited to the private realm of maternal care and domestic duty. Assessments of gender in *The Grapes of Wrath* tend to maintain traditional separations between public/private spaces and gendered relationships to them, treating such spaces in the text as intact categories intensified by the economic circumstances of the 1930s.[2] However, much of the novel complicates such a dichotomy by collapsing traditional separations of public/private space. It also alters gendered relationships to those spaces, revising the concept of the domestic sphere. Though Steinbeck builds upon traditional patriarchal and matriarchal models, *The Grapes of Wrath* breaks down the walls of the domestic sphere by linking the daily work of the private and public, creating multiple gendered domesticities, and showing that human caretaking—the necessary force for survival in an age when patriarchal, capitalist individualism has failed—crosses gendered boundaries.

Steinbeck does not appear to be trying to rewrite gender roles or shift power along the binary to privilege women over men and create a matriarchal utopia. After all, at the close of the novel, Tom Joad remains a heroic figure of masculine independence, leadership, and self-sacrifice. Rose of Sharon is portrayed as the inheritor of Ma Joad's matriarchal wisdom and power, able to give restorative life to an ill man, whose "lips came together" as she "smiled mysteriously" with the hint of sexual promise (455). Yet Steinbeck complicates a depiction of Rose of Sharon as a coming-of-age matriarch whose powers are located in traditional feminine and maternal roles: she gives birth to a stillborn baby, and her "mysterious" smile holds as much threat as it does allure. Steinbeck is writing beyond conventional forms of masculinity/femininity and the spaces that have traditionally defined them. As Richard Astro, Warren Motley, and Nellie McKay have pointed out, in writing *The Grapes of Wrath* Steinbeck was influenced by anthropologist Robert Briffault's theories on the matriarchal origins of society, the sometimes devastating effects of patriarchal individualism, and the potentially restorative effects of matriarchal collectivism and communal care.[3] Motley has examined Ma Joad's role as a matriarchal leader and "goddess" figure associated with the rhythms of nature ("From Patriarchy to Matriarchy," 405)—a woman who promotes a new order of humanism and collective concern. McKay, however, critiques the association between women's supposed "natural" domesticity and the ways that such views limit women's social agency to the roles of "happy-wife-and-motherdom," observing that Steinbeck's expansion of Ma Joad's social power does not "extend to an awareness of women's lives and identities beyond the domestic sphere, other than that which has a direct relationship on the survival of the family" ("Happy[?]-Wife," 66).

Steinbeck indeed dramatizes the centrality and power of Ma Joad's caretaking role. However, in *The Grapes of Wrath*, multiple characters engage in multiple forms of caretaking, redefining definitions of caretaking and redefining the spaces in which that caretaking occurs. Steinbeck's expansion of Ma Joad's power, of caretaking, and of the domestic thus extends beyond re-visioning society as a matriarchal culture or limiting women's power to mothering roles. Similarly, as Steinbeck expands the domestic sphere, he also extends the boundaries of "family" to individuals with whom the Joads interact and assist (when they can often least afford to) but who are not actually related to them. Thus, the actions of the Joad family and the education and expansion of caretaking become a microcosm for the kind of social caretaking that Steinbeck envisions as necessary for human survival in a capitalist society in which the emphasis has previously (and harmfully) been individual greed and self-advancement.

Steinbeck's consideration of precapitalist matriarchal forms of power led him to consider the interconnectedness of the domestic and the public realms as well as the power dynamics inscribed in gender. Thus, while Steinbeck may not have been a proto-feminist able to envision women's power beyond forms of caretaking, he seems to be working against the limitations inherent in gender binaries and considering the ways in which caretaking and the domestic sphere may be expanded beyond the feminine and private and into the realm of the public, patriarchal world. In this way, Steinbeck questions what it means to be a man when traditional, patriarchal methods of defining manhood are unavailable. Similarly, he broadens definitions of womanhood and matriarchy by extending forms of caretaking beyond the confines of the family and domestic ritual. In *The Grapes of Wrath*, Steinbeck establishes the importance of domestic space in the lives of both men and women, supporting his overarching theme of human connection as being necessary for collective survival.

From the Home to the Open Road: Expanding the Sentimental Domestic Tradition

For a text so focused on a critique of capitalism and its devastating effects on those most vulnerable to market forces, much of the novel's action takes place in private, domestic spaces. Through their migration west, the Joads re-create a home site in every place that they stop, literally moving the domestic scene across the landscape of the country. Their efforts enmesh the domestic with their search for work and economic security. To emphasize the difficulty of finding employment, only two scenes of the Joads at work occur in the text. Steinbeck instead offers detailed portrayals of the daily domestic work of packing, setting up, cleaning, cooking, and maintaining campsites, as well as preserving the family's meager resources. By connecting the Joads' domestic world with their public world, Steinbeck—much like women proletarian writers Meridel Le Sueur, Tillie Lerner Olsen, and Grace Lumpkin, to name a few[4]—reveals the often hidden domestic labor that burdens working-class women. However, by transforming Ma Joad's position within the family hierarchy, Steinbeck places more value on domestic work, the domestic space in which the work occurs, and the women who engage in that work.

Motley argues that in placing this value on domestic work, Steinbeck "follows Briffault's argument that economically productive labor is a woman's source of power" ("From Patriarchy to Matriarchy," 406). Motley and Briffault identify women's social power as that generated by their "productive" domestic labor. This analysis of power and domestic labor, however, requires further examination because of the gendered classification of that social power and the socially proscribed sites of work. As McKay points out, the traditionally "powerful" nurturing roles of wife and mother prohibit women from access to masculine forms of power by limiting them to caretaking positions that serve and support the men who engage in public labor outside the home.

Steinbeck's text, with its roots in both sentimentalism and literary realism, reveals a struggle to navigate the idealized humanism promoted by Briffault's matriarchal theories and the ensuing alteration of gender roles and gendered forms of power. With the expansion of domestic space, Steinbeck must account for the shift in relationships that represent and influence individual identity, gender identity, and community identity. Because of traditional associations among masculinity, labor, and the land, Steinbeck's extension of domestic space (in the context of 1930s social upheaval) complicates his characters' readings of their own identities. As the novel progresses, the Joads are forced to challenge traditional gender roles in order to maintain the family in the midst of economic hardships.

Although *The Grapes of Wrath* is not a domestic novel in a traditional sense,[5] its focus on the home and on Ma Joad's ability to maintain her family both materially and emotionally may be read in view of the political and social aims of that genre. Nancy Armstrong argues that authors of earlier domestic fiction sought to represent human value in terms outside of available politicized literary discourse and thus represented "an individual's value in terms of his, but more often in terms of *her*, essential qualities of mind" ("Introduction," 622). Domestic fiction, according to Armstrong, "seized the authority to say what was female . . . in order to contest the reigning notion of kinship relations that attached most power and privilege to certain family lines" (623). Novels such as Emily Brontë's *Wuthering Heights* (1847), Charlotte Brontë's *Jane Eyre* (1847), and William Makepeace Thackeray's *Vanity Fair* (1848) brought order to social relationships by subordinating all social differences "to those based on gender." By representing psychological motives such as emotional connection, individual desire, and moral value, they countered prevailing social hierarchies and "exalted the domestic woman over and above her aristocratic counterpart.... [T]he female was the figure ... on whom depended the outcome of the struggle among competing ideologies."

The domestic novel's impact should not be underestimated, for as it progressed it "helped to formulate the ordered space we now recognize as the household, made that space totally functional, and used it as the context for representing normal behavior" (637). Further, nineteenth-century sentimental fiction in the United States to which *The Grapes of Wrath* has already been linked draws from this tradition. B. R. McElderry Jr., in his essay "*The Grapes of Wrath*: In the Light of Modern Critical Theory," is untroubled by sentimentality in the novel, writing that it "is vigorously sympathetic to the 'open' society" and that it "skillfully communicates attitudes of a relatively inarticulate group or type.... Sentimentality may impair, but does not cancel, its value" (313). Numerous critics have alternately praised and panned sentimentality in the text, but the exchange grew a bit more involved with the traditions of sentimental literature after Leslie A. Fiedler denounced *The Grapes of Wrath* as "maudlin, sentimental, and overblown" ("Looking Back," 55). John Seelye defends the novel against Fiedler's charges by comparing *The Grapes of Wrath* to *Uncle Tom's Cabin*, declaring Steinbeck's novel "the greatest sentimental novel of protest of the twentieth century" ("Come Back," 13).

Jane Tompkins, Shirley Samuels, and Nina Baym argue that, like domestic fiction, sentimental fiction uses gendered discourse to enact new political and cultural ideologies, and Ann Romines examines the significance of what she terms the "domestic ritual" of housework in such novels. Whereas nineteenth-century literature by men gave domestic work "almost no serious consideration," Romines argues that women writers used portrayals of sentimental heroines who engage in the habits of housework, or "domestic ritual," to push "back confusion daily, to create [their] own domestic sphere," and to participate "in an enterprise connected with the continuity of a common culture and the triumph of human values over natural process" (*Home Plot*, 10, 13). Similarly, women writers of the 1930s frequently used domestic ritual or focused on domestic scenes and female protagonists in their social protest writing. The presentation of domestic life allowed these writers to show working-class women's connection with common (i.e., middle-class) culture and to emphasize working-class female struggles for survival against the chaos of the capitalist system. In developing shared domestic sympathies, and by contrasting the daily work of the domestic with the ideology of "home," women proletarian writers could argue for "the triumph of human values over natural process" or reveal the human tragedy created by a capitalist system that thwarts triumph at every turn. Tillie Lerner Olsen and Josephine Johnson are two such authors who focus simultaneously on class and gender concerns, undermining classic capitalist mythologies through the individualized experiences of female protagonists.

Olsen, in her unfinished novel *Yonnondio: From the Thirties*, not only reveals "poverty's arithmetic" and the Holbrook family's desperate attempts to survive on Jim's intermittent, meager salary, but she also carefully parallels work done in the home with work done in the farm and factory (23). In one memorable scene, Anna Holbrook cans peaches in the kitchen and worries over her children's heat-stroke symptoms when the narration cuts to the slaughterhouse, where conditions are hellish and a boiler explodes, scalding workers—particularly women: "[T]he main steam pipe breaks open. . . . Peg and Andra and Philomena and Cleola directly underneath fall and writhe in their crinkling skins, their sudden juices" (181). The description of the accident not only evokes the appalling conditions of the slaughterhouse, but the "crinkling skins" and "sudden juices" also reference the peaches Anna is canning, imparting weight, danger, and a heightened sense of desperation to her labor. Johnson's novel, *Now in November*, is set on a mortgaged midwestern farm, where the entire Haldmarne family must work together for survival. The family's three daughters share in the constant toil of both farm and home, and each female pays a high personal price for the failure of traditional patriarchal protections—without ownership of the land, without financial security, without marriage, there is no safety for them or for the family itself. The mother is fatally burned fighting a field fire, the oldest daughter goes mad and commits suicide, and the two youngest daughters, Marget and Merle, shoulder the burdens of the entire family, as Marget describes: "I saw Father with awful clearness as he would be soon. Old and querulous and able only to shell beans in the sun. And I saw how the debt would be Merle's and mine to carry by ourselves—how many years I do not know, but for a long and uncounted time" (230).

While woman proletarian writers have represented women's "hidden" domestic work to analyze the influence of public space on private home life, to equate women's work with industrial or agricultural work, or to break down capitalist mythologies, Steinbeck in *The Grapes of Wrath* draws from multiple domestic and sentimental traditions, reinvesting domesticity with symbolic matriarchal power and the ability to reinforce human connection. Thus, in the social and political upheaval of the 1930s, Steinbeck draws again upon the female figure and the domestic realm to redefine human value and enact the working-class struggle. To draw his characters realistically and argue for their humanity, Steinbeck essentializes human difference to gender and seeks to define social constructs, thereby working against the dehumanizing forces of capitalist "machines" that perpetuate the "causes" leading to social inequality and unrest (32, 150).

The Constant Value of Domesticity

"And all of them were caught in something larger than themselves," Steinbeck writes of the landowners evicting their tenants, though the idea expands to encompass the men and women evicted (31). The owners of the land "take no responsibility for the banks or the companies because they were men and slaves" and "the banks were machines and masters all at the same time" (32). In a world where men and masculinity are defined by their labor and land ownership, to take both away is to thrust men into more than just economic crisis—it is to remove the signifiers of masculinity, the most basic premise of their identities. "Grampa took up the land, and he had to kill the Indians and drive them away. . . . [I]t's our land. We measured it and broke it up. We were born on it, and we got killed on it, died on it. Even if it's no good, it's still ours. That's what makes it ours—being born on it, working it, dying on it" (33). They don't just own the land; owning the land is defined by their lives just as it helps to define their lives.

All men are subject to the overwhelming forces of the capitalist bank, and yet "the bank is something more than men" (33). For Steinbeck, when masculinity falters, femininity remains steady, necessary for everyone's survival. In the aftermath of the owners' visit, in the midst of male confusion, the women know intuitively that confusion can turn to aggression, for "a man so hurt and so perplexed may turn in anger, even on people he loves" (34). The women—practical and forward-thinking—question the men about the future, but receiving no answer, they retreat with the children to the work of the house. While the men have been failed by the market, failed by the public realm, and failed by capitalist forces, the domestic realm is the constant to which Steinbeck returns. There, the women continue with the ongoing work of the household and the ceaseless labor of survival larger than any suffering of the self.

Steinbeck's turn to the domestic allows him to explore the human consequences of a broken socioeconomic system, linking *The Grapes of Wrath* to traditions in women's writing that reveal ideologies embedded in representations of the life of the home. Jennifer Haytock, in her examination of modern war and domestic novels, observes that such texts offer insight far beyond their surface concerns: "Domestic writing is more than a private record of an individual woman's life in her home; it is the representation of the power dynamics and social inscriptions that structure the life of the home, for women and for men" (*At Home*, xiii). For Steinbeck, too, the revolutionary power of the domestic sphere is symbolic of essential human value and social progressivism. However, while Steinbeck achieves his humanist presentation by converting public space to domestic space and transforming traditional gender roles, he fails to break the limitations of gendered divisions of power and the discourse of domestic ideals.

The Grapes of Wrath's opening scenes conflate natural, agricultural, and domestic elements, cutting across the ideological and physical barriers that define them as separate. The crop-killing dust that "settled on the corn, piled up on the tops of fence posts, piled up on the wires . . . blanketed the weeds and trees" draws attention to the natural world and its associations with agricultural production and public labor (3). But this dust also invades homes where men and women "huddled," though houses "were shut tight, and cloth wedged around doors and windows. . . . [I]t settled like pollen on the chairs and tables, on the dishes. The people brushed it from their shoulders." The apocalyptic dust chokes the crops outside and menaces the people who have sought shelter together in houses, showing that everyone takes refuge in the home—regardless of gender—but that this space is vulnerable to the same forces that threaten to destroy both their land and their economic security. Thus, Steinbeck's all-pervading dust hints at the fragility of social, ideological, and gendered barriers that define these spaces as separate and unconnected. The first chapter's final scenes depict a return to gendered divisions of labor, family role, and emotional (dis)connection as Steinbeck reinforces his critique of the instability of social ideologies that define men and women through separated public and private spaces.

In these early pages, men, women, and children occupy specific spaces; they observe each other to determine appropriate reactions to tragedy. Men "stood by their fences and looked at the ruined corn," women "came out of the houses to stand beside their men" and looked at the men's faces, while children "stood near by, drawing figures in the dust with bare toes," sending "exploring senses out to see whether men and women would break" (3). Steinbeck concludes the opening chapter by placing these anonymous figures in separated, gendered spaces: "The women went into the houses to their work, and the children began to play.... The men sat in the doorways of their houses; their hands were busy with sticks and little rocks. The men sat still—thinking—figuring" (4). This placement prefigures the scene in chapter 5 in which men, women, and children react to the news that the owners will evict them from their land. The women return to the home, the children return to play in the yard, and the men return to "squatting in the dust" (35). However, Steinbeck prepares the reader for a new understanding of domestic space through the Joads' journey to follow with his placement of these symbolic figures. The first chapter's closing image of the men sitting in the doorways of their homes fidgeting with "sticks and little rocks" gestures at their transitional status. The literal movement of the men from agricultural and natural space toward domestic space hints at the failure of traditional patriarchal protections and at the refuge offered by both matriarchal nurturing and the constant value of domestic space.

It is the home space that Tom Joad seeks at the beginning of the novel when he is released from prison, meets up with Reverend Jim Casy, and heads toward the former Joad homestead. Though many readers focus on the Christlike, self-sacrificial journeys of these two men, it is important to observe the spaces that Steinbeck creates around them. Tom has just been released from the McAlester correctional facility, which he describes as a de facto home and domestic space where "[y]ou eat regular, an' get clean clothes, and there's places to take a bath" (26). Although the all-male facility does not meet the sexual needs of the incarcerated men—prompting Tom's wry remark that it "[m]akes it hard not havin' no women"—the domestic certainties of McAlester are so appealing that Tom tells of a man who deliberately violates parole in order to be returned to prison: "Says he come back where they got a few conveniences an' he eats regular. He says it makes him feel lonesome out there in the open havin' to think what to do next. So he stole a car an' come back."

Tom, however, believes he has a home and family to which he can go and thus, upon his parole, immediately travels to find it. But because this home has been displaced, Tom's journey becomes a quest for home. Not only does he share the expansion of domestic space that occurs as his family establishes temporary homes throughout their migratory travels, but he also seeks to recover the economic and emotional security of the domestic ideal. Tom's dream changes from the Joads' empty "unpainted house ... mashed at one corner ... pushed off its foundations so that it slumped at an angle, its blind front windows pointing at a spot of sky well above the horizon" to one in which he shares with Ma Joad "one a them white houses with orange trees all aroun'" (40, 99).

Similarly, Reverend Casy's journey is grounded in and influenced by the domestic. His first appearance in the novel as a wanderer sitting "on the ground, leaning against the trunk of the tree" connects him to nature and to the agricultural space that fails to provide men with work or security (18). Casy not only accompanies Tom to the abandoned Joad homestead and the temporary home the family occupies, but he asks the family members if he can join them on their venture to California. In so doing, Casy doesn't just ask if he can tag along or share the Joads' food supplies but requests a position within the family structure itself: "He knew the government of families, and he knew he had been taken into the family. Indeed his position was eminent, for Uncle John moved sideways, leaving space between Pa and himself for the preacher. Casy squatted down like the others, facing Grampa enthroned on the running board" (103). Thus, not only is room physically made for Casy in the masculine space of the family, but, like Tom's journey, his becomes the expanded domestic journey of the entire Joad family.

Steinbeck emphasizes that Casy's developing revolutionary consciousness is awakened in two primary domestic spaces: the Hooverville camp and the jailhouse. Casy first kicks a deputy to prevent him from attacking migrants in a Hooverville camp and then sacrifices himself to save Tom and his family from persecution: "Casy said softly, 'If you mess in this your whole fambly, all your folks, gonna get in trouble ... your ma and your pa, they'll get in trouble. Maybe they'll send Tom back to McAlester'" (266). When Tom is later reunited with Casy and discovers his involvement in the peach workers' strike, Casy describes his time in the jailhouse after his arrest as a pivotal moment in which he learns about other men's troubles and begins working on their behalf: "Jail house is a kinda funny place.... Here's me, been a-goin' into the wilderness like Jesus to try find out somepin. Almost got her sometimes, too. But it's in the jail house I really got her.... Great big ol' cell, an' she's full all a time. New guys come in, and guys go out. An' 'course I talked to all of 'em" (381). It is not alone in the wilderness as a Christlike, masculine wanderer but in jail that Casy's revolutionary consciousness wakens and that he finds the human connection he seeks throughout the novel. Despite its obvious negatives, the jailhouse represents a domestic ideal because of its emphasis on daily household concerns: regular beds, regular meals, regular baths, and the uninterrupted care of bodily needs. Because domestic work in a patriarchal system is traditionally women's work, an all-male domestic site becomes, for Steinbeck, a domestic ideal because the men experience having their needs taken care of without participating in the work behind the caretaking. This situation, then, leaves them with time to talk, develop, and connect. Both Tom and Casy experience this all-male domestic space as an opportunity for creating human bonds; unlike the house yards where anonymous men think alone and figure silently, the men in these all-male domestic sites have time and space to talk to each other and establish relationships that lead to unity and action.

Not Just for Men: Domesticity and Power

Steinbeck, however, is not just concerned with creating a new domestic ideal or inventing a masculine domestic realm. While the jailhouse presents an alternative location for idealized male connection, Steinbeck also acknowledges the domestic as a potentially revolutionary space reserved for, and run by, women. Furthermore, he presents the domestic as the universal experience connecting all human beings through the ceaseless work required to meet basic requirements for shelter and food, the need to maintain family units for survival, and the emotional connection developed through the domestic's emphasis on meeting the needs of others. Because their land and jobs have been lost, men who would leave the domestic now stay in it, relocating the center of the novel's action to this site. Men, who would leave their families and their houses to work fields, sell crops, move livestock, or perform other work, now either sit in yards or help their families pack meager possessions and set up camps as they migrate across the American landscape. The male Joads even sell the tools of their labor—horses, a wagon, and farming implements—while domestic items such as pans, dishes, and utensils are carefully saved for the trip ahead. Steinbeck, thus, not only transfers power to the domestic sphere as the sustaining force for the Joad family but also uses migration to compel the relocation of home sites across the entire country, transforming the landscape from one of agricultural and industrial opportunity to a series of domestic scenes. Focusing on the Joads' domestic life enables Steinbeck to draw them as a microcosm of the working-class family, subject to a machine of dehumanizing socioeconomic forces but urgent and relevant to a reader who sympathizes with their basic human plight.

As Motley rightly points out, Steinbeck's portrayal of Ma Joad and her domestic work differs from "classical accounts of the pioneer wife" and "does not take the diurnal chores and unending childbearing as signs of [her] oppression" ("From Patriarchy to Matriarchy," 406). However, while Motley reads these signs as Steinbeck's embrace of Briffault's argument that economically productive labor is a woman's source of power, Steinbeck's use of this labor must also be read in light of the female sentimental domestic tradition in its various forms. What is new about Steinbeck's use of the domestic is not that he ascribes female power and idealizes feminine strength within this particular—and as McKay notes, limited—realm. Instead, it is Steinbeck's expansion of the domestic sphere and the redefinition of this space through domestic work that is innovative and revealing. Rather than confine women to the home and circumscribe women's power to the confines of caretaking within the walls of the home, Steinbeck has removed the physical and metaphorical walls of the domestic sphere that confines and defines women. Steinbeck pushes at the limitations of domestic power, highlighting it not only as a primary force for human survival but also as a connecting force that allows an individual or a family unit to bond with another. Through the domestic, Steinbeck emphasizes this message of group caretaking—a moral responsibility to care for others and to expand the definition of "family" to include all members of the social group—as a necessary force for modern survival in the face of a failing capitalist system that emphasizes patriarchal individualism over collective care. Ma Joad's power increases and her influence grows as her world expands through the literal cross-country journey. The Joads not only establish temporary homes in multiple—usually un-walled—sites, but they also create connections with other families through these domestic spaces.

Ma Joad doubtless is the maternal "goddess" figure Motley and others have praised and criticized as sentimental, matriarchal, and highly feminized. In her first appearance, she cooks breakfast inside Uncle John's kitchen: providing food is one of her primary activities throughout the text. As Ann Romines observes in her study on domestic ritual in women's writing: "A woman who ... made effective ritual of her housekeeping was taking on godlike status, as she pushed back confusion daily, to create her own domestic sphere. Establishing an awareness of the ever-lurking threat of chaos, should a housekeeper let down her guard, seems to have been an essential part of a girl's education" (*Home Plot*, 10). While Steinbeck indeed describes Ma Joad as a "goddess" whose "position as a healer" and "arbiter" made her "remote and faultless in judgment," his lofty accolade may also reflect the type of chaos-control through domestic ritual that Romines describes (74). However, Ma takes the use of domestic ritual to control chaos a step further by using domestic routine to counter external socioeconomic threats to the survival of the family. With no land, no work, and virtually no money, the Joads' lives have been thrown into confusion, and the establishment of small daily normalities is necessary to keep the family going. Ma literally creates—or directs the creation of—the family camps by routinely laying out bedding for sleeping, boxes for sitting, and dishes for eating at each site, but she also uses the ritual of cooking to control the threat of chaos to her own family. Because this ritual is so ingrained in normal daily activity and so thoroughly ascribed to Ma as her responsibility, no one recognizes that this ritual becomes a method of controlling chaos or asserting authority. Yet, even as Ma Joad automatically cooks for her family—and they automatically expect her to—she is also able to use the practice of feeding them to calm or comfort them or to exercise control by using food preparation or the need to eat to influence family decisions.

In this way, disordered, threatening events are contrasted by the seemingly mundane routine of preparing and eating a meal, balancing confusion with the domestic stability Ma Joad alone provides. She monitors resources and the consumption of food as a measure of their health, emotional well-being, and ability to survive. Ma both capitalizes on expected economic windfalls and uses food to urge hopefulness that they will find jobs and security: she cooks pork and greens before they slaughter the pigs and depart for the West, she splurges on neck meat for stew on their arrival at Hooverville, and she cooks hamburger, fried potatoes, and coffee on the first night of picking peaches. After Al, John, and Pa grow discouraged from the lack of work opportunities at Weedpatch Camp, she encourages faith: "Ma pulled herself together. 'John, you go find Pa. Get to the store. I want beans an' sugar an'—a piece of fryin' meat an' carrots an'—tell Pa to get somepin nice—anything—but nice—for tonight. Tonight—we'll have—somepin nice'" (324).

The domestic stability Ma Joad offers increasingly contrasts the instabilities of the outside world. A microcosm of the soothing that food provides is the Hooverville episode in which Ma cooks a stew that attracts a group of hungry children from the camp. In this highly sentimental event, Ma is unable to refuse the children's needs, rationing a small portion of the family's meal to them: "I can't he'p it. Can't keep it from you" (258). Thus, Steinbeck extends the definition of family to include all of these stray children through Ma's empathetic domestic caretaking.

Even as Ma makes difficult decisions that have an impact on her family's resources, her authority in this realm provides her with the opportunity to influence decisions beyond the domestic sphere. Her influence extends past matters of the home and household to any decision that affects the family at large. Ma, at times, urges the family to pause the journey and find a place to stop and prepare a meal: "Maybe we better fin' a place to stop 'fore sunset,' she said. 'I got to get some pork a-boilin' an' some bread made. That takes time'" (133). However, while Ma begins by influencing the pace of the trip, she eventually begins to control the direction and movement of the entire family. Though safe at Weedpatch Camp, Ma worries about the men's unemployment and subsequent inability to buy quality food. She insists that the family leave to find work:

> "Now you figger," Ma said. "I ain't watchin' this here fambly starve no more..."
> "This here hot water an' toilets—" Pa began.
> "Well, we can't eat no toilets.... I don' care what the pay is. We're a-goin'." (355)

Similarly, Ma refuses to allow Tom to leave the family after Casy's death:

> Listen to me... I'm gettin' cornmeal today. We're a-gonna eat cornmeal mush. An' soon's we get enough for gas, we're movin' away. This ain't a good place. An' I ain't gonna have Tom out alone. No, sir. (391)

Ma Joad connects her authority over food to her decision-making agency, even when it contradicts the wishes of the men.

However, while many of Ma Joad's assertions of authority occur in domestic scenes or directly relate to household concerns, Ma does not appear to be a figure whose power is entirely located within and limited by the domestic sphere. Steinbeck's expansion of the domestic sphere itself appears less a limitation on the world of the Joads than an acknowledgment of the interconnectedness of the public and private realms that patriarchal ideologies have tended to view as separate. While Ma initially draws much of her authority from the domestic and her matriarchal stature, Steinbeck's expansion of the domestic sphere for all of his characters and the relocation of gendered spaces creates tension in his presentation of gender identity and power. When traditional forms of masculinity fail, when men are failed by the bank, the master, and the machine, Steinbeck seems to ask, how do men and women negotiate the space to be human?

Transitional Figures, Domestic Spaces, Collective Survival: Redefining Masculinity and Caretaking

Steinbeck's spatial representations are key to understanding the tensions his novel creates. Even as he expands the domestic sphere to encompass the American landscape, he is cognizant of the meanings inherent in other spaces occupied by his characters. Just as anonymous men, women, and children move through yards, doorways, and houses to represent both their traditional roles and their uncertain new relationships, the Joads begin the narrative in traditional relationships that are altered as family authority shifts and gender identities are newly complicated.

Uncle John's yard serves as a masculine, public space. When Tom Joad and Reverend Casy first enter this space and meet Pa, Steinbeck maintains the house/yard dichotomy and establishes the yard and the truck as both masculine and public. It is significant that Tom finds Pa Joad working on the truck, hammering rails on its sides; the scene reinforces the associations among yard, vehicle, work, male identity, and patriarchal authority. Ma is inside cooking, and the men are able to play a brief joke on her because of her position in the house. She literally can't see Tom's face as he stands in the doorway: "She looked out the door, but the sun was behind Tom, and she saw only a dark figure outlined by the bright yellow sunlight" (73–74). Once again, Steinbeck's spatial placement symbolizes the gendered power structure of the family—Pa is the patriarch working outside, Ma is the matriarch working in the home, and Tom stands in the doorway as a transitional figure. Steinbeck initially follows traditional spatial designations by assigning the public yard as masculine and the private domestic as feminine; those who occupy those spaces perform the traditional gender roles associated with them. However, as Steinbeck moves the Joads away from the yard, expands the domestic sphere, and complicates the spatial representation of the truck, the gender roles of those who occupy those spaces change.

In the absence of work or land to define masculinity and in the face of an expanding domestic sphere, Steinbeck relocates masculine space to the truck. As Tom and his brother Al are unable to find jobs, they instead help the family by driving and maintaining the truck. The young men feel responsible for this part of the family's survival: the truck and their ability to keep it running is a symbol of their masculine identity and authority: "[T]his was [Al's] responsibility, this truck, its running, and its maintenance. If something went wrong it would be his fault, and while no one would say it, everyone, and Al most of all, would know it was his fault. And so he felt it, watched it, and listened to it. And his face was serious and responsible. And everyone respected him and his responsibility. Even Pa, who was the leader, would hold a wrench and take orders from Al" (96–97). The truck allows Tom and Al a way to define their masculinity through their knowledge of and their responsibility for the machine. Tom, who learned to drive and repair cars while in prison, initially dismisses his younger brother as a "squirt" but begins to accept him when Pa assures him that Al "worked for a company. Drove truck last year. He knows quite a little.... He can tinker an engine, Al can" (82). Al, meanwhile, idolizes Tom for his experience and prison reputation—"his brother had killed a man, and no one would ever forget it"—and feels his failures even more deeply in contrast to his brother's masculinity (84).[6]

Steinbeck also uses the car space as an opportunity for connection, particularly among men. Scenes of car repair often parallel domestic scenes or create supplementary masculine spaces within the domestic campsites. For example, the Joads first meet the Wilsons in a domestic setting because they stop to camp in the same site, but Al's offer to repair the Wilsons' car connects the two families. Al is also able to extend a masculine form of hospitality to repay the Wilsons' domestic hospitality during Grandpa Joad's illness: "Al said, 'I'll fix your car—me an' Tom will.' And Al looked proud that he could return the family's obligation" (139). The Wilsons' car troubles offer Tom and Al the opportunity to be masculine providers, suggesting that the two families travel together: "Tom and Al went silent, each waiting for the other. 'You tell 'em,' Al said finally. '... [M]aybe it ain't the same thing Al's thinking. Here she is, anyways. We got a overload, but Mr. and Mis' Wilson ain't. If some of us folks could ride with them an' take some a their light stuff in the truck, we wouldn't break no springs an' we could git up hills. An' me an' Al both knows about a car, so we could keep that car a-rollin'. We'd keep together on the road an' it'd be good for ever'body'" (148). Significantly, Tom and Al treat each other as equals, with equal claim to the idea and equal control—drivership and responsibility for a vehicle. They offer a shared responsibility for the welfare of both families, acknowledging that their best chance for survival is to combine resources. Similarly, in Hooverville Tom and Al become acquainted with Floyd Knowles while he repairs his old Buick. Knowles tells them about the dangers of California and first suggests the need for workers to organize.[7] Thus, like the jailhouse experience that educates Casy, the masculine space of the car offers men a place to talk and connect.

Yet even as Steinbeck creates the truck as a space in which men can define their masculinity and create connections, he complicates this masculine space by connecting it with the domestic that serves as the family center. The truck not only carries the family and all of their possessions, but it is also at times a makeshift shelter. Given a significant position within the family hierarchy, the truck becomes a meeting site: "The house was dead, and the fields were dead; but this truck was the active thing, the living principle. The ancient Hudson ... was the new hearth, the living center of the family; half passenger car and half truck, high-sided and clumsy" (99–100). While Robert DeMott critically stresses Steinbeck's use of the domestic term "new hearth" and views the truck as "the site of matriarchal wisdom and the center of domestic relations" (Introduction, xv), Steinbeck clearly emphasizes the hybrid nature of the vehicle by placing it between a dead house and dead fields. It is a mixture of passenger touring car and work truck, embodying the domestic caretaking of the hearth while also representing the masculine agency of the work truck.

The family's placement around and in the truck is significant, providing insights into the convergence of the public and domestic spaces as well as the shifting power dynamics and gender roles. During the family council, Pa, Uncle John, and Grandpa Joad—who form "the nucleus" of the family—squat in a semicircle facing the truck. The women stand behind the men, and the children stand silently with the women. Al squats with the men for the first time, as "[a]lways he had stood behind with the women before," signifying his acceptance as a man and his promotion to a man's level of authority (100).

However, Steinbeck quickly begins to undermine that division, and the family council is twice interrupted by Ma Joad's return to the stove: "Ma went to the house again ... and the yellow light flashed up in the dark kitchen. When she lifted the lid on the big pot, the smell of boiling side-meat and beet greens came out the door. They waited for her to come back across the darkening yard, for Ma was powerful in the group" (103). Her physical movement between female domestic space and male public space—accepted and causing a pause in the discussion—underscores her stature within the family as well as her transitional status. The tacit acknowledgment of Ma's power interrogates the family's physical placement around the truck, revealing that power dynamics within the family are more complex than simple gender divisions. By moving between the family and the house to tend the meal they will eat before leaving, Ma wordlessly emphasizes her importance in the decision-making process.

Ma Joad's pivotal confrontation with Pa about the separation of the family occurs in front of the truck as she wields a jack handle. After the truck breaks down, Tom proposes that the family temporarily split, leaving Tom and Casy to find parts and make repairs with the intention of catching back up with the rest of the family farther along the road. Although Pa supports the plan and assumes the authority as male head of the family to approve this course of action, Ma recognizes the danger of the proposed separation and the likelihood that a temporary split will become a permanent separation. She stands at the center of her family group rather than at the edge, in front of the vehicle that symbolizes both domestic and masculine space. In this scene, Ma enacts her idealized matriarchal role by protecting her family's interests, but she inverts the behaviors to which women are assigned when she threatens violence to the head of her family. She not only stands up to all the men in the family, but she also shames Pa and emasculates him in front of them: "An' I'll shame you, Pa. I won't take no whuppin', cryin' an' a-beggin'. I'll light into you. An' you ain't so sure you can whup me anyways" (169). For Steinbeck, the convergence of the feminine and masculine is necessary for the family's survival, but it carries costs. To increase matriarchal power is to decrease patriarchal authority: to increase Ma Joad's influence is to masculinize her, and to decrease Pa's influence is to emasculate him.

By the close of the novel, Ma Joad and Tom replace Pa's patriarchal leadership in the family. He can resist only by withholding approval or threatening violence, a traditional form of control that no longer holds power over Ma. He threatens: "Seems like times is changed.... Time was when a man said what we'd do. Seems like women is tellin' now. Seems like it's purty time to get out a stick" (352). Yet an unimpressed Ma observes the connection between his inability to work and his diminished authority, underscoring her point as she continues with her labor: "Ma put the clean dripping tin dish out on a box. She smiled down at her work. '... [Y]ou ain't a-doin' your job, either a-thinkin' or a-workin'. If you was, why, you could use your stick, an' women folks'd sniffle their nose an' creep-mouse aroun'. But you jus' get you a stick now an' you ain't lickin' no woman; you're a-fightin', 'cause I got a stick all laid out too'" (352). Pa Joad, significantly, regains some of his lost authority—and his masculinity—in the final pages of the text, in a futile attempt to save both the Joads' boxcar home and their truck. By organizing a group of men to build a bank against rising floodwaters in the hope of protecting their homes and their cars, Pa emphasizes the need for unified action in the face of overwhelming forces. The men fight to save both the home sites and the cars, reinforcing the balance between domestic and masculine space as necessary for survival. Though the levee is ultimately broken by a tree, Pa's efforts signify his awakening consciousness and his refiguration as a transitional character.

In *The Grapes of Wrath*, the two figures that increase authority in the text are the two figures that successfully transition between domestic space and masculine space. While the roots of their authority are grounded in more traditionally defined gender roles, both Ma Joad and Tom shift between these spaces. Tom's masculinity is reinforced by his ability to repair and maintain the truck, which is viewed as a form of caretaking. Further, Tom values the home—upon his release from prison and his discovery that "home" is gone, he joins forces with Ma to preserve the family, sharing Ma's dream of an idealized physical home with white picket fences and orange trees and supporting the domestic principle that the home is ultimately the family. Thus, Tom's domestic education teaches him to value humanist ideals, which become his impetus for movement toward collective action and self-sacrifice on behalf of the working class.

Steinbeck draws Ma Joad as a domestic authority who moves beyond maternal caretaking to occupy male spaces and take on masculine authority. Yet Steinbeck also seems to struggle with the ways in which Ma's expansion of power operates. Though she grows in authority and directly challenges the men of the family for control, her expressions of traditional masculine behavior are brief, and she quickly returns to her nurturing role. After the jack handle confrontation, she "looked in astonishment at the bar of iron" and her hand trembles before she drops it to the ground (170). Similarly, she attributes her shaming of Pa to a caretaking impulse: "[I]f you can take an' make 'im mad, why, he'll be awright" (352). Given the pervasiveness of traditional forms of female caretaking, Steinbeck seems uncertain how to illustrate a sustained extension of women's power. Admittedly, there are times in *The Grapes of Wrath* when feminine power appears potentially threatening. Ma Joad's strength is unassailable; though her position is both "great and humble," she is "the citadel of the family, the strong place that could not be taken" (74). It is through her that the family finds its will to survive, which means that she can choose its fate. Just as simply by refusing to acknowledge her husband's manhood, she can take it away. A similar ambivalence, thus, appears in the final scene of the text where Rose of Sharon's self-actualization and nurturing gesture is left deliberately sensual and vaguely threatening, an ambiguous commentary on whether her inheritance of Ma Joad's power and authority should be viewed positively.

Ultimately, Steinbeck privileges an expansion of the domestic realm because he views it—and its caregiving associations—as a stabilizing and sustaining social force. However, while Steinbeck was led to consider the gendered implications of expanding domestic caregiving and the public/private realm, he seems unable to move beyond those correlations to deeper assessments of femininity and masculinity or to deconstruct associations of "women's work" and "men's work" even within the domestic realm. As McKay has pointed out, only one scene demonstrating an awareness of the gendered divisions of domestic labor occurs in the text. When Casy offers to help salt pork prior to the family's departure, Ma Joad doesn't seem to understand why he would offer assistance on this particular task:

> She stopped her work then and inspected him oddly, as though he suggested a curious thing.... "It's women's work," she said finally.
> "It's all work," the preacher replied. "They's too much of it to split it up to men's or women's work. You got stuff to do. Leave me salt the meat." (107)

Thus, while Steinbeck is breaking down divisions of gendered space, it seems that he isn't redefining the work that goes on within those spaces—after all, there are no scenes of the male Joads cooking meals, washing dishes, or participating in other "women's work" in the text. Steinbeck instead appears to be trying to adapt forms of female caretaking for men, attempting to redefine masculinity by turning to the stability of what has traditionally defined women: caregiving. Steinbeck's model is not necessarily a new matriarchal order, nor is it a glorification of traditional female domesticity. Instead, Steinbeck is recovering and redefining masculinity because traditional, patriarchal signifiers of manhood have failed to define men in the crisis of capitalist failures. Women, for Steinbeck, become more masculine in the face of this male crisis and because, out of necessity, their authority expands as they become more equal participants in the collective effort to lead and survive.

Sentimental proletarianism is concerned with redrawing the boundaries of the American family to include the working class; in so doing, it highlights the injustices of an unfair and unequal capitalist system that not only prevents certain families from surviving but blames them for their suffering and their failures. By drawing parallels between mothers who love their children, workers who sympathize with others' suffering, the vulnerability of families, and forms of caretaking that expand the definition of family/social groups, sentimental proletarian literature argues not only that working-class families deserve sympathy but that the result of that sympathy should be a revolutionary consciousness that results in social change.

While sentimental proletarian literature—particularly in texts written by women—at times addresses racial difference, proletarian authors primarily focus their arguments for sympathy upon class difference and upon the economic structures that separate them from the middle class. Although there is vigorous and valid debate about an American class (or caste) system, class difference in America is still seen largely as a question of skill, work ethic, earning potential, and choice rather than birth or origin—a belief that is foundational to capitalist mythologies and the American Dream. Sentimental proletarian literature attempts to address a sentimental ideal that equates the performance of class—in which occupying a certain class position requires the demonstration of certain behaviors and the consumption of particular material goods—with interior morality. However, most proletarian authors cannot fully deconstruct the racial dimensions of sentimental ideals because the majority of writers are members of and working within the dominant racial group, focusing on the white working class.

Sentimentalism and race became inextricably linked in the nineteenth century because sentimentalism was first defined by whiteness and later used to argue for the legitimacy of African American personhood. In the twentieth century, neo-slave narrative authors not only return to this paradox but also build on proletarian critiques that separate moral, interior worth from the results of systemic forces. Because of the racial and gender ideals that undergird the sentimental mode, African American authors also critique sympathy as a tool, aware of its ability to move audiences but skeptical of its power to enact real social change. The upcoming authors in this study build on the history of the sentimental mode in order to contextualize America's slave history and legitimize African American suffering but remain cautious about their ability to gain full inclusion in the American family through sympathy.

5 / Margaret Walker's *Jubilee*: "Forged in a Crucible of Suffering"

When *Jubilee* was first published in 1966, it was hailed as a welcome addition to the Civil War novel genre. Winner of the Houghton Mifflin Literary Fellowship Award, it was described on its dust jacket as "inevitably being called the Negro *Gone with the Wind*," a comparison that would today be troubling. It not only invited Margaret Mitchell's vast readership to pay attention to Margaret Walker's work, but it also suggested that *Jubilee* offered an alternative perspective to white Civil War fiction narratives, which had previously been all that was available. *Jubilee*, however, did far more than just offer a fictionalized narrative from the perspective of Mammy and Prissy about what they really thought of their captivity and of mistresses like Scarlett O'Hara. Noting its "evocation of the folk experience and folk attitudes of Southern Negroes on the plantations," reviewer Abraham Chapman declared that the novel brought a welcome breath of innovation to "a thoroughly quarried, frequently hackneyed genre of writing" that had been "the source of some of the crudest stereotypes of Negro characters in American fiction" ("Negro Folksong," 43). Chapman praises Walker for presenting the "little-known everyday life of the slaves" including their behavior, speech patterns, emotions, frustrations, and aspirations: "As it unfolds one sees plantation life as it was seen by Negro slaves, feels the texture of American history as it was felt by Negro slaves." Jane E. Oppenheim in her review praised *Jubilee* for contributing "more than just historical value. It has great sociological significance" (229).

Because Walker incorporated her family's oral history as well as research into nineteenth-century slave narratives and because her groundbreaking novel approached the subject of slavery from the perspective of those "looking up from the bottom rather than down from the top," Walker has been repeatedly credited with creating the genre of the neo-slave narrative ("How I Wrote," 64). The novel defined "a subject of representation that would come to predominate in the African American novel for the rest of the twentieth century. Literally dozens of novels about slaves and slavery appeared in the wake of *Jubilee*" (Rushdy, "Neo-Slave Narrative," 87). Although, as Ashraf H. A. Rushdy observes, it would take five more years before the second novel in this genre appeared with Ernest Gaines's *The Autobiography of Miss Jane Pittman* (1971) and four more years for the third with Gayl Jones's *Corregidora* (1975), and "an African American novel about slavery would become almost annual fare thereafter."

Jubilee, like the other two neo-slave narratives in this study, is based on real-life figures and slave history. Deriving her historical novel from the narrative passed down from her grandmother, Walker not only shares an African American perspective of Civil War history, but she also traces the connection between twentieth-century American culture and its past. By appropriating and reimagining historical narratives, Walker asserts the value of African American womanhood, history, community, and voice. Her historical novel draws from and critiques the nineteenth-century sentimental tradition in order to promote a humanist philosophy that acknowledges African American suffering and suggests a new way forward. In Walker's rendering, African American suffering takes on a divine purpose that teaches a sentimental message of love, forgiveness, and redemption. Thus, the African American woman, who is placed at the center of both family and community, has the power not only to endure suffering but also to teach others how to extend sympathy and healing. Thus, Walker creates a sentimental female lineage that promotes African American community, connecting contemporary racial problems with the past while also finding hope for the future.

Jubilee follows the life of Vyry, a light-skinned, light-haired enslaved woman born in the novel's opening pages to Sis Hetta (who dies in childbirth) and her white master, John Morris Dutton. Vyry grows up on a Georgia plantation, where she is raised by a caring mammy, benevolently neglected by her father, and tormented by his jealous wife. Dutton and his wife have a son, Johnny, and a daughter, Lillian, who closely resembles Vyry in age and physical appearance. Vyry eventually falls in love with Randall Ware, a dark-skinned freeman, with whom she has two children, Jim and Minna. When Randall is forced to leave Georgia before the Civil War, he asks Vyry to leave her small children behind and escape with him, but she refuses to do so and is caught attempting to flee. After years of hardship during the Civil War, soldiers eventually arrive and free the slaves, but Vyry waits in vain for Randall's return while caring for her sister, Lillian. She eventually marries Innis, a freed slave, with whom she has a son. The family leaves the plantation and travels throughout Georgia and Alabama attempting to find a place to settle but find difficulty everywhere because of racial tension. They finally settle near a town where Vyry's midwifery skills are valued by the white townspeople. Randall eventually finds them, which allows Vyry, Innis, and Randall to share their past experiences and realize that the marriage between Vyry and Randall is truly over. The novel closes with Vyry contentedly preparing for the arrival of another child with Innis.

Because Walker's narrative so faithfully follows her own grandmother's biography and because of the extensive historical context provided in the novel, there exists some critical debate as to whether *Jubilee* should be classified as a neo-slave narrative or a transitional text that signals a shift from nineteenth-century straightforward oral narrative to the "fictionalized slavery and freedom literature of the late twentieth century" (Beaulieu, *Black Women Writers*, 15). Phyllis Rauch Klotman deplores early comparisons between *Jubilee* and *Gone with the Wind*, arguing that Walker's novel is not historical romance because it does not conjure up the "tightly girdled, hoop-skirted lilies" of white plantation tradition and instead records black folk history ("Oh Freedom," 139). Babacar Dieng argues that *Jubilee* is a historical novel that gave rise to the neo-slave narrative in its present form, an "ancestor of a wave of neo-enslaved narratives and African-American historical fictions ... a product of the thirties which gave impetus to the revisionist movement reclaiming African-American history" that didn't take hold until the 1960s ("Reclamation," 117). Holly Martis credits the work as a historical novel that was "truly groundbreaking work" for its subject matter and for "giving rise to a whole cultural industry" ("Lineages," 49). Begun in 1934 and completed in 1965, Walker's novel understandably makes use of multiple literary traditions. However, few if any scholars have recognized its incorporation of the sentimental mode.

Walker wrote *Jubilee* over the course of thirty years, drafting portions of the initial manuscript while a senior at Northwestern University in 1934, researching slave narratives and the history of the Civil War throughout her life, and completing the manuscript as her doctoral dissertation at the University of Iowa (1962–65). She first began thinking about writing a novel and her personal connection to African American history during her adolescence. The novel is largely based on the life and experiences of her maternal great-grandmother. Walker learned about her great-grandmother's life through her grandmother, Elvira Ware Dozier, who lived with her family until Walker was an adult.

Walker recalls in her essay "How I Wrote *Jubilee*" that her parents often came home late at night and found her "enthralled in [her] grandmother's stories" (51). When Walker's parents called the stories "tall tales," her grandmother protested that she was "not telling her tales; I'm telling her the naked truth." For Walker, *Jubilee* began in her childhood, while listening to her grandmother's stories of slavery: "I promised my grandmother that when I grew up I would write her mother's story." For Walker, however, simply relating her personal family story was not enough. She knew that she had received an invaluable oral history: "I was . . . determined to substantiate my material, to authenticate the story I had heard from my grandmother's lips. I was using literary documents to undergird the oral tradition" (56). Walker wanted to prove that the stories passed down to her were authentic and accurate. She spent thirty years researching *Jubilee*, reading Civil War histories and novels; accounts of Southern history, laws and slave codes; congressional investigations of the Ku Klux Klan; plantation account books, diaries, letters, bills of sale, and other personal papers; and nineteenth-century slave narratives. What Walker found, she writes, "further corroborated the most valuable slave narrative of all, the living account of my great-grandmother, which had been transmitted to me by her own daughter" (57).

Her grandmother's stories offered Walker a deeply human, family-based perspective on the effects and costs of slavery that went further than records of battles and troop movements. Her oral history gave names and faces to the human suffering of centuries of slavery, extending beyond partisan abolitionist debates and connecting the seemingly distant past to the contemporary struggle for African American equality. Researching the history of slavery and confirming her grandmother's story gave Walker a more acute awareness of the relationships among all people. The Nuclear familial relationship became a microcosm for the human family, which in turn became the sentimental structure for her novel. "The story," as Walker's grandmother told it, "reflected the relationship of my great-grandmother to all people around her, black and white" (53).

Walker, however, also highlights the feminine structure of this humanist perspective, one that has traditionally linked both the sentimental novel and slave narratives: sentimental novels realign families and American culture around women and the home, while female-authored slave narratives often associate women with maintaining family and community in the face of social forces that sought to tear them apart. "I think you recognize the humanistic value of Vyry," Walker observes in an interview with Lucy Freibert, "because whether it's Aunt Sally or Mammy Sukey, whether it is Miss Lillian or Miss Lucy, you see the kinship of women" ("Southern Song," 53). In writing her neo-slave narrative, Walker not only connects humanism to feminine sympathy but develops an ancestry that has been passed down through the female line of her family: "I realized when I finished the book that I had never known Vyry, but I knew her daughter, and she was like Vyry. My mother said, 'Oh, you've got my grandmother down. She was just like that.' I said, 'But you know I was really using grandma.' Then she said, 'Well Mamma was like grandma.' And I said, 'And my mother was like her mother.' I'm like my mother. The older I get, the more I look like my mother and I think like my mother. My grandmother was just like her mother. Women are like their mothers" (53). Walker, in essence, is able to appropriate the voice of her ancestors because they have the same voice. By developing this lineage, Walker not only creates the authority to speak for and as her own female ancestors, but she suggests that all women are similarly connected to their own female lines: "Women follow the pattern of women who have gone before them." By understanding this process of lineal sympathy and shared experience, then, women are able to connect to each other and develop community. Just as Walker's historical research supports the veracity of her grandmother's narrative, Walker's sympathetic lineage provides her with the authority to write Vyry as a voice that speaks generally for African American experience, offering a humanist philosophy based on sentimental kinship.

Walker strongly values this sense of lineage, viewing her work as deeply connected to both the past and present: "[F]or black people, the 20th century has been a century of protest. And in all my work I look first at the historical perspective. I'm always looking back in order to understand what's happening today, and what may happen tomorrow" (Graham, "The Fusion," 280). Like the sentimental literature of the past, Walker's writing attempts to bring readers closer to the history she represents in order to influence them toward social change: "I attempted to understand what it meant to have social change and its benefits for black people and their rights.... [S]ome of us are too old to understand the kind of social change we need in this country, but our children are not too young. We owe them another world; we owe them another mind to face the future.... Black women writers, and particularly myself, have faced three main problems or conflicts in all our work: racism, fascism, and sexism. I think I have been fighting them all my writing career" (284). Storytelling not only shaped Walker but also revealed a strong female lineage capable of survival, leadership, and social change. Thus, Walker, by inviting readers into her family history, also asks them to experience a larger shared history as an epic, redemptive journey toward freedom.

Suffering and Divine Agency

Scholars have noted that Walker's portrayal of Vyry as a perpetually optimistic and fortunate individual despite her experiences in slavery seems, at times, unrealistic or exaggerated. Hortense J. Spillers criticizes the novel for an allegorical propensity, arguing that "Walker adopts a syntax and semantics whose meanings are recognizable in an explanation of affairs in human time. But these delegated efficacies register at a deeper level of import so that 'nature,' for instance, is nature and something more, and character itself acts in accordance with the same kind of mystical or 'unrealistic' tendencies" ("Hateful Passion," 301). Walker, however, has defended her portrayal, explaining that although she has taken "the license of the imaginative worker," she has "tried to be honest" in portraying her great-grandmother, who "was shaped by the forces that dominated her life. In the Big House and in the Quarters, she was raised according to Christian ethics, morality, and faith, and she could not react any other way. Her philosophy of life was a practical one, and she succeeded in getting the things she wanted and prayed for. She realized that hatred wasn't necessary and would have corroded her own spiritual well-being" ("How I Wrote," 62–63). Suffering—learning through suffering and reader sympathy attained through suffering—is a key aspect of the sentimental mode. While in *Charlotte Temple* or *The Coquette* errant young women are punished for mistakes by suffering dire consequences, later sentimental novels show that suffering is instructive and brings the sufferer closer to God and family, as in *The Wide, Wide World* and *The Lamplighter*. As a woman who suffers through no fault of her own and is the victim of mistreatment due to her enslavement and to others' maliciousness, Vyry's misery eventually brings her to an understanding of

God and humanity akin to the experiences of nineteenth-century sentimental heroines. Although protected as a child from physical abuse, when Vyry enters the home of her master and father as a servant, she is exposed to his benign neglect and his wife's malicious assaults. Finding fault with Vyry's every attempt to serve, Salina Dutton kicks her, slaps her, throws a pot of urine in her face, and hangs her by her thumbs from hooks in a closet: "Vyry's toes barely touched the floor.... [W]ith her arm-pits hurting so bad, she lost consciousness of everything and did not know how long she hung there in torture" (32).

Although Vyry is persecuted for her light skin and her too-close resemblance to Lillian, Walker is careful to connect Salina's vengeful abuse to the abuse all slaves suffer at the hands of their owners. While John and Salina Dutton contradict claims that the slaves are unhappy and assert that only abolitionist ideas might upset them—"[t]hey are all well treated, and we love them and take good care of them just like a part of our family. When they are sick we nurse them back to health. We feed and clothe them and teach them the Christian religion" (82)—Vyry witnesses field hands whipped to death, watches Salina slap and kick servants and force cooks to drink ipecac to make sure they aren't eating the food, and sees the overseer brand a runaway slave on her face with the letter *R*. Slaves die of plague and lack of medical care and are punished for stealing food when they don't have enough to eat. The overseer violently murders slaves who are torn between following Dutton's orders and the overseer's because their "resistance" makes him angry. And while Dutton grows incensed when the overseer kills a slave, Salina points out that he's "the best overseer in the county.... He knows how to handle nigras, and a good driver is hard to find. You'd better leave him alone" (135).

When Vyry is caught attempting to escape with her children, she is whipped like any other runaway. Returning to the plantation, she knows that her father, who was often away, will not interfere: "[T]here would be no compassion. It was a well-known fact that if a slave ran away and was caught in the act, flogging was the punishment" (171). Vyry is tied to a whipping post, naked to the waist, with hands and feet "stretched as far as they could without touching the earth beneath her ... or reaching beyond the post" (172). A guard "who was generally hired to whip slaves"—a man whose main job was to inflict these kinds of beatings—lashes Vyry with "a raw-hide coach-whip used to spur the horses." The description of Vyry's whipping is graphic, focusing equally on her pain and on the cuts to her flesh: "The whip burned like fire and cut the blood out of her and stung like red-hot pins sticking in her flesh while her head was reeling and whirling. It hurt so badly she felt as if her flesh were a single molten flame, and before she could catch her breath and brace herself again, he had wrapped the whip around her the second time. . . . She was whirling around in a cutting, fiery wind while the fire was burning her flesh like a tormenting fever and she kept sinking down in the fire and fighting the blackness until every light went out like a candle and she fainted" (172–73). After Vyry wakes, cut loose from the whipping post and lying on the ground—other slaves collect her and tend to her after dark for they are fearful of openly showing care for her—she wonders why she has survived and asks herself, "Why has God let me live?" and prays, "*Lawd, have mercy, Jesus! Send somebody to get me soon, please Jesus!*" (174). By posing such a question immediately after a horrifically rendered flogging, Walker implies that Vyry's suffering does indeed have a godly purpose, although what that purpose is will not be revealed until later in the novel. It also implies a connection between Vyry and Jesus Christ, as her position on the wooden post suggests.

Although Vyry does not ask if God has forsaken her, as Christ does before his crucifixion, both questions link bodily suffering with divine purpose and spiritual redemption. On the cross, Christ asks, "My God, my God, why hast thou forsaken me?" shortly before dying (Matt. 27:46, King James Version), which many biblical scholars believe is a reference to Psalm 22. The psalm begins with the exact question and, written six hundred years before the crucifixion, appears to predict some of the suffering Christ experienced such as dehydration, pierced hands and feet, and the Roman guards dividing his clothing by casting lots.[1] When Christ's question is interpreted as an acknowledgment of prophecy and his own role in fulfilling it, his suffering becomes *necessary* to the redemption of mankind. Through this acknowledgment, Christ reminds witnesses of his agency because he repeatedly accepts his pain and determines that it shall be transformed into forgiveness and redemption (of himself and others). Thus, Walker suggests that African American suffering under slavery is part of a larger divine destiny, and this parallel is significant because Vyry's suffering is necessary to her understanding of herself and the world. She develops a Christlike philosophy of suffering, forgiveness, and love that provides agency through the acceptance of suffering.

A Legacy of Suffering

The implication of an "unfolding of the Divine Will" in *Jubilee* is precisely what Hortense J. Spillers describes in her essay "A Hateful Passion, a Lost Love" (299). Drawing on Paul Tillich's definition of a *theonomy* in which "[h]uman history is shot through with Divine Presence so that its being and time are consistent with a plan that elaborates and completes the will of God," Spillers argues that "in Walker's novel agents (or characters) are moving and are moved under the aegis of a Higher and Hidden Authority." Spillers contends that Walker's "characters are larger than life; that they are overdrawn, that, in fact, their compelling agency and motivation are ahistorical, despite the novel's solid historical grounding" (301). Vyry and her family "become the privileged center of human response," and through them the novel becomes "an interrogation into the African-American character in its poignant national destiny and through its female line of spiritual descent" (299, 305). It is important to recognize, however, that Walker is doing more that just arguing for a Divine Presence or Plan behind Emancipation and Reconstruction while tracing a female lineage for African American cultural survival. Walker is also drawing upon a history of sentimentalism that connects suffering to moral redemption and places women at the center of a new world order; she rewrites this moral order with an enslaved African American woman at its center. In Walker's novel, the heroic, individualistic African American male ends up alone, isolated from his family, clinging to his militant views. Meanwhile, the white female heroine, destroyed by her suffering, loses her mind. It is only the African American woman who both suffers and embraces sentimental ideals and who interprets a divine purpose from that suffering that is able to lead her family—and by extension her community—forward.

After the Civil War, Vyry experiences new forms of suffering because freedom from slavery does not mean freedom from discrimination and abuse by whites. Industrious and hopeful, Vyry and Innis Brown look for a piece of land to farm and to build a house for their growing family, but they experience constant setbacks. When they first set up a small farm on the low country land of the Chattahoochee River in Alabama, they believe they have a chance to realize their dreams. Innis, however, quickly realizes that "they would be better off the less they went into town," where he had encountered a white man who "talked pretty rough" to him and told him that "niggers was made to work for white folks and all this free nonsense warn't agoing to work" (328). Although

Innis and Vyry are puzzled that the man didn't object to their settling near the river, they discover why he acted "kinda satisfied" about their location when their land floods dangerously that spring. The family is trapped in the loft of the house for three days, losing their cow and all of the newly planted crops. As they wait for the water to recede, Vyry tells the children the story of Noah and the ark, closing with the ominous prophecy that "God told Noah by the rainbow sign / No more water, but the fire next time" (336).

In their search for a new home, Innis and Vyry are next fooled into taking over a sharecropper's lease despite their hopes of living an independent life, free of white control. They find a white family on a failed farm who claim to be moving and willing to let the family take over the house and land. After settling in, however, Vyry and Innis are surprised by the appearance of a white man who claims the property and forces them to sign a sharecropping contract. Neither can read or write, but Innis makes his mark, and the family does its best to farm the hardscrabble land without purchasing any seed or provisions from the sharecroppers' store. However, at the end of the year, the white landowner claims that they've taken a large amount of store credit and adds the amount to the money he insists is owed. Despite knowing they are being cheated, they are forced to accept a debt that is added to "next year's bill" and sign another contract (361). Vyry and Innis realize that they have been trapped into the cycle of work and debt that maintains a form of economic servitude akin to slavery: "That white man means trouble, and we ain't never gwin git outen his debt. Another year he'll tack on some more, and knowing us is ignorant will just make it worser.... Lawd, we ain't staying on this here bad land and letting that white man get us more and more in debt until we can't even much eat."

Vyry and Innis escape to Troy, Alabama, where Vyry finds work cooking for the Jacobsons, a wealthy white family that owns many properties. Although Vyry is concerned about the rowdy behavior of local African Americans and the presence of the Ku Klux Klan, the Jacobsons help the family secure a tract of land outside of town. However, once Vyry and Innis build a house and begin to focus on farming, the family's growing independence removes them from the Jacobsons' protection and puts them at risk for Klan vengeance. Vyry angers Mrs. Jacobson when she stops cooking for them to focus on caring for her own home and newborn child, angrily telling her that "you colored people don't want to work the way you useta.... [Y]ou need not come back" (373–74). Shortly thereafter, while Vyry's daughter Minna is home alone, three white boys enter the house, threatening her and baby Harry with a razor. The boys are startled into leaving when Innis, Vyry, and their oldest son come home, but a few days later they see the Ku Klux Klan burn down their house as they return from Sunday evening church services. After losing her home and possessions, Vyry falls into a deep depression, wondering if her family's continuous suffering is a message from God: "I done tried and tried. We is done from pillar to post, and just when I thought we was bout to git us a home at last, they done burned all we got to the ground. Why, Lawd? Just tell me, why? . . . What is I done to them white folks? Lawd, what is I done? Is you punishing us, and is I just ungrateful?" (379).

Once again, Vyry and Innis search for a place to safely settle. With help from the Union army and the Freedman's Bureau, they claim a farm outside of Greenville, Georgia. Vyry, however, is reluctant to rebuild—insisting that the family live in a tent—because she continues to sense white resentment against African Americans. However, once Vyry demonstrates her abilities as a midwife, the members of the town ask the family to stay because they need her services. The white townspeople hold a house-raising and a quilting bee in order to help the family get started, and Vyry feels a sense of "friendship and understanding from their new neighbors" (441). So, while Vyry and Innis believe they have finally found refuge and relief from white violence and discrimination, Vyry is deeply disturbed when tensions between her oldest son and husband erupt into physical violence. Jim had accidentally let the sow—an important investment for the family—die, so Innis whips Jim. Stepping into the middle of the fight, Vyry defends her son from further beating, arguing with Innis about the use of physical punishment on her children: "[Y]ou ain't gwine browbeat and mistreat nobody here, not long as I'm living and I can help it" (449). The fight upsets her, not only because of the strife between her son and husband, but because

> all that confusion in her house yesterday went back to something in her life that she thought she had forever escaped. It brought back all the violence and killing on the plantation when Grimes was driving and beating the field hands to death. It brought back the horror of the deaths of Mammy Sukey, and Grandpa Tom, the branding of Lucy, and burning the old men to death, the plague, and the hanging, murder, and fire, when the slaves all knew their lives were not worth a copper cent with a hole in it. . . . Now this awful hatred and violence was threatening to destroy her happy home and her loving family. It was in her own brand-new house. (453)

Vyry realizes that the violence of the past continues to haunt her present, not just in the form of the Ku Klux Klan and white discrimination, but within her own family and its potential to act out of the pain and trauma that was inflicted by those who have mistreated them. "Deeply shocked," Vyry "knew she herself had been capable of killing Innis Brown" out of her anger and her desire to protect her children (454), thus acknowledging that the capacity for violence is in her as well. Like the emotional numbness that mothers experience in proletarian literature, as well as the fathers who lash out, this capacity for violence is a consequence of a legacy of suffering. In the sentimental paradigm, it is the mother's sensibility that enables her to recognize this cycle and her moral role to prevent it.

Redemptive Forgiveness as an African American Sentimental Model

Vyry, "sick of killing and violence . . . sick of the hate that went with it," asks, "Was this kind of evil going to follow her all the days of her life?" (454). Vyry's question has relevance for both her time and generations of African Americans living with a legacy of slavery and racial violence into the twentieth century and beyond. Each of the three neo-slave narratives under discussion in this study deals with the contemporary legacy of slavery, the ways that the wounds of the past contribute to the realities of the present, both in white and African American communities. But in *Jubilee*, Vyry presents a model of learning through suffering, an African American destiny in which suffering of biblical proportions can either be absorbed within and perpetuated by those who were victims of it or be transformed into redemptive love and forgiveness that has the power to help them survive.

Vyry, therefore, turns to God and goes to the woods to pray, just as Jesus frequently withdraws himself from friends and disciples to refresh himself and find guidance in prayer.[2] In the woods, Vyry falls to her knees and tells God, "I'm suffering so, Lord, my body is heavy like I'm carrying a stone. I come to ask you to move the stone, Jesus." Vyry prays, "We can't go on like this no longer, Lord. We can't keep on a-fighting, and a-fussing, and a-cussing, and a-hating. . . . I'm asking you to let your forgiving love cover our sin" (454–55). Relieved of her burden—whether that stone represents trauma, pain, suffering, guilt, or all of it—Vyry believes that forgiveness and love are the only way forward. She tells her son to let go of his anger against Innis, a metaphor for the larger anger they've held inside for the abuses they suffered in slavery and from racist whites: "Keeping hatred inside makes you git mean and evil inside. We supposen to love everybody like God loves us. And when you forgives you feels sorry for the one what hurt you, you returns love for hate, and good for evil. And that stretches your heart and makes you bigger inside with a bigger heart so's you can love everybody when your heart is big enough. Your chest get broad like this, and you can lick the world with a loving heart!" (457). Vyry argues that by returning love for hate, forgiveness for violence, people not only avoid being poisoned by the violence done against them, but they become stronger than those who commit the violence.

Although the family has been "from pillar to post," Vyry recognizes that God has not been punishing them, and this belief allows her to have faith in human goodness regardless of skin color:

> I don't believe the world is full of peoples what hates everybody. I just doesn't believe it. I knows lots of times folks doesn't know other folks and then they gits to thinking crazy things, but when you gits up to peoples and gits to know them, you finds out they's got kind hearts and tender feelings just like everybody else. Only ways you can keep folks hating is to keep them apart and separated from each other. Of course I knows they's plenty evil peoples in the world, look like they's just born evil and the devil's they companion, but I just doesn't believe its cause they's white or black. I doesn't believe every white person's evil and every black person's good. (474)

Vyry argues for a view of humanity that looks beyond race, offering a hopeful vision of the world that suggests racial division arises from a lack of sympathy—from the fear and jealousy that occurs from not knowing others as human beings.

Vyry's views are contrasted with those of her ex-husband, Randall Ware, who has become embittered and militant because of his own suffering, such as his expulsion from the legislature and loss of the vote, the forced sale of his land to whites, and the beatings and intimidation by the Ku Klux Klan. Ware's anger not only prevents him from overcoming the suffering he has experienced, but it causes him to distance himself from God and adopt color-line divisions that embrace a "with us or against us" mentality: "You can keep your white Christian God along with all your good white friends because I never could stand hypocrites. . . . You got his color and his blood and you got his religion, too, so your mind is divided between black and white" (480). Through Ware, Walker acknowledges the historical controversy within the African American community regarding the ways that religion has been used as an oppressive force as well as the desire to adopt a militant stance against white violence and discrimination.

Ultimately, the message of forgiveness and sympathy prevails. Vyry argues against Ware, claiming that she "ain't gwine try to beat the white man at his own game with his killing and his hating" (482). Adopting the commonly used metaphor of the Jewish slaves' liberation from Egypt, Vyry declares: "We's done come through slavery and we is free at last. I knows we's got to wander a while in the wilderness just like the children of Israel done under Moses, but when the battle's over we shall wear a crown" (483). Likening their suffering to a period of confusion and wandering provides a divine meaning to their suffering, shaping it into a journey with both a purpose and an end. After cataloging a list of abuses she has experienced, Vyry tears off her blouse to show her scarred back, weeping to show that she has indeed suffered a great deal. But she then returns to her message of forgiveness, concluding that if one of her abusers were to ask for food, she would not deny him or her: "I would feed em. God knows I ain't got no hate in my heart for nobody.... I believes in God and I believes in trying to love and help everybody, and I knows that humble is the way.... [T]hat's my doctrine and I'm gwine to preach it to my childrens, every living one I got or ever hopes to have" (485).

Vyry's sentimental message is so strong that when she shares her views with Jim, she convinces him to forgive Innis despite his resentment and anger. As a result, she realigns the emotional center of the family: "The tension in the house began to ease.... The charged feelings in the house were dissipated as once again the family life revolved around the quietly confident Vyry, whose presence exuded her own inner peace" (458). Not only does Walker demonstrate the power of forgiveness, but she also draws Vyry as the ideal sentimental woman who both embodies Christian sympathy and serves as the emotional and moral center of her family. "[T]ouched with a spiritual fire and permeated with a spiritual wholeness that had been forged in a crucible of suffering," Vyry was "only a living sign and mark of all the best that any human being could hope to become. In her obvious capacity for love, redemptive and forgiving love, she was alive and standing on the highest peaks of her time and human personality. Peasant and slave, unlettered and untutored, she was nevertheless the best true example of the motherhood of her race, an ever present assurance that nothing could destroy a people whose sons had come from her loins" (486). Vyry's doctrine is that love and sympathy will overcome all racial strife and difference, and will eventually overcome evil. The overall moral message is that good will overcome evil if the majority of those who suffer learn to hold onto God's love and forgive. Thus, there is a use and a purposefulness in suffering, which allows Vyry to serve as the emotional and spiritual leader of her family. In the same manner that sentimental novels reposition the mother and wife as central to the world order, the African American mother is positioned as central to the post-slavery world.

While *Jubilee* writes a new world order that is both spiritual and matriarchal and that connects women to their history through a female lineage, Octavia Butler's *Kindred* addresses a world in which African Americans have become disconnected from their shared history. In Butler's historical and cultural matrix, contemporary readers need the vehicle of sympathy to understand the present and cannot heal or effectively move forward without recognizing the strengths and the sacrifices of those who suffered before them. In drawing her presentation of American slave history, Butler not only demonstrates the power of sympathy but also reveals what happens when sympathy is lost—an individual becomes less than whole, disconnected from the self and from the family to which he or she assumes belonging.

6 / Octavia Butler's *Kindred*: "My Face Too Was Wet with Tears"

Octavia Butler is arguably best known for her novel *Kindred*, published in 1979. She was the first African American woman to make a name for herself writing science fiction and remains one of the few African American writers—along with Samuel R. Delany—to have achieved success in the field. After developing a love of reading and an interest in science fiction as a child, Butler was inspired to try her hand at writing after watching a bad science fiction movie on television and deciding that she could write something better herself. Over the course of her career, she published eleven novels as well as numerous short stories and nonfiction pieces. Although Butler, who died in 2006, achieved a successful career in science fiction, winning some of the most prestigious awards in the field, including multiple Hugo and Nebula awards as well as a MacArthur Foundation "genius" grant, she always resisted being pigeonholed as a genre writer. Not only did she complicate the science fiction genre by consistently including African American women as empowered characters whose social position challenges American racial stereotypes, but the themes of her novels and stories also frequently deal with issues of bondage and freedom. Butler's work often drew from her experiences growing up in a working-class African American community during the civil rights period and is frequently rooted in African American history and literature.

In an interview with Charles Rowell, Butler describes the origin of her idea for *Kindred*, relating an anecdote in which, during the Black Power movement of the 1960s, she heard a young man giving remarks at Pasadena City College. The speaker said, "I'd like to kill all these old people who have been holding us back for so long. But I can't because I'd have to start with my own parents" (79). Butler was so struck by his statement that she "carried that comment ... for thirty years," believing that the young man "was still blaming [older generations of black people] for their humility and their acceptance of disgusting behavior on the part of employers and other people.... He felt so strongly ashamed of what the older generation had to do, without really putting it into the context of being necessary for not only their lives but his as well." Butler's goal, in *Kindred*, was to work against this shame and anger by teaching readers to feel sympathy for enslaved African Americans and their descendants. Butler's intention was not to create pity for previous generations' suffering but to demonstrate the ways in which their suffering and their survival required strength, enabling the survival of their descendants.

Kindred uses a time-travel plot device to bring the protagonist, Dana, in close contact with her literal past—both by forcing her to interact with her ancestors and by placing her, as a modern-day African American woman, in the conditions of antebellum slavery. Science fiction thus becomes a sentimental vehicle for confronting the legacy of slavery in the United States and pushing at the limits of sympathy. By collapsing the boundaries between past and present, Butler awakens Dana—and the modern reader—to the experiences of her enslaved ancestors. Whereas nineteenth-century sentimental novels drew metaphors of equation to show that unlike groups suffer in similar or parallel ways (i.e., white women understand enslaved women because the death of a child is like the loss of a child to a slave sale), Butler's *Kindred* shows that Dana suffers in the same way as her ancestors given like conditions. She moves Dana from being an observer of suffering to a suffering subject. This breaking of boundaries enables Butler to collapse history and show the close linkage between past and present attitudes toward race and gender.

Butler long maintained that *Kindred* is actually fantasy, rather than science fiction, because no science is involved in the time travel that occurs in the novel. *Kindred* is also a neo-slave narrative because it tells the story of a young African American woman who is trapped in bondage to a Maryland planter. The twist, however, is that Butler centers her story around a contemporary woman, Dana, who lives in California in the year 1976 but is called back in time, repeatedly, to the early 1800s to save the life of a white ancestor and slave owner. Dana, who is a writer and is married to a white man, one day disappears from her home and finds herself on the banks of a river. She realizes that a white boy is drowning and saves his life, returning to her own time when the boy's father arrives and threatens her with a gun. A series of jumps in time ensue, and Dana realizes that she may only be home in California for hours or days but can return to Maryland at a time years after her previous visit. Similarly, she can spend weeks or months in antebellum Maryland, living as a slave, and be returned to her home only hours after she disappears.

The problem for Dana is that she has no control over her trips in time; with her returns to the past, she realizes that the boy—who gradually grows into an adult—is Rufus Weylin, a man who will eventually father one of her female ancestors. Although neither Rufus nor Dana knows how she is called back in time, Dana arrives each time Rufus is in mortal danger, and she realizes that she must keep him alive so that Hagar Weylin may one day be born. This situation places Dana in a difficult position because she comes to feel familial affection toward Rufus, although she abhors enabling the awful things he does as a white slave-owner. Even as Dana brings modern views of her own identity, equality, and humanity with her to the past, she is forced into the role of a slave in order to survive the nineteenth century. Dana also develops strong friendships with other household slaves and feels conflicted and confused, caught between her outrage at their treatment and her relationship with Rufus. *Kindred* concludes when Hagar is finally born, but Rufus wants to force Dana into a sexual relationship. Dana had felt protected by her relationship with Rufus and her own modern perspective, and when Rufus attempts to rape her, Dana kills him, sending her home for the final time and permanently releasing her from her bondage.

Like many neo-slave narrative authors, Butler drew from personal family history and historical accounts of the antebellum period to provide details for her narrative. Although *Kindred*, unlike *Jubilee*, does not attempt to re-create through fiction her mother's or grandmother's lives, Butler's admiration for previous generations of African Americans and her interest in the relationship between contemporary and slave history was informed by her family heritage. Butler was raised by her mother, who spent her early childhood on a sugar plantation in Louisiana: "From what she's told me of it, it wasn't that far removed from slavery" (Kenan, "Interview," 496). As Butler recalls, "My mother's life and my grandmother's life and the little bit I know of her ancestors' lives were very hard and very terrible. . . . [Butler's grandmother] chopped sugar cane, and she also did the family laundry, not just her own family but also the white family for whom they worked. . . . That was hard, physical labor" (Rowell, "Interview," 50). Butler also repeatedly witnessed racism against her mother, who worked as a domestic servant: she was required to enter the back doors of houses and was spoken to "in ways that were obviously disrespectful" (51). Like the young college speaker, Butler at first was angry at her mother for accepting such treatment: "As a child I did not blame them for their disgusting behavior, but I blamed my mother for taking it. I didn't really understand. This is something I carried with me for quite a while, as she entered back doors, and as she went deaf at appropriate times." She came to realize, however, not only that her mother's actions enabled her own survival—"I ate because of what she did"—but also that her anger and shame were a common response: "I spent a lot of my childhood being ashamed of what she did, and I think one of the reasons I wrote *Kindred* was to resolve my feelings.... *Kindred* was a kind of reaction to some of the things going on during the sixties when people were feeling ashamed of, or more strongly, angry with their parents for not having improved things faster, and I wanted to take a person from today and send that person back to slavery" (Kenan, "Interview," 496). To diffuse the anger for what young people perceive as a history of "accommodationist" behavior and to unburden present generations of the shame of a history of abuse, Butler had to find a way to develop sympathy between African Americans of the past and present.

As a science fiction writer, her unique solution came through the narrative device of time travel. This plot device enabled Butler to force her protagonist—and her readers—to cross time and inhabit that perspective of the slave. In an interview with Nick DiChario for *Writers and Books*, Butler acknowledged that the methodology of *Kindred* "was to make people feel the book" ("Conversation," 206). By "taking a modern day black person and making her experience slavery, not just as a matter of one-on-one but going back and being part of the whole system," Butler provides readers with a protagonist who represents themselves, with whom they have much in common and who would react as they would and feel as they would feel when placed in similar circumstances (207). Thus, readers share in feeling distance from the past as well as Dana's change in subject position, as the suffering she experiences moves them closer in sympathy for the enslaved. As Butler makes clear to her interviewer, she is not trying to make readers "understand what it felt like to be a slave" or attempting to present an anthropological or historical description of a past period. Instead, she is attempting to "confront a modern person with that reality of history": "It's one thing to read about it and cringe that something horrible is happening. I sent somebody into it who is a person of now, of today, and that means I kind of take the reader along and expose them in a way that the average historic novel doesn't intend to, can't." This confrontation both closes the distance between past and present and acknowledges that a persistent gap exists—Dana, after all, does return to 1970s California to live out the rest of her life. However, she is forever changed by having come into contact with her past.

Butler's preparatory research for writing *Kindred* taught her that she would need to push the boundaries of the slave narrative in order to bring readers close to the experience of slavery: "[O]ne of the things I realized when I was reading the slave narrative ... was that I was not going to be able to come anywhere near presenting slavery as it was. I was going to have to do a somewhat cleaned-up version of slavery, or no one would be willing to read it. I think that's what most fiction writers do. They almost have to" (Kenan, "Interview," 497). Butler sought to reach beyond historical fiction in order to present a narrative that did not pose a "version" of history so much as provide a vehicle for connecting contemporary readers to the past, to help them inhabit history while overcoming the disjuncture that occurs when one cannot comprehend another's suffering. Butler is able to exploit this disjuncture to her advantage, drawing from the conventions of science fiction to create a space in which readers accept the combination of multiple realities. As a genre, science fiction is generally focused on the future, not the past, so it is a startling choice to combine it with the historical genre of the slave narrative. Of course, Butler has always insisted that *Kindred* is more a fantasy than science fiction since the operations of the time travel aren't a focus of the novel, but the semantics may be largely irrelevant. *Kindred*, like most science fiction, offers "zones of possibility" because it bends, alters, or rewrites accepted rules of reality; science fiction is a literature where "almost any formulaic deformations are possible" (Landon, *Science Fiction*, 17). Incorporating time travel into the neo-slave narrative allows Butler to make slavery "possible" for contemporary readers. Whereas historical fiction acknowledges that its narrative events happen in the past and allows readers emotional distance from the events described, Butler's combination of genres actually thrusts the issue of slavery forward, into the present, allowing her to collapse the emotional distance for readers.

Beverly Friend reads the conclusion of *Kindred* as a failed commentary on women's agency, arguing that its overall message is that "contemporary woman is not educated to survive, that she is as helpless, perhaps even more helpless, than her predecessors.... Men understand how the world is run; women do not. Victims then, victims now" ("Time Travel,"

55). Elizabeth Ann Beaulieu, however, argues against this "pessimistic feminist reading," citing Dana's trip to Maryland with her husband, Kevin, after she has healed (*Black Women Writers*, 130). Dana looks up records of what happened to the enslaved men and women on the Weylin plantation after she killed Rufus and disappeared, finding sales records for many of them, which deeply saddens her. Beaulieu points out that while Dana questions why she wanted to return to Maryland, where "slavery had touched her—firsthand," Kevin reminds her, "You probably needed to come for the same reason I did. . . . To try to understand. To touch solid evidence that those people existed" (Beaulieu, *Black Women Writers*, 130; Butler, *Kindred*, 264). Dana could not save the people she cared for, and her actions caused more suffering for them since killing their master resulted in the sale of his slaves, but Dana's affectional connection allows her to draw a direct line between their lives and her own. And this is much of Butler's moral imperative: that modern-day African Americans should acknowledge the suffering as well as the strengths experienced by their predecessors, which contribute to their own abilities to survive. As Beaulieu points out, "Dana finally accomplishes the difficult task of individuating herself as a black woman in twentieth-century America, discovering a sense of personal history and developing a more intimate relationship with the black ancestors to whom she owes her existence" (130). Dana develops this intimate relationship through shared suffering, and it is through readers' sympathy with that suffering that a sense of understanding and historical reconnection is established.

Collapsing History, Questioning Sympathy

Butler's novel addresses similar historical themes to Walker's *Jubilee* insofar as both authors confront the legacy of American slavery in the twentieth century. However, while Walker writes a historical novel set in the nineteenth century that takes the modern reader back in time, Butler's narrative moves the protagonist back and forth across the historical distance, straddling both the past and the contemporary eras. By doing so, *Kindred* more directly links twentieth-century racial attitudes and cultural perspectives to their formation in slavery while also revealing the ways in which members of American society—both black and white—have developed a cultural amnesia that erases the origins of their beliefs as well as the humanity of their ancestors. Dana, at the beginning of the novel, "has virtually no historical awareness" (Beaulieu, *Black Women Writers*, 118). Realizing how little she understands about the nineteenth century, Dana tries to increase her knowledge of the historical period during the brief times she is back home: "I read books about slavery, fiction and nonfiction. I read everything I had in the house that was even distantly related to the subject—even *Gone With the Wind*, or part of it. But its version of happy darkies in tender loving bondage was more than I could stand" (116). Dana often finds this book knowledge insufficient or inaccurate in comparison to her real-life experiences. References to Margaret Mitchell's "loving bondage" are contradicted by clear physical and emotional abuse, and even Frederick Douglass's 1845 *Narrative* fails to accurately represent her experience, such as when she sees that children on the Weylin plantation are fed in the cookhouse: "I was glad to see them there because I'd read about kids their age being rounded up and fed from troughs like pigs" (72). Dana can't even rely on a family oral history, which is often a strong component of African American family and culture. When trying to discern her connection to Rufus Weylin, she eventually puzzles out that he must be an ancestor because she remembers the last name of a distant great-grandmother born Hagar Weylin, whose parents are listed in the family Bible as Rufus Weylin and "Alice Green-something Weylin" (28). But Dana wonders, "[W]hy hadn't someone in my family mentioned that Rufus Weylin was white? If they knew. Probably they didn't."

Furthermore, even though Dana lives in an era of growing freedom, her entire approach to history as well as her perspective on her time in the nineteenth century is different from that of her husband—who is white—because of their differing skin colors. Kevin is progressive and antiracist; he loves his wife and wants to protect her from harm. When he is pulled back in time with Dana, he gets into trouble because "he couldn't tell the difference 'tween black and white" (150). But although Kevin abhors slavery, his relationship to it is different because he is never subject to being made a slave himself. His masculinity and his white privilege protect him, affording him far greater agency than those whose skin color relegates them to a status with fewer—if any—social rights and freedoms. Kevin initially thinks that the chance to view history up close could be fascinating, telling Dana that it "could be a great time to live in" because a person could "go West and watch the building of the country, see how much of the Old West mythology is true" (97). When Dana points out that the West is "where they're doing it to the Indians instead of the blacks," she highlights a significant difference in their perspectives: Kevin thinks of history from a position of white privilege that does not consider the subjugation of other peoples, whereas Dana is sensitive to nonwhite perspectives about the period. Kevin takes the role of Dana's master when they are together in antebellum Maryland, assuming this right by skin color alone, and there are no restrictions on his freedom to leave Maryland when he is left behind and must wait for Dana to return.

Sentimental novels operate by developing emotional bonds and affective communities in order to extend sympathy across social divisions and reveal moral truths, particularly through shared experiences of suffering. *Kindred* simultaneously employs and critiques sentimentalism. It creates emotional connection across the lines of history to explore the legacy of American slavery while acknowledging the flaws in a system that teaches moral truths through assuming sympathetic identification with an Other whose experiences cannot fully be understood. On the one hand, *Kindred* shows that it is impossible for an individual of privilege to truly understand the suffering of another: an individual with social protection or status is always inhibited and limited by those very benefits from truly understanding the suffering of one without that protection. Thus, privilege in *Kindred* includes whiteness, maleness, and wealth, as well as the privilege of having lived in a post-slavery period with additional freedoms.

One of the ways *Kindred* mimics the sentimental novel and invites sympathy across these boundaries is through the technique of character doubling. Butler takes great pains to show physical similarities between Dana and Alice, the woman who will become the mother of Hagar Weylin. A patroller who mistakes Dana for Alice's mother exclaims, "You could be her sister, her twin sister, almost" (41). The two women grow as close as sisters during Dana's time in Maryland; Dana nurses Alice from near death to full health, and the two of them spar frequently, fighting and making up. Dana and Alice are also both closely connected to Rufus, who involves Dana in his coercion of Alice and is emotionally attached to both women. He calls them "[o]ne woman. Two halves of a whole," and attempts to rape Dana after Alice's death because he believes he can substitute Dana for Alice (257). Rufus and Kevin are also paralleled, and while there are significant differences between the two, the doubling implies an alignment of racial power and sexual access between the past and the present. Both Rufus and Kevin claim ownership of Dana; although Kevin serves as Dana's master for appearances and protection while they are in antebellum Maryland, he has the "right" of ownership because of his race and gender. This role puts him in the same category as Rufus, who views him as competition because he intends to claim those rights to Dana in Kevin's absence. Dana feels the slippage between the role of husband and master when she and Kevin want to maintain their marital relationship. Since their marriage is not recognized during that time, they maintain the "charade" that Kevin, as Dana's master, has taken her to bed. Except, in that time, no one believes it is pretending, and Dana feels disturbed, "almost as though I really was doing something shameful, happily playing whore for my supposed owner" (97).

The parallel, as well, between Rufus's ownership and sexual contact with Alice—Dana's double—and Kevin's "ownership" and sexual contact with Dana suggests that power dynamics within modern relationships are still subject to a racialized and sexualized historical imbalance of power that cannot yet be forgotten. When Dana first meets Kevin, she is working for a labor agency that workers refer to as a "slave market," and when they first have lunch together, a white male coworker harasses Dana, repeatedly whispering that the two writers are going to create porn together, "[c]hocolate and vanilla porn!" (56). The harassment suggests that Dana, as a black woman, is still subject to sexual objectification by white males, who assume a right of sexual access, even if that only means through fantasy or observation. Even within her relationship with Kevin, who treats her with respect, Dana is acutely aware of power dynamics. After they are living together, Dana is concerned about maintaining her independence and continuing her career as a writer. Kevin assumes that Dana will type his manuscripts—a subservient, feminized role—particularly after they are married. Dana reluctantly types them at first, but then refuses, irritating Kevin but establishing a more equal power dynamic within the relationship. Although Kevin does not assume rights of ownership to Dana, he does make gendered assumptions, and Dana feels compelled to protect her agency and equality within the relationship—her position is defensive, whereas Kevin has the position of privilege and needs only to be reminded to respect her rights and independence. Such negotiations reveal that the historical imbalance of power remains in place and has deep roots, despite contemporary gains.

Exploring the Limits of Sentimental Identification

Dana begins the novel unable to comprehend the suffering she witnesses. Although she responds to others' suffering, her reaction is to pull away and separate herself because she cannot comprehend it. When Dana witnesses white patrollers beating a man in front of his wife and child, she is faced with a reality that is too horrific for her to process: "I could literally smell his sweat, hear every ragged breath, every cry, every cut of the whip. I could see his body jerking, convulsing, straining against the rope as his screaming went on and on.... I shut my eyes and tensed my muscles against an urge to vomit" (36). She has a physical and emotional response to the man's suffering—she feels sick and terrified—but she closes her eyes to try and stop her witnessing. She also recognizes that nothing has prepared her for this reality, so she is unable to process it. No experience from her life would have allowed her to comprehend this man's suffering because what she has witnessed only imitated suffering: "I had seen people beaten on television and in the movies. I had seen the too-red blood substitute streaked across their backs and heard their well-rehearsed screams. But I hadn't lain nearby and smelled their sweat or heard them pleading and praying, shamed before their families and themselves. I was probably less prepared for the reality than the child crying not far from me. In fact, she and I were reacting very much alike. My face too was wet with tears. And my mind was darting from one thought to another, trying to tune out the whipping" (36). Imaginative identification does not compare to the reality before her. Her own response is to "tune it out," but like the child with her, she is overwhelmed by her witnessing and reduced to tears. One of the critiques of sentimentalism is that it prioritizes emotion over reality, separating the two and resulting in melodramatic emphasis in emotional scenes that lack realism. In this moment, Dana recognizes that twentieth-century cinematic portrayals of this kind of suffering not only lack the reality of what she has just witnessed—using "too-red blood" and "well-rehearsed screams"—but they also lack the human being's physical and emotional context. By smelling the man's sweat and hearing his breath, she understands that the man's suffering is real. By witnessing the child's tears and seeing the man's wife refuse to watch the beating, she recognizes that pain is emotional as well as physical, that those who love the sufferer are hurt by his pain. Thus, it is not glamorized suffering or melodramatic emotion but this connection—the affective bond that transfers pain between the sufferer and those who care for him or her—that enables sentimental identification to occur.

Despite her dark skin and her attempts to fit in, Dana is marked as an outsider to the plantation culture. Not only do plantation residents expect her to appear and disappear at random intervals, never aging while the rest of them grow older, but Dana is also visually set apart because she wears twentieth-century clothing—jeans or pants during a time when women wore only dresses. She also speaks without a Southern accent, tells Rufus not to call her a "nigger" because the term is offensive, and behaves—at least in private with Rufus—as an equal to whites. According to Rufus, Dana doesn't "talk right or dress right or act right" (30). Although she tries to explain her accent by claiming to come from New York—a free state—Dana's speaking style is a liability in nineteenth-century Maryland because it indicates her education to whites who worry about her ability to read and her likely abolitionist ideas. Thus, Nigel warns Dana that she sounds "[m]ore like white folks than some white folks" and that the master "don't want no niggers 'round here talking better than him, putting freedom ideas in [their] heads" (74). Whites aren't Dana's only problem: many African Americans aren't sure where her loyalties lie because of the long-standing association between education and whiteness. Thus, when Dana tries to help Alice and her husband, Isaac, escape from Rufus, Isaac is distrustful, saying, "She sure don't talk like no nigger I ever heard. Talks like she been mighty close with the white folks—for a long time" (119). Later, when Dana helps Alice recover from the terrible wounds of being punished for her escape attempt, Alice lashes out in anger and pain over losing Isaac and her freedom, calling Dana "doctor-nigger": "Think you know so much. Reading-nigger. White-nigger! Why didn't you know enough to let me die?" (160).

As an outsider to the nineteenth-century world, Dana's first instinct is one of survival, to get out of the past and back to her own time alive and unharmed. She makes numerous references to survival, believing that a "slender . . . fine-boned" woman like Alice's mother was "probably not as strong as she needed to be to survive" in that era. "But she was surviving, however painfully. Maybe she would help [Dana] learn how" (38). Because of her precarious position as an African American woman in a white-ruled world, needing to be "owned" in order to be protected, Dana feels sure that she won't make it without the guardianship of either Kevin or Rufus: "I don't think I have much chance of surviving here alone" (82). Dana thinks primarily of existence and escape, of the hardships and suffering that African Americans—herself included—face. When she tells Kevin her fears and he points out that her ancestors had fewer advantages but still lived through it, Dana responds: "Strength. Endurance. To survive, my ancestors had to put up with more than I ever could. Much more" (51). Dana suggests that there are limits to her suffering, implying that she could neither endure nor fully understand the lives her ancestors experienced. Not only does Dana reveal a broad gulf between her understanding of modern-day and historical suffering, but such a view indicates a limit to sympathetic identification: if a person places limits on his or her ability to suffer, can that person sympathize with another's suffering if it exceeds those limits?

Because of those limits, Dana recognizes that she—and Kevin, during his first weeks there—relate to the people and the period from a distance, as though they are playing parts: "I began to realize why Kevin and I had fitted so easily into this time. We weren't really in. We were observers watching a show. We were watching history happen around us. And we were actors. While we waited to go home, we humored the people around us by pretending to be like them. But we were poor actors. We never really got into our roles. We never forgot that we were acting" (98). Dana recognizes the distance she has placed between herself and the people of the past; although subject to the same abuses, the same treatment, the same limits to her agency, she views her suffering as temporary and not a part of her true reality. She doesn't acknowledge that she shares the suffering and experiences of others, placing distance between herself and them by anticipating an escape from that suffering. This gap allows her to maintain assumptions about the people she befriends and comes to care for, still viewing them with the judgment of a person who maintains twentieth-century agency and sees nineteenth-century people as stereotypes instead of individuals. Responding to "Aunt" Sarah's fear of talking about freedom and her assertion that she "can get along" because "[t]hings ain't bad here," Dana believes that Sarah "had done the safe thing—had accepted a life of slavery because she was afraid.... She was the kind of woman who would be held in contempt during the militant nineteen sixties. The house-nigger, the handkerchief-head, the female Uncle Tom—the frightened powerless woman who had already lost all she could stand to lose, and who knew as little about the freedom of the North as she knew about the hereafter" (145). Feeling "[m]oral superiority" over "someone even less courageous" than she was, Dana doesn't yet understand why someone would appear to choose her position in slavery and judges her with the disdain of a different era.

Shifting Subject Positions: Acquiring Sympathy through Shared Suffering

Dana eventually confronts her judgments, her inability to understand her past and the people in it, because she comes to care for Sarah and the others, seeing them as individuals. She also shares their suffering. The pain of labor and physical abuse, combined with the suffering caused by fear for the welfare of those she loves, moves Dana from her subject position—from the distant inheritor of slave history into the subjectivity of a slave. By repeated exposure to history, Dana changes from observer to sufferer. Her first transitional step occurs when she realizes that Rufus's most effective means of control over her—since he chooses not to abuse her physically—is through her sympathy with others. Rufus forces Dana to help him manipulate Alice into sex by threatening to hurt Alice (more than he already has), knowing that causing her additional pain will hurt Dana, too. When he asks Dana to convince Alice to go to him, Dana at first refuses, so he threatens, "You want her to get hurt?" (163). Then, to further convince her, he threatens Dana directly: "You talk to her—talk some sense into her—or you're going to watch while Jake Edwards beats some sense into her!" Rufus doesn't need to beat Dana herself, merely force her to watch Alice being beaten, causing her to feel as though she were responsible for Alice's beating and suffer for the pain experienced by another. Although Dana is horrified by participating in the rape of another woman—that she terms it "rape" is a clear indication of how she views the coerced sexual relationship—she does see her role in convincing Alice as a way to mitigate at least some of her suffering: "I couldn't refuse to help the girl—help her avoid at least some [of the] pain" (164).

Slaves are equally—if not more—afraid of separation from their families than they are of physical abuse, and Dana's experience teaches her the strength of this threat. Her jumps back into the past mirror, in some ways, the risk and uncertainty of men and women whose marriages were not legally recognized, people who never knew if they would suddenly lose each other to sale or death. While sentimental novels often achieved sympathy for the enslaved by equating the separation of slave families through sale to the separation of loved ones through death (more familiar to white, middle-class readers), Butler places twentieth-century Dana in the position of experiencing this form of suffering firsthand. Dana is separated from Kevin each time she is sent back into antebellum Maryland, leaving her uncertain whether she will return to him in the twentieth century. But when Kevin is brought back with her—he is touching her when Rufus "calls," so he time travels with her—her experience more closely parallels other enslaved African Americans because she leaves him in the past and doesn't know if she will find him again. When Dana comes back to 1970s California without him, she later returns to antebellum Maryland to discover that five years have passed and Kevin has left for the Northern free states. She doesn't know if she will be able to get word to him or whether they will be reunited because she is dependent on Rufus to send a letter and because she isn't sure where to find Kevin. Dana is not a free woman: the Weylins accept that Kevin is her "owner," and she has the status of a slave and is not allowed to act or move freely (even though Rufus knows the truth, his attachment to her means that he would prefer that Kevin not claim her so that he can "keep" her). Dana quickly learns the pain of separation as well as how difficult it would be to reunite with a loved one in "this horse-and-buggy era" (162) where African Americans are not supposed to be able to write and are barred from mailing letters, letters travel slowly or are lost, and journeys take months. Such difficulties make the pain of separation more acute: beyond the incredible barriers of slavery itself, if someone is sold or sent a long distance away, it would be highly unlikely for him or her to find family or loved ones again.

Although Rufus and his father are often indifferent to the sale of slaves when the purpose is financial, their knowledge of the pain it causes enables them to exert control in another manner beyond physical abuse. Dana experiences this when Rufus uses the threat of permanent separation from her husband to get what he wants from her: "You threaten me, I'll threaten you. Without me, you'll never find Kevin" (125). He knows that Dana will accede to his demands in the hope that he will help her find her husband. However, he further controls Dana by actively preventing her from contacting Kevin (he hides the letters she writes instead of mailing them). By lying to Dana, Rufus obtains her obedience as she awaits word from her husband, as well as virtual ownership over her, a situation that is disrupted only when Alice reveals the letters hidden in Rufus's bedroom. Dana's love for her husband and her fear of never seeing him again allow her to better understand others' suffering. She develops a deeper sympathy for Alice because, after she and her husband fail to escape, Isaac is sold to traders taking slaves to Mississippi. Rufus gains control of Alice through the sale, as Dana had anticipated: "Rufus had done exactly what I had said he would do: Gotten possession of the woman without having to bother with her husband" (149). But Dana recognizes the depth of Alice's suffering when she and her own husband are reunited, for she realizes that Alice will never experience this outcome: "She was watching us—watching dry-eyed, but with more pain than I had ever seen on another person's face. My husband had come to me, finally. Hers would not be coming to her" (184). Rufus pushes Alice too far, however, when he makes her believe he has sold her children. After Alice attempts to escape, Rufus tries to control her through the threat of separation and sends the children to his mother's sister in Baltimore "[t]o make her see what could happen ... if she tried to leave [him]" (251). But Alice has suffered too much at Rufus's hands and hangs herself. Disgusted and angry, Dana accuses Rufus of murder, telling him: "You killed her. Just as though you had put [a] gun to her head and fired."

Similarly, Dana more fully sympathizes with others' experience of separation each time another person is sold. She is shocked to return to the plantation and find that Luke, a friend who works in the fields, had been sold because of his recalcitrant attitude. Dana is saddened by Luke's loss and surprised that his son Nigel hadn't run away, but Rufus points out that although Nigel had attempted to escape and been brought back, he is now married: "Man marries, has children, he's more likely to stay where he is" (139). As a slaveholder Rufus acknowledges that slaves develop emotional ties that create a strong impetus to stay in slavery, while also providing slaveholders with additional leverage to maintain control over them. This understanding gives her a new perspective about Sarah's apprehension of freedom talk (and the threat of discovery), allowing Dana to sympathize with her fear and find parallels between their situations: "He [Rufus] had already found the way to control me—by threatening others.... It was a lesson he had no doubt learned from his father. [Tom] Weylin, for instance, had known just how far to push Sarah. He had sold only three of her children—left her one to live for and protect" (169). In addition to reminding each slave about personal vulnerability, each sale also reopens the wounds of past losses. When Sarah tells Dana to watch what she says, Dana realizes that Sarah is even more careful than she had been before: "Luke's being sold must have frightened her badly. He used to be the one who hushed her" (150). And after Alice's suicide, Sarah tells Dana that it was incredibly painful for her to take care of Alice while she mourned for the loss of her own children: "I didn't want to even be close to her. When Marse Tom sold my babies, I just wanted to lay down and die. Seeing her like she was brought all that back" (250).

The physical abuse Dana experiences brings her closer to an understanding of the impact of suffering on African Americans who lived under slavery. While the emotional suffering of others deeply troubles Dana, the physical experiences of her time in the nineteenth century bring a new level of awareness: "Rufus's time was a sharper, stronger reality. The work was harder, the smells and tastes were stronger, the danger was greater, the pain was worse.... Rufus's time demanded things of me that had never been demanded before, and it could easily kill me if I did not meet its demands" (191). Although her first whipping sends her back to her own time, allowing her to escape briefly into the present-day, later abuses are not life threatening. They do, however, cause her to question her assertion that she would be able to escape or resist abuses that she feels she would be unable to tolerate. Dana quickly loses the knives she carries back with her for protection and is unable to use them to defend herself because she hesitates to use violence against another human being—"Now I would be sold into slavery because I didn't have the stomach to defend myself in the most effective way" (42)—or because she is easily disarmed. Although Dana constantly asks herself whether she has the strength and resolve to escape to freedom, each beating reduces her distance from the experience of being a slave and makes her feel the imposed limits on her agency.

Dana frequently thinks about returning home, and if she can't return home, escaping north, suggesting a strong parallel between the two. Regardless of her means of escape, Dana is in bondage and sees escape as the principal means of long-term survival, which is a primary reason why she questions other slaves' (seeming) acceptance of their subjugation. Dana is unsure whether she has the skills and fortitude to successfully achieve her goal and makes reference to famous fugitive slaves such as Frederick Douglass, Sojourner Truth, and Harriet Tubman, who not only found freedom but also published narratives about their experiences. Yet, while these exemplars became enshrined in American history, their narratives do not tell the story of others who were unable to follow in their footsteps. Dana's attempt to run away teaches her that the narrative of escape is far more complex—and bound with suffering—than history and literature might convey. When Dana is caught running away from the plantation, she is surprised when Rufus tells her, "You're going to get the cowhide.... You know that" (176). She finds it difficult to accept that she will receive another whipping: "Somehow, I hadn't known. His gentleness had lulled me." Dana is stripped naked and tied with her hands above her head, then whipped severely by Rufus's father. Although Dana tries to convince herself that she is dying in order to trigger a jump in time, she knows that it is "only punishment... Nigel had borne it. Alice had borne worse. Both were alive and healthy" (176). After the beating, Dana is in pain but also conflicted at the new fear she feels: "[W]hy was I so frightened now—frightened sick at the thought that sooner or later, I would have to run again?" (177). Dana knows that others have experienced such pain—or worse—and begins to recognize how physical abuse instills fear and circumscribes personal agency: "The pain of my body was enough for me to contend with. But now there was a question in my mind that had to be answered. Would I really try again? Could I? . . . See how easily slaves are made?"

Not long after Dana's beating, the overseer Edwards decides to make a show of his power and forces Dana to do the washing, labor for which she has not sufficiently recovered. Although Dana feebly protests, she quickly gives in to his demands because he threatens her with his lead-weighted whip: "I went out, God help me, and tried to do the wash. I couldn't face another beating so soon" (182). Some months later, Rufus sends Dana to the fields to punish her for something beyond her control—his father died of an illness and Dana could not save him. The labor itself is hot and exhausting; the field overseer, Evan Fowler, whips Dana to force her to work more quickly, lashing her shoulders at random intervals: "He did that all day. Coming up suddenly, shouting at me, ordering me to go faster no matter how fast I went. . . . He didn't hit me that often, but he kept me on edge because I never knew when a blow would fall. It got so just the sound of his coming terrified me" (213). Although Dana at first considered resisting, by the end of the day the constant pain of the work and the beatings overwhelms her: "After a while, it was more painful for me to push myself than it was for me to let Fowler hit me. After a while, I was so tired, I didn't care either way. Pain was pain. After a while, I just wanted to lie down between the rows and not get up again." Although Rufus shows remorse for Dana's treatment—he has her wounds treated and restores her to a household serving position—the threat of returning her to the fields is another form of control over her. When Rufus tries to make amends and she angrily turns to go, he tells her, "You walk away from me, Dana, you'll be back in the fields in an hour!" (214). Stunned, Dana realizes that his threat is real, that although they have a special bond, Rufus "meant it": "He'd send me back out. I stood staring at him, not with anger now, but with surprise—and fear."

Dana's suffering—both physical and emotional—brings her so fully into the subject position of a slave that she worries that she has lost her twentieth-century identity and become the nineteenth-century slave. When Alice criticizes her for what she sees as an attitude that is too accommodating toward whites—"You run around fetching and carrying for that woman like you love her. And half a day in the fields was all it took" (220)—Dana worries that her suffering has made her too submissive, has taken the resistance out of her. She realizes, "Once . . . I had worried that I was keeping too much distance between myself and this alien time. Now, there was no distance at all. When had I stopped acting? Why had I stopped?" (221). A short time later Dana discovers her friend Tess and two other slaves being sold and placed in a coffle: she is so distraught that she wonders if she should have let Rufus die after all. Sarah's daughter Carrie, however, comforts Dana by pointing out that her actions have the ability to influence all of the African Americans enslaved on the plantation—if Rufus dies, it is not just Dana's ancestral line that suffers. All of the slaves will be sold, which means families will be separated and perhaps sent to worse conditions. Although Dana experiences guilt over her feelings toward Rufus, forgiving his abuses and unable to hate him, she recognizes that her complicated relationship also affects African Americans she cares about and that she is entangled in a complex relationship with both whites and blacks. When Dana mentions, "I can see why there are those here who think I'm more white than black," the mute Carrie gestures at her with an annoyed expression, wiping the side of Dana's face with her fingers (224). Nigel, Carrie's husband translates: "She means it doesn't come off, Dana.... The black. She means the devil with people who say you're anything but what you are." Dana is thus brought into sympathetic alignment with the enslaved people with whom she has developed deep affectional bonds in a way that acknowledges her as a member of this community and allows for the complexity of her position.

Although Dana develops her sympathy through identification with suffering, it is also clearly important that *Kindred*'s readers learn to view African Americans of the past not only with sympathy but also with an understanding of their agency: survival in an extremely oppressive system *is* agency. Dana learns this lesson, discovering that enslaved African Americans have found multiple ways to resist and survive, despite the risks. Luke demonstrates a form of passive resistance, espousing the ideology that you "[d]on't argue with white folks.... Don't tell them 'no.'... Just say 'yes, sir.' Then go 'head and do what you want to do" (96). He also shows that even passive resistance can have serious consequences when he is sold for his attitude. Similarly, when the slaves find out that Dana can read and write, many of them ask her to teach them in secret, even though the penalties are severe if they are caught. *Kindred* also reveals that enslaved African Americans develop other methods of resistance, which largely have to do with taking care of each other and protecting each other from further suffering. When Dana is forced to do the washing by the overseer but is not physically recovered to handle the labor, Alice insists on taking over and sends her back to the cookhouse. Worried about the consequences, Dana protests, but Alice declares,

"He knows where I sleep at night" (183). Although Alice's relationship is coerced, she knows that she can use Rufus's power against the abuses of other white men and can extend that protection to Dana. Sometimes, protecting each other means disciplining one of their group, as when the women beat up Liza, the sewing woman, who reported Dana's escape attempt. Liza refuses to tell on her attackers, claiming that her bruises and lost teeth are the result of a fall, and as Alice tells Dana, "She'll keep her mouth shut next time.... We let her know what would happen to her if she didn't. Now she's more scared of us than of Mister Tom" (179).

Through *Kindred*, Butler appropriates the sentimental mode to connect contemporary readers to the past. Her aim is to help those who have become removed over time from their cultural history, to overcome the disjuncture that occurs when one cannot comprehend another's suffering. For Butler, understanding past suffering is foundational to understanding present suffering; developing sympathy for distant ancestors will generate sympathy for closer ones. This process is key to regenerating a cohesive African American cultural group with the power to heal from the past and generate effective social change, a group that is recognized through affectional bonds and sympathetic identification. Although her focus is primarily on an African American linage—connecting contemporary African Americans to their historical roots and to their ancestors' struggle for freedom and equality—*Kindred* deliberately intertwines white and black experience. It literally re-creates a mixed-race American familial lineage that is first linked by blood and then linked by sympathy. Dana is a vehicle for contemporary African American consciousness as well as for the general modern reader, and her ancestors, she discovers, are made up of both white and African American members.

However, *Kindred* also makes clear that white readers have a much greater gap of sympathetic identification to work through and greater responsibilities toward Others who have suffered. Dana develops her sympathy through firsthand experience—most often at the hands of her own white ancestors—while Kevin's privilege protects him and slows his ability to fully comprehend the suffering of those around him. He cares primarily about Dana and his inability to protect her; it is only after he is left behind alone that he is forced to truly inhabit the antebellum world, attempts to help slaves escape, is accused of plotting a slave rebellion, and suffers over the pain he witnesses. In addition to experiencing fears of permanent separation and a lack of agency, Kevin must overcome the privilege that inhibited his ability to recognize the suffering of others and that makes his personal suffering different. Through his firsthand experiences, Kevin develops a fuller sympathetic identification with Dana and with enslaved African Americans.

Ultimately, Dana bears both physical and emotional scars of her experience, and Kevin shares her desire to understand what she has been through, prompting their visit to modern-day Maryland to explore historical records and find out what happened to the people who lived on the Weylin plantation. Their shared sympathy, and their sympathy for the suffering of others, brings them to a new understanding of their past and present. *Kindred* projects a hopefulness that this sympathy will engender new understandings of history, suffering, and the present that will generate new opportunities for healing. While *Jubilee* and *Kindred* suggest that sympathy is required for African American healing and progress, other neo-slave narrative authors question the meaning of sympathy and the process by which sympathetic healing can occur. Toni Morrison, in *Beloved*, complicates the focus on sympathy's healing properties by shifting the lens to the requirement for suffering in order to generate that sympathetic identification. Morrison questions whether African American communities require suffering in order to receive sympathy and whether overcoming or healing from the American history of slavery actually comes at the cost of sympathy.

7 / Toni Morrison's *Beloved*: "Feeling How It Must Have Felt to Her Mother"

> *I was big, Paul D, and deep and wide and when I stretched out my arms all my children could get in between . . . there wasn't nobody in the world I couldn't love if I wanted to.*
>
> —TONI MORRISON, BELOVED (162)

In a scathing 1987 review of *Beloved*, Stanley Crouch angrily accuses Toni Morrison of writing melodramatic sentimental fiction that is "designed to placate sentimental feminist ideology," making sure that "the vision of black woman as the most scorned and rebuked of the victims doesn't weaken" ("Aunt Medea," 67). Equally offensive to this critic is that he believes Morrison "lacks a true sense of the tragic," and he criticizes the author for what he feels is an omission of realistic and complicating detail about experiences of slavery, such as African participation in the slave trade. Thus, Crouch asserts, Morrison "only asks that her readers tally up the sins committed against the darker people and feel sorry for them, not experience the horrors of slavery as they do." While he praises Morrison's musical structure and her deft use of images, he criticizes her "maudlin ideological commercials" and deems the text largely "portentous melodrama" (68, 71). Asserting that *Beloved*'s primary flaw as a novel is that it does not "transcend race" in order to focus upon the larger concerns of the human condition, he continues, "*Beloved* fails to rise to tragedy because it shows no sense of the timeless and unpredictable manifestations of evil that preceded and followed American slavery, of the gruesome ditches in the human spirit that prefigure all injustice" (71, 68).

This critic's accusations are, unfortunately, familiar. Echoing the criticisms of realists and modernists who accuse sentimentalism of being unable to portray both real experience and true feeling, Crouch describes *Beloved* as suffering "from the failure of feeling that is sentimentality"

(69). And yet, this criticism seems oxymoronic because of sentimentality's very claims upon feeling. Morrison's critic argues that it is not enough for her to write a text that causes readers to "feel sorry" for those who experienced slavery but that the novel must cause readers to "*experience* the horrors of slavery." And yet, one might argue, that is exactly sentimentalism's aim: to cause the reader to sympathize with the plight of enslaved persons, to feel what they are feeling in order to come to sympathy with them. If feeling, according to Crouch and critics like him, is a failure of realism, one might ask, how is a text that attempts to portray extreme suffering to do so "realistically"? When the experience of slavery is so horrific as to have traumatized generations of families; to have perpetuated countless rapes, physical assaults, and murders; to have resulted in a war, decades of racial violence, social and economic oppression, and cultural beliefs that are based in centuries-old racial stereotypes; how is a text to make a contemporary reader, more than one hundred years removed, "experience the horrors of slavery"?

In the twentieth century, Morrison continues the sentimental critiques of many nineteenth-century African American women's slave narratives in her neo-slave narrative *Beloved*, which was published in 1987, won the Pulitzer Prize in 1988, and has become, arguably, one of the most discussed novels in contemporary literature. Despite Crouch's assertions about the "failures" of feeling within the text, Morrison's *Beloved*, like Harriet Jacobs's *Incidents in the Life of a Slave Girl* or Harriet E. Wilson's *Our Nig*, adopts the style of sentimental fiction to capitalize on familiar cultural tropes and reader sympathy while simultaneously critiquing the racial and gender ideologies embedded in sentimental narrative. However, as a contemporary author, Morrison not only uses the forms of sentimental fiction to increase sympathy for her seemingly unsympathetic protagonist—a mother who murders her own child—and to capture reader sympathy for the past suffering experienced by millions of enslaved persons, but she also incorporates critiques of sentimentality. Those criticisms enable Morrison to present African American slave history as a form of trauma with a living legacy and to reveal that contemporary views of African American identity are shaped by a cultural history that is deeply informed by our shared history of slavery as well as suffering itself. In this postmodern neo-slave narrative, Morrison appropriates the real-life historical narrative of Margaret Garner's tragic story, as well as of sentimental fiction and nineteenth-century slave narratives, to comment upon a history of suffering and the ways in which cultural views of sympathy and suffering contribute to ongoing racial and gender ideologies.

Although Morrison's novel explores multiple forms of trauma created by the experience of slavery, one of the most recognizable sentimental tropes in *Beloved* is the separation of families and the development of kinship communities that extend beyond blood ties. This theme is integral to Harriet Beecher Stowe's antislavery argument: the loss of family is a form of suffering that is presented again and again in slave narratives throughout the nineteenth century. The prevalence of this theme in *Beloved* is both appropriate because Morrison's novel focuses upon a family and a community heavily traumatized by the abuses of slavery, of which separation and loss of family was common, and ironic because the text's protagonist is a mother who murders her own child. Morrison's central character, Sethe—the fictional counterpart to the real-life Margaret Garner, who also killed her child when faced with a return to slavery—could be viewed as utterly unsympathetic in the eyes of a reading public that deems motherhood an essential aspect to womanhood. Both in Garner's time and in Morrison's twentieth century—a culture that remains heavily influenced by the legacy of sentimentalism's gender roles—women are placed at the moral center of the family: their highest priority is considered to be the love, care, and protection of their children. For Sethe to kill one of her children is a violation of all that makes her a mother and a woman in the eyes of a culture that holds the mother-child relationship sacrosanct. In fact, during the nineteenth century, pro-slavery arguments often pointed to enslaved women's lack of mother-child relationships as evidence of their lack of humanity, neglecting to acknowledge that such ties were often severed through sale or that women were unable to care for their children because they were forced to labor in fields or service while children were supervised by a designated caregiver. For Morrison to write a neo-slave narrative that violates the mother-child relationship so obviously is to risk alienating her readers' sympathies and reinforcing such stereotypes. Working against the murder, however, is a narrative of maternal love that seeks to reclaim African American motherhood and familial structures. Morrison shows that Sethe kills her daughter out of love and the desire to protect, connecting this extreme response to the suffering experienced by every member of her family and community. This perspective calls attention to the maternal and familial ideology inherent in sentimentalism, as well as assumptions about selfhood, race, and class that are foundational to that ideology. As even members of Sethe's community struggle with her actions—both before and after she commits the murder—the novel provides a meditation on suffering itself, revealing layers of pain within a traumatized community and questioning the effectiveness of sympathy as an affective tool. Inviting the reader to consider the nature of sympathy, love, and affective connection, Morrison asks readers how much suffering is *required* in order to receive sympathy and whether overcoming or healing from suffering comes at the cost of sympathy.

Rebecca Wanzo, in *The Suffering Will Not Be Televised*, asks a key question confronting writers who seek to portray suffering, "particularly black writers who represent the history of black struggle": "How do you represent suffering in a way that people will not dismiss as sentimental?" (95). Many novels that attempt to represent slavery have often been criticized for being melodramatic or sentimental, and Wanzo cites a John Updike review of Tom Wolfe's novel *A Man in Full* (1998) in which he praises the white author's "attempt at the great black novel without 'the usual mooning about slavery'" (95). What Crouch comes close to arguing, and what Wanzo suggests is the challenge for authors who wish to write about slavery and suffering, is that "the mere existence of the representation is sentimental . . . representations of suffering that are not ironic, minimalist in their representation, and that represent women are always vulnerable to being accused of sentimentality. Representing tears, inviting sympathy from the reader, inviting identification or self-examination in relationship to a representation of pain—any of these is routinely read as sentimental" (96).

The caveat that "good literature" must "transcend race" suggests a perspective of hegemonic privilege, one that assumes that the human condition is both raceless and ungendered, represented accurately only by the white male writer. When critics like Updike praise novels by suggesting that they "transcend race," they indicate that such texts are "closer to 'reality,'" a reality that is "far from sentimental and feminist readings of racial and gendered injustice" (95). As Wanzo rightly points out, these critics do not offer a clear definition of what "good" African American literature is, but they are clear that it should not contain portrayals of excessive suffering. Such writing should demonstrate the ways in which "black people have some responsibility for their suffering" (97). It should not "focus on violence against black women" and should not "treat black people as victims or as suffering from 'cruel determinism.'" To write about specific forms of suffering in gendered and raced bodies and to write about the conditions that bring about the suffering of those bodies calls into question the ideologies that undergird beliefs about a universal subjectivity represented by male whiteness.

In retrospect, then, it should be clear that when women began to write sentimental fiction, they placed themselves at the center of a new social order that valued female subjectivity and argued for the recognition of women as valuable cultural subjects. However, women who wrote nineteenth-century sentimental fiction tended to be white, Protestant, and middle-class. As African American authors began to tackle the ways in which human identity was constructed as white, they wrote narratives that argued first for black humanity—because cultural definitions designated citizens as white and persons with black skin as chattel/property—and later for their gender identities—African American men sought to prove that they were just as much "men" as white men by acquiring literacy, property, and the respect of their communities, and African American women showed the ways that they met the definitions of white "womanhood" while simultaneously being prevented from doing so because of their social conditions.

Challenging the Universal: Maternal Love, Loss, and Selfhood

Critics have extensively discussed maternal love as a significant theme in *Beloved*, noting the ways that Morrison's presentation of Sethe's "too thick love" (165) dramatizes the psychological struggles of identity that motherhood in slavery entails. Critics have examined the psychological and cultural meaning of Morrison's presentation of motherhood in the novel from a variety of positions. Barbara Offutt Mathieson offers a psychoanalytic analysis of the novel, in which she delineates the stages of child development and argues, through an examination of Sethe's psychological scars, that there is a correspondence between memory and maternal love. Stephanie A. Demetrakopoulos reads the novel through C. G. Jung, examining the "dark and painful side of mothering, the fact that mothering can extinguish the developing self of the mother, sometimes even before that individuation can really begin" ("Maternal Bonds," 51). After reviewing the extent to which "Sethe's maternal bonds almost destroy her," Demetrakopoulos concludes that Sethe is denied "normal motherhood by the culture that envelops her," which causes her to carry "mother instinct to an absurd and grotesque length" and eventually requires "the death of the maternal" in order for her whole self to live (55, 58). Meanwhile, Jean Wyatt offers a Lacanian analysis, examining the discursive position of the maternal symbolic, interpreting Morrison's use of language and metaphor and arguing that the novel "reconstructs the acts of maternal heroism as the reproductive feats of the maternal body" ("Giving Body," 213). Such heroism appears as an alternative to the system of master definition, a patriarchal symbolic order. Colleen Carpenter Cullinan examines the Christian tradition that links motherhood and redemption, or "more specifically, speaks of the maternity of Christ," in order to discuss the "discourse of redemption voiced by the mothers of *Beloved*" and the ways that maternal voices respond to suffering and sin ("Maternal Discourse," 78).

While these readings offer insightful ways to understand the significant symbolic place motherhood holds both in American culture and in *Beloved*, another context in which to understand Morrison's attention to maternal care is its ability to convey a universalized sense of suffering. To extend sympathy across social boundaries, sentimental novels often focus on experiences that are thought to be universal, such as death, the loss of a child, or separation from family. Sentimental novels frequently focus upon the severing of ties between parent and child. Such fiction is rife with orphans who are made vulnerable to the horrors of the world by the loss of a parent—such as Gerty and Ellen Montgomery—as well as parents who suffer over the loss of their children—such as Ruth Hall and Eliza. Both Lauren Berlant and Rebecca Wanzo, drawing from Adam Smith, have discussed the philosophy of liberalism that underpins Enlightenment sensibility which argues for the "naturalness and universal nature of sympathy" but which has also been criticized for a universality that is based in a white, Westernized, masculine subjectivity that does not acknowledge limits on agency (Wanzo, *The Suffering*, 23, 20–21). Although critical of the use of "conventions and clichés as placeholders for the universal," Berlant points out that nineteenth-century American sentimental writers "generate an affective and intimate public sphere that . . . sanctifies suffering as a relay to universality in a way that includes women in the universal" (*Female Complaint*, 12). To cross the racial divide that excluded enslaved African American women from this affective, feminine sphere, Stowe in *Uncle Tom's Cabin* focused upon the universality of losing a child. Wanzo contends that the slave mother's experience "of her child being sold into slavery would not be the same as a white woman's suffering in the face of the death of her free white child. The two events would not evoke the same feelings. Nonetheless, Stowe uses this homogenization of suffering to encourage empathy" (25). Because white female readers could understand the horror of losing a child, they would sympathize with Eliza's plight as a mother and a woman.

Just as Berlant is critical of sentimental stereotypes and clichés, Wanzo points out that such an assumption of universal suffering "comes at the cost of dehumanizing other black women" (25). By ignoring the real ways in which being sold into slavery is not the same as death and by refusing (or being unable) to acknowledge the differences in their suffering, nineteenth-century sentimental novelists privilege white suffering and white identity. Stowe's novel recognizes that African American women are mothers and are women who suffer, "but their suffering is not framed as resembling the suffering of the imagined ideal white reader. Rather, their pain is presented as suffering that should be prevented by people who have Christian compassion for others." Such differences are what led to a preference in race-themed sentimental texts for light-skinned mulatto heroines, protagonists who more closely resemble the ideal white reader, resulting in a colorism that maintains connections between whiteness and strong moral character. *Uncle Tom's Cabin* has been extremely influential, and while not alone in privileging whiteness, its legacy "has haunted numerous African American women who are viewed as far from white feminine ideals when they try to illustrate that they should receive sympathy" (26).

Sethe, then, is a deliberately problematic sentimental protagonist, simultaneously drawing from and disrupting traditional narratives of maternal loss and suffering. Morrison positions Sethe to receive sympathy through accepted beliefs about universal suffering through her love of her children, her fear of losing them, and her pain over the loss of her daughter. However, Morrison also positions Sethe to challenge assumptions regarding universal suffering because, as a fugitive slave, Sethe's circumstances are unique and utterly unavailable to the modern reader. Readers are constantly reminded of Sethe's non-idealized body—her skin is dark and heavily scarred—and she crosses acceptable social barriers by killing her own child. Sethe's suffering is not framed as the same as or equal to that of the "imagined ideal white reader" but instead challenges readers to sympathize with her pain while recognizing the vast differences that exist between them. By engaging members of the text's African American community in a confrontation with their own beliefs about suffering—who deserves sympathy for their suffering, comparisons of suffering, and whether one continues to deserve sympathy if suffering ceases—Morrison demonstrates that suffering is both universal and individualized, that a sympathy based only on perceived similarity and universality (and doesn't allow for difference) is limited and ineffective. However, if sympathy with acknowledgment for difference is achieved, it can provide opportunities for healing.

In the moments leading up to and during Sethe's attempt to kill her children—resulting in the death of only one—she isn't angry or sadistic. These are not the actions of a depraved or indifferent mother. Instead, Morrison makes clear that Sethe loves her children even more than herself, connecting her escape and her act of violence to her love and her desire to protect her children from the horrors she experienced in slavery. Sethe's love is an act of rebellion against a system that actively works to inhibit all affective and familial relationships for African Americans, particularly that of mother-child. Baby Suggs, Sethe's mother-in-law, exemplifies this experience. She bore eight children to six fathers, and all of her life, "men and women were moved around like checkers. Anybody Baby Suggs knew, let alone loved, who hadn't run off or been hanged, got rented out, loaned out, bought up, brought back, stored up, mortgaged, won, stolen, or seized.... What she called the nastiness of life was the shock she received upon learning that nobody stopped playing checkers just because the pieces included her children" (23). After two daughters are sold before she even knew they were gone and after sleeping with a straw boss in exchange for keeping a son who is sold anyway, Baby Suggs becomes pregnant again but finds it too painful to love children that are repeatedly taken from her: "That child she could not love and the rest she would not."

Sethe was kept on the same plantation as her mother, but they did not have a relationship because her mother was forced to work and Sethe was raised by another woman: "I didn't see her but a few times out in the fields and once when she was working indigo" (60). Later, when her mother is hanged for some unknown offense, an enslaved woman named Nan tells Sethe that she was the only child her mother had chosen to keep—she "threw away" the babies conceived out of rape—and that she had named her for the black man she had chosen to love: "The others she did not put her arms around. Never" (62). Sethe struggles to interpret these acts as signs of her mother's love, and she questions her mother's feelings for her, wondering if she had been hanged because she had been caught escaping and had left her daughter behind: "No. Not that. Because she was my ma'am and nobody's ma'am would run off and leave her daughter, would she? . . . Even if she hadn't been able to suckle the daughter for more than a week or two and had to turn her over to another woman's tit that never had enough for all" (203). Knowing the emotional costs of motherhood in slavery, Paul D worries about Sethe's attachment to her children, believing that disconnection is the only way to protect the self from additional harm: "The best thing, he knew, was to love just a little bit; everything, just a little bit, so when they broke its back, or shoved it in a croaker sack, well, maybe you'd have a little love left over for the next one" (45).

Sethe, however, rejects the idea that one can protect the self or alleviate suffering by withholding. While Paul D replaces his heart with a rusted "tobacco tin" in order to survive brutalities, losses, and disillusionments, Sethe conflates her identity as a mother with her selfhood, both of which require freedom and agency (72). Like Walker's Vyry in *Jubilee*, Morrison's Sethe cannot contemplate escaping Sweet Home without her children. The act of fleeing is both a protective act for her children and a declaration of selfhood: "I did it. I got us all out.... Each and every one of my babies and me too. I birthed them and I got em out and it wasn't no accident. I did that. I had help, of course, lots of that, but still it was me doing it; me saying, *Go on*, and *Now*. Me having to look out. Me using my own head. But it was more than that. It was a kind of selfishness I never knew nothing about before. It felt good. Good and right" (162). A modern reader would have a hard time interpreting Sethe's actions as selfish because she saved her children from slavery and risked herself in the process. But her contemporaries could construe her actions as selfish because to love her children was a fundamentally selfish act. To save her children is to save herself, both because it defies a system that denies African American motherhood and because it was her first claim of ownership to her freed self. Claiming affective bonds is a method of claiming the self, and those bonds are strongest with family, the relationships that are most assiduously denied by the system of slavery. In the twenty-eight-day period after her escape, Sethe bonded with the free black Ohio community members and participated in "[d]ays of healing, ease and real-talk... feeling their fun and sorrow along with her own" (95). Developing these affective bonds allows Sethe, "along with the others," to claim herself, because "[f]reeing yourself was one thing; claiming ownership of that freed self was another." The acts of loving and feeling sympathy toward others are acts of selfishness because they require a sense of *self*.

Milk-Love: Reclaiming Body, Self, and Familial Relationships

The connection between Sethe's suffering, her love for her children, and her desire to prevent their suffering is exemplified in repeated references to her mother's milk. Sethe connects her ability to nurse her children both literally and metaphorically with her role as their caretaker and mother—a role that is impossible if one is prevented from possessing one's body and selfhood. When she is sexually assaulted by Schoolteacher's nephews at Sweet Home, boys who hold her down and drink the milk from her breasts, the violation is both physical and psychological because of the trauma it induces and its participation in a history of separating enslaved women from their children, not just through sale, but also by severing their emotional relationships and treating the women as chattel. The preservation of Sethe's milk is symbolically the ownership of her own body and her exclusive relationship to her children:

> Nobody will ever get my milk no more except my own children. I never had to give it to nobody else—and the one time I did it was took from me—they held me down and took it. Milk that belonged to my baby. Nan had to nurse whitebabies and me too because Ma'am was in the rice. The little whitebabies got it first and I got what was left. Or none. There was no nursing milk to call my own. I know what it is to be without the milk that belongs to you; to have to fight and holler for it, and to have so little left. (200)

When Sethe recalls the abuses she suffered at Sweet Home, she repeatedly points to the mammary rape as the worst assault perpetrated against her. Although Paul D is mortified that Schoolteacher whipped Sethe, she repeatedly interjects, "And they took my milk!" (17). Thus, during her escape, Sethe focuses on bringing her milk to her children because she needs to provide actual nourishment for her nursing baby and because it symbolizes the unique relationship only she, as their mother, has with them: "All I knew was I had to get my milk to my baby girl. Nobody was going to nurse her like me. Nobody was going to get it to her fast enough, or take it away when she had enough and didn't know it. Nobody knew that she couldn't pass her air if you held her up on your shoulder, only if she was lying on my knees. Nobody knew that but me and nobody had her milk but me" (16). Sethe's need to reunite with her children motivates her to survive the horrors of the final days at Sweet Home and the extreme hardship of her escape: "What I had to get through later I got through because of you. Passed right by those boys hanging in the trees. One had Paul A's shirt on but not his feet or his head. I walked right on by because only me had your milk, and God do what He would, I was going to get it to you" (198).

Milk becomes a metaphor for Sethe's ability to love and designate who is a member of her family. As Sethe seeks to remind Beloved, after coming to believe that she is her daughter, when she arrived in Ohio, exhausted, with her back torn from the whipping at Sweet Home, and having given birth to Denver on the way: "You remember that, don't you. . . . That when I got here I had milk enough for all?" (198). Although Sethe had two older boys who were too old to nurse and needed only to have enough milk for the newborn Denver and the infant "crawling-already?" daughter, the ambiguity of the indefinite pronoun "all" (in lieu of "both") suggests that she includes all of her children. As Sethe comes to recognize Beloved as her daughter, returned in human form, she begins to associate her with milk. When Beloved kisses her neck in the clearing after the mysterious choking incident, Sethe separates herself from Beloved and "later believed that it was because the girl's breath was exactly like new milk" (98). The milk smell on Beloved's breath connotes nursing, linking Beloved to the dead infant and reincorporating her into Sethe's family circle. Poetic segments that hint at both Beloved's stream-of-conscious memories and conversations with Sethe show that—after becoming convinced that Beloved is her daughter—Sethe asks her to remember the milk, to remember being included in this circle of familial love:

> You rememory me?
> Yes. I remember you.
> You never forgot me?
> Your face is mine.
> . . . .
>
> I have your milk
> I have your smile
> I will take care of you
>
> You are my face; I am you. Why did you leave me who am you?
> I will never leave you again
> Don't ever leave me again
> You will never leave me again
> You went in the water
> I drank your blood
> I brought your milk
> . . . .
>
> I waited for you
> You are mine
> You are mine
> You are mine (215–17)

Sethe identifies herself to Beloved as the one who has her milk and shares her face—imagistic representations of motherhood—and, therefore, is the one who protects and cares for her. Because of the narrative fragmentation, "I drank your blood" suggests that Denver is included in the circle of relationships, but Sethe metaphorically drank Beloved's blood by cutting her throat. By declaring "I brought your milk," Sethe reasserts her role as life- and love-giver, the one who designates family bonds. Thus, "you are mine" is ambiguous as both Beloved and Sethe claim ownership of each other.

Much as she does with her older children, however, Sethe does not limit the metaphor of milk-love to literal nursing, nor does it indicate only which children are part of her family. She expands the idea of having "enough milk" as a metaphor of inclusion, designating Paul D as part of her familial circle as well. When Sethe chooses to include Paul D as part of her family, she associates her decision "to launch her newer, stronger life with a tender man" with her mother's milk (99). When she enters the house thinking about the special meal she plans to make for Paul D, she finds him bathing in a tub in the kitchen. As he pulls her against his wet, naked body, the talk about her cooking becomes foreplay, and Sethe thinks, "There was no question but she could do it. Just like the day she arrived at 124—sure enough, she had milk enough for all" (100). With her children long grown, Sethe is not physically nursing or producing milk; instead, having enough milk is metaphor for her choice to extend her love to him and designate him as a member of her family.

Sethe's milk-love allows her to reconstruct her familial and affectional bonds in opposition to destructive societal pressures under slavery, reclaiming her body and placing the African American mother at the center of the African American family. What is interesting about this construction of family is its combination of both consanguinity, to use Cindy Weinstein's term, and affective choice. What *Beloved* shares with sentimental fiction is a focus on the construction of the family. Weinstein argues that the primary task of sentimental literature is to redefine the family "as an institution to which one can choose to belong or not" (*Family, Kinship*, 8). Nineteenth-century sentimental fiction constitutes an "interrogation and reconfiguration of what constitutes a family . . . replacing it with a family that is based on affection and organized according to a paradigm of contract," by which Weinstein generally means adoption or marriage (9). Sentimental fiction challenges the consanguineous relations—or blood ties—that bind biological families together.

Although nineteenth-century sentimental novels promote mother love as an antidote to paternal failure, children in sentimental fiction are often left motherless, a factor that "demands that the possibilities for who counts as family be expanded. In the process, the criterion by which families are deemed capable (or not) to raise a child shifts from considerations of economy to those of affection. Sentimental fictions are about finding the right place where sympathy flourishes and understanding that place and those people as one's home and 'family'" (9). Sentimental literature, however, focuses on middle-class white families where the ties of consanguinity are socially and legally validated; altering that family structure becomes a way to reorganize national social structures and emphasize affection as a new hegemonic moral and familial order. As an enslaved African American woman, Sethe's consanguineous ties to her children are neither socially nor legally recognized. Furthermore, African American women's affective ties to their children have traditionally been ignored. Rather than focus on a child left vulnerable and needing to expand the definition of family by affective bonds, *Beloved* focuses on a mother who as a child was made vulnerable by the system of slavery that denies all ties of biology and affection and who then demands recognition for that relationship by rescuing her own children. Thus, Sethe's combination of both the physical and the emotional—milk and love—reclaims both African American consanguineous family structures and the sentimental affective process that legitimizes a mother's role in determining the structure of the family.

The Demands of Sympathy: Suffering as a Reflection of the Self

Sethe attempts to kill her children, succeeding only in killing her daughter, because she is protecting them from the abuses and dehumanization that she knows they will experience under slavery and because she is refusing to relinquish her familial rights to Schoolteacher's control. When she recognizes the hat of her former master, "She just flew. Collected every bit of life she had made, all the parts of her that were precious and fine and beautiful, and carried, pushed, dragged them through the veil, out, away, over there where no one could hurt them" (163). As James Berger has pointed out, this reference to the veil evokes W. E. B. Du Bois's *The Souls of Black Folk*, in which the veil is a metaphor for both American racial separation and African American double consciousness. Berger interprets this moment as an apocalyptic revelation of "continuing white racism and of African American self-destruction" ("Ghosts of Liberalism," 410). However, one must also consider Du Bois's connection between double consciousness and selfhood. In *Souls*, Du Bois writes that African Americans are "born with a veil, and gifted with second-sight in this American world," that they can achieve "no true self-consciousness" but can only "see [themselves] through the revelation of the other [i.e., white] world" (364). Sethe claims herself through her escape, through her children, and through her sympathetic connections with African American community members during her month of freedom. Her desire to push her children "through the veil" can be read as the wish to place them firmly in a consciousness where selfhood is not determined in relation to white consciousness or the white world. Although violent, her act is not so much self-destructive as it is radically rebellious and protective. Because the white world is dominant—everything and everyone is defined through or against white norms—Sethe's reality demands that African Americans maintain double consciousness, and only death will free her and her children from defining themselves in this divided manner, from existing as Others. Although Paul D protests that what she did was wrong and points to the aftermath of her actions, she declares, "I stopped him.... I took and put my babies where they'd be safe.... They ain't at Sweet Home. Schoolteacher ain't got em" (164–65). Regardless of the costs and the judgment of her community, Sethe maintains that her actions were protective. Although only her daughter died, Sethe's actions prevented all of her children from returning to slavery; they were allowed to remain within the African American community and claim a greater chance for self-definition.

In drawing this bloody line, Sethe's actions render her unsympathetic and incomprehensible to both the white and the African American communities. When Schoolteacher enters the woodshed and sees what she has done, he realizes "that there was nothing there to claim," comparing her to a mishandled horse or hound "if you beat it beyond the point of education" (149). Schoolteacher's statements are highly ironic. Throughout the narrative, his assessments of Sethe's and other slave's bodies or "characteristics" have degraded and dehumanized them. Though the previous owner and master of Sweet Home promoted the view that slaves were men and women, thus treating them in a more human fashion, Schoolteacher works against such an idea, classifying them as more animal than human. Such treatment creates a crisis of conscience that causes Paul D to despair over his manhood and Sethe to go to violent extremes to save her children. And yet, Schoolteacher views her act as proof of a complete lack of humanity—there is "nothing there to claim" because he sees a mother's murdering her children as evidence that all of her humanity has evaporated. What he doesn't recognize is that he sought to reclaim ownership of a woman, not a beast, one who "made fine ink, damn good soup, pressed his collars the way he liked." But what Schoolteacher and his nephews find is a woman who has violated what a socially defined woman should hold sacrosanct—she has killed her own children—leaving them too stunned to understand her motivations, asking repeatedly, "What she go and do that for?" (150). As they leave, the men avoid the eyes of the community members who have gathered, feeling disturbed by all the "nigger eyes" and recalling the children's staring eyes in the sawdust. Children—even "nigger" children that they prefer to view as property or animals—invoke in these men a sympathetic response that they wish to ignore. Sethe's eyes particularly trouble them because it "looked like she didn't have any. Since the whites in them had disappeared and since they were as black as her skin, she looked blind." Sethe's eyes evoke another animalistic image because many animals—such as horses and dogs—don't show the whites, but the image also gives the impression that she is possessed or overcome by something unnatural.

Schoolteacher and his nephews are not the only ones disturbed by Sethe's eyes. When Paul D reunites with Sethe, he recognizes her face despite the passage of eighteen years, recalling that the irises of her eyes are "the same color of her skin, which, in that still face, used to make him think of a mask with mercifully punched-out eyes" (9). The violence of this image—the term "punched-out" generally refers to a mechanized process that creates holes, but the use of "punched" also connotes the violence of a physical blow—suggests that Sethe's eyes reflect a sadness or suffering that has resulted from her experiences. However, the "punched-out eyes" can also suggest blindness, that the eyes have been removed, and Paul D seems to find this "merciful" because it is a way to protect Sethe from witnessing or experiencing things that would hurt her further.[1] Eyes are often metaphorically viewed as windows to the soul—a way to glimpse a person's interiority—and as mirrors—a person can view himself reflected in another's eyes. It may be merciful for Paul D not to see himself in Sethe's eyes because they confront him with their shared suffering as well as suffering he cannot understand. Sitting by a fire at Sweet Home, telling Paul D that her children had been sent north and of her own plans to run, "her eyes did not pick up a flicker of light. They were like two wells into which he had trouble gazing. Even punched out they needed to be covered, lidded, marked with some sign to warn folks of what that emptiness held" (9). Sethe's eyes are disturbingly empty because others see only emptiness: they do not see themselves reflected back.

This affirmation of suffering—a sympathy that depends on identification with the sufferer in a way that reflects one's own experience—is precisely what this African American community struggles with throughout the novel. Even prior to the killing, Morrison points to problems of sympathy that inhibit community members from overcoming or healing from their traumatic past. Although the novel does not advocate forgetting the past—as its emphasis on "rememory" and the return of Beloved attest—the novel emphasizes that the ongoing suffering of those who have experienced trauma must be acknowledged and addressed in order for healing to occur. Even more important than *why* Sethe killed her daughter is the effect it has on her community and people's capacity to extend sympathy to her despite their inability to understand her choice. *Beloved*'s concern is less with how a mother can kill her daughter—for as Morrison points out, this happened more frequently than contemporary readers realize because women with no other options were desperate to free their children from slavery[2]—than with questions about whether community members can extend sympathy to those who have suffered *differently from them* and facilitate healing. Focusing on a catalog of hurts and asking whether one individual or group suffered more or less than others actually magnifies isolation and suffering and does not allow for a true recognition of pain or the costs of that suffering.

Paul D breaches Sethe's isolation and becomes someone who shares her grief, but his ability to sympathize with Sethe is sorely tested when he is confronted with the story of her violent actions. After their reunion, Paul D and Sethe share their stories of Sweet Home—to Denver's irritation—and find comfort in their common past because it enables them to sympathize more fully with each other's pain. After telling the story of her assault, whipping, and escape, Paul D comforts Sethe by standing behind her, tracing the "chokecherry tree" of scars on her back, and cupping her breasts in his hands: "Behind her, bending down, his body an arc of kindness, he held her breasts in the palms of his hands. He rubbed his cheek on her back and learned that way her sorrow, the roots of it; its wide trunk and intricate branches" (17). In addition to listening to her story, Paul D's physical contact allows him to come closer to her sorrow, bringing him in greater sympathy with Sethe to provide her comfort. His sympathy causes Sethe to wonder if she could "just stand there a minute or two, naked from shoulder blade to waist, relieved of the weight of her breasts, smelling the stolen milk again and the pleasure of baking bread? Maybe this one time she could stop . . . and feel the hurt her back ought to. Trust things and remember things because the last of the Sweet Home men was there to catch her if she sank?" (18). As a Sweet Home man, Paul D understands her past experiences; by temporarily taking the burdens of those sexual/maternal memories and supporting her through her pain, he demonstrates that he shares her suffering. Sethe believes that Paul D is "someone to share [her grief]," making up for the loss of the friends in the community who had turned away from her years ago (96).

However, Paul D cannot sympathize with or accept Sethe when he learns that she obtained her family's freedom by killing one of her children. After loving and sympathizing with her, Paul D experiences a process of physical and emotional displacement that distances him from Sethe. When Stamp Paid shows Paul D a newspaper clipping and tells him what happened, he at first insists that the story isn't about Sethe because he doesn't recognize her face in the picture: he repeatedly asserts, "This ain't her mouth" (156). However, he sees Sethe in the drawing's eyes, noticing that they are "almost as calm as hers," and in the woman's posture, noting that her head "was turned on her neck in the manner he loved so well." Denying the news because he wants to love her, Paul D refuses to acknowledge the face as Sethe's because he knows that African Americans appear in newspapers only when the news about them is terrible, "something out of the ordinary—something whitepeople would find interesting, truly different." He is afraid that what he will learn about Sethe will make her unrecognizable and unsympathetic to him. Indeed, when he goes to Sethe and shows her the clipping, he begins to feel disoriented as she circles the room and explains: "It made him dizzy . . . listening to her was like having a child whisper into your ear so close you could feel its lips form the words you couldn't make out because they were too close" (161). Paul D finds her words incomprehensible and discovers that he can't follow her story from their shared past at Sweet Home to her desperate act in Ohio.

When Sethe expresses being unable to fully love while enslaved, Paul D believes he understands, relating her suffering to his own experiences as a prisoner, where the men learned that "you protected yourself and loved small. . . . A woman, a child, a brother—a big love like that would split you wide open in Alfred, Georgia. He knew exactly what she meant: to get to a place where you could love anything you chose—not to need permission for desire—well now, *that* was freedom" (162). However, when Sethe describes gathering her children, putting her babes "where they'd be safe," Paul D feels a "roaring" in his head and finds her unrecognizable from the woman he had known at Sweet Home: "This here Sethe was new.... This here Sethe talked about love like any other woman; talked about baby clothes like any other woman, but what she meant could cleave the bone. This here Sethe talked about safety with a handsaw. This here new Sethe didn't know where the world stopped and she began. Suddenly he saw what Stamp Paid wanted him to see: more important than what Sethe had done was what she claimed. It scared him" (164). The repetition of "this here" and "new" indicates that Paul D sees Sethe not just in a new light but as a completely different person, someone with whom he has no shared past, someone with whom he cannot sympathize. Unlike white culture, which views Sethe's actions as inhumane or as proof of her lack of love, Paul D understands her violent actions as the "claim" of love between mother and child. But for Paul D, who has survived by claiming nothing, this declaration is too dangerous. Paul D tells Sethe that her love is "too thick," indicating that a separation of self from what that self loves is necessary for both to survive. But when Sethe scoffs, "Love is or it ain't. Thin love ain't no love at all," Paul D finds no other rebuttal than to fall back upon the cultural narrative that asserts that it is always wrong for a mother to kill her child. Thus, Paul D declares, "You got two feet, Sethe, not four," judging her actions, as Schoolteacher had, as indicative of a bestial, less-than-human nature (165). Sympathy is breached, and "right then a forest sprang up between them; trackless and quiet," separating Paul D from the affectional family Sethe has created.

"Don't Talk to Me": Comparative Suffering and the Failure of Sympathy

Baby Suggs, who appears to be a model for love and sympathy in *Beloved* and is a leader within her community, also fails in this regard and, therefore, retreats to isolation, grief, and death. Baby Suggs seems to understand the healing power of sympathy and, after being freed, conducts holy services to which she invites all members of the free black community. She commands children to laugh, men to dance, and women to cry, which results in an emotional outpouring, sympathetic sharing, and community affective bonding: "It started that way: laughing children, dancing men, crying women and then it got mixed up. Women stopped crying and danced; men sat down and cried; children danced, women laughed, children cried until, exhausted and riven, all and each lay about the Clearing damp and gasping for breath. In the silence that followed, Baby Suggs, holy, offered up to them her great big heart" (88). As the men, women, and children blend through their shared actions, they also share one another's emotional responses. Preaching that "they [whites] do not love your flesh ... don't love your eyes ... do not love your hands," Baby Suggs tells the crowd: "*You* got to love it, *you!* ... Flesh that needs to be loved. Feet that need to rest and to dance; backs that need support; shoulders that need arms, strong arms I'm telling you ... and the beat and beating heart, love that too." This community is made up of people who have been subject to enslavement and abuse because of their bodies—as Cheryl I. Harris argues in "Whiteness as Property," the non-whiteness of African American bodies is what makes them legally susceptible to being categorized as property, treated inhumanely, and subject to white people's hate and fear—and Baby Suggs offers her heart because love is an antidote to suffering. She urges them to love themselves as a process of discovering selfhood.

However, while Baby Suggs preaches love and while she cares for her daughter-in-law and grandchildren, she judges Sethe's suffering against her own. When Sethe once suggests that they move to escape the wrath of the baby ghost inhabiting 124, Baby Suggs scoffs, "Not a house in the country ain't packed to its rafters with some dead Negro's grief.... Don't talk to me. You lucky. You got three left. Three pulling at your skirts and just one raising hell from the other side. Be thankful, why don't you? I had eight. Every one of them gone away from me. Four taken, four chased, and all, I suspect, worrying somebody's house into evil" (5). Baby Suggs continuously mourns the loss of her children and her inability to know them despite refusing to allow herself to attach to them because it had been too painful to love them only to have them taken from her.[3] By suggesting that all enslaved people suffer but some in greater measure, Baby Suggs implies that greater suffering imparts more legitimacy to that suffering. She admonishes Sethe to "be thankful" because she has children left alive and with her and has never faced having any of them sold away, which implies that her suffering is not as great as what Baby Suggs herself has experienced. Baby Suggs's response minimizes Sethe's pain and suggests a difference between their experiences that separates them: Sethe can't "talk to" Baby Suggs because she can't understand Baby Suggs's loss. Like Paul D, Baby Suggs understands Sethe's love for her children but not her intense attachment to them or the connection between her children and her selfhood. Baby Suggs "didn't approve of extra" and would advise others that "[e]verything depends on knowing how much.... Good is knowing when to stop" (87).

Baby Suggs advocates a lifestyle of moderation, but she extends this to emotional experience, a logical response given her coping method of reducing her attachment to her own children. Thus, when Sethe explains, "I wouldn't draw breath without my children," Baby Suggs "got down on her knees to beg God's pardon" for her (203). Baby Suggs believes that Sethe's intense focus on her children requires forgiveness because it violates the message of grace and love—to love yourself—which she has been preaching. It also goes against Baby Suggs's own forced separation from her children: she has had to survive, to "draw breath" without them because she had no other choice. To do so, she has separated herself from them, although her separation has not lessened her suffering. A mother who was allowed to be a mother to only one of her children, Baby Suggs continues to grieve for her children throughout her life, clinging to the remnants of small features that she recalls about those she lost—a lisp, a skin color, a dimple, a love for burned bread. Thoughts of finding her scattered children are among her first thoughts in freedom—"[W]here do I start? Get somebody to write old Whitlow. See who took Patty and Rosa Lee. Somebody name Dunn got Ardelia and went West, she heard. No point in trying for Tyree or John" (143)—and she claimed to "feel" the death of each one of her children.[4] As a result, Baby Suggs believes that "the sadness was at her center, the desolated center where the self that was no self made its home. Sad as it was that she did not know where her children were buried or what they looked like if alive, fact was she knew more about them than she knew about herself, having never had the map to discover what she was like" (140). Despite believing that the loss of her children has contributed to her loss of self, Baby Suggs reproaches Sethe because she believes their situations are comparative—they have both lost children—and "knowing when to stop" separates Baby Suggs from Sethe.

Thus, Baby Suggs, who has connected self-identity, love, and community sympathy with holy redemption feels betrayed—indescribably broken—by Sethe's violent act. Baby Suggs values the mother-child relationship, but despite grieving for her own children and because she survived by distancing herself from them, she cannot comprehend Sethe's "claim" either. It is she who recalls Sethe from her shock, reminding her of her maternal role when she enters the woodshed and begins to care for the survivors. She tells Sethe, "It's time to nurse your youngest," coaxing Sethe to exchange the dead child for the living (152). However, when Sethe attempts to nurse Denver without first washing her older daughter's blood off her chest, "[t]hey fought then. Like rivals over the heart of the loved, they fought. Each struggling for the nursing child. Baby Suggs lost when she slipped in a red puddle and fell. So Denver took her mother's milk right along with the blood of her sister." Baby Suggs's fight with Sethe represents a conflict between their belief systems—Baby Suggs attempts to separate Sethe's maternal love from what it cost to assert and maintain that familial and affectional tie. When Baby Suggs slips in the baby blood, she not only loses the battle, but her action reveals her inability to understand both the price and the gains of what Sethe has done. Denver drinks both milk-love and the blood of her sister, representing the extreme cost to African American women in asserting this claim over their bodies and their families: both substances are fundamental to her survival.

After these bloody events, Baby Suggs loses her faith and retreats to the bedroom to ponder color. Because she could not protect her family through the sympathetic love she has preached in the Clearing and because she does not agree with Sethe's behavior, she questions the usefulness of sympathy itself. Helpless to prevent Schoolteacher from entering her yard and saddened by what she believes is disapproval in the African American community that prevented anyone from warning them, Baby Suggs is confronted with her own powerlessness and the seeming passivity of sympathy: "The heart that pumped out love, the mouth that spoke the Word, didn't count. They came in her yard anyway and she could not approve or condemn Sethe's rough choice" (180). Although she had urged love as an antidote to suffering and encouraged sympathy as a way to create kinship, Baby Suggs believes that members of her community see her love as pride, holding back from protecting her family and drawing further away when they are shocked by Sethe's actions: "After sixty years of losing children to the people who chewed up her life and spit it out like a fish bone . . . to belong to a community of other free Negroes—to love and be loved by them, to counsel and be counseled, protect and be protected, feed and be fed—and then to have that community step back and hold itself at a distance—well, it could wear out even a Baby Suggs, holy" (177). Because love is not enough, and it now appears that sympathy is not enough, Baby Suggs "believed she had lied. There was no grace—imaginary or real—and no sunlit dance in a Clearing could change that. Her faith, her love, her imagination and her great big old heart began to collapse twenty-eight days after her daughter-in-law arrived" (89). She is convinced that "[h]er authority in the pulpit, her dance in the Clearing, her powerful Call . . . all that had been mocked and rebuked by the bloodspill in her backyard. God puzzled her and she was too ashamed of Him to say so" (177). Baby Suggs's "great big old heart" loses the ability to create or maintain affectional bonds; she is left isolated and alone, feeling that "[h]er past had been like her present—intolerable—and since she knew death was anything but forgetfulness, she used the little energy left her for pondering color" (4).

When Baby Suggs and Sethe first arrive among the Ohio free black community, they find friendship and sympathy among the people there. But because individual members of the community engage in comparisons of their suffering—either measuring their experiences of slavery and abuse against each other's or feeling unable to appreciate someone else's suffering as equal in depth to their own—their ability to maintain affectional bonds and create community kinship is inhibited. Members focus on differences in suffering, insisting not only that each person must experience pain of acceptable depth but also that this pain be ongoing—to receive sympathy, one must demonstrate that one *continues* to suffer. The community considers anyone who shows freedom from suffering as prideful, punishing that person through isolation. It is not until members of the community acknowledge Sethe's continued pain and overcome their aversion to her actions—accepting the difference in her choice and her experiences—that they are able to extend sympathy. With Denver acting as a bridge in this process, the community serves as a catalyst for the release of the ghost (or demon, depending on how one interprets Beloved's presence) and brings Sethe back into a unified community that has the potential to heal beyond its suffering.

Earlier, members of the community perceive Baby Suggs as suffering in the ways that they do, when she preaches out of her pain and gives them her "great big heart," the group establishes sympathy and kinship. Deriving authority from their shared experiences—the loss of loved ones and the loss of a self created in slavery—and her deep understanding of their suffering, Baby Suggs becomes the central figure that binds the community together. More than a preacher, she is also a symbolic mother to the entire kinship group, which has been affectionally bonded in the style of an extended sympathetic family. Her home—a spatial symbol of family organization—becomes a "cheerful, buzzing" center of activity, where she "loved, cautioned, fed, chastised and soothed" just as a mother provides love and moral guidance and cares for the bodily needs of her children (86–87). This kinship is extended outside of the established community to other African Americans, as "strangers"—fugitive slaves—are invited to rest at her home, and individuals freely leave messages there, "for whoever needed them was sure to stop in one day soon" (87).

A party spontaneously grows out of Baby Suggs's joy at Sethe and her children's arrival and Stamp Paid's spontaneous gift of fresh blackberries, because she quickly determines that they have too much food "to keep for one's own" (136). While recognizing the primary needs of her immediate family—"one's own"—Baby Suggs's maternal impulse is also to share her good fortune and her happiness with her extended kinship circle, so that what starts out as a few blackberry pies transforms to "a feast for ninety people." Although members of the community "ate so well, and laughed so much" at the party, when the next morning they consider the bounty and merriment on display, they grow angry at what they term Baby Suggs's pride. Exaggerating the amount of food to mythical proportions—"three (maybe four) pies grew to ten (maybe twelve) . . . two hens became five turkeys. The one block of ice . . . [b]ecame a wagonload of ice cakes"—the townspeople imagine that Baby Suggs and her family have far more material resources than anyone else in town (137). They angrily question Baby Suggs's authority as the bonding agent of their kinship circle: "Where does she get it all, Baby Suggs, holy? Why is she and hers always the center of things? . . . Giving advice; passing messages; healing the sick, hiding fugitives, loving, cooking, cooking, loving, preaching, singing, dancing and loving everybody like it was her job and hers alone." Suddenly, Baby Suggs's loving heart and her gifts to the community become signs of privilege, which set her apart and above the group she seeks to unite. Her reunion with and joy in her biological family cause her affectional family to question the strength of their ties, and they feel insecure about the source of her authority as well as their places in the kinship circle.

Equally significant is the fact that Baby Suggs's happiness in this moment makes them forget about her suffering, causing them to lose sympathy for her. Although they acknowledge that she has also lived in slavery, they begin to concentrate on the differences of their experiences, minimizing her suffering to the point of negating it. Comparing their own experiences in slavery against what they imagine to be hers, they picture her as "an ex-slave who had probably never carried one hundred pounds to the scale, or picked okra with a baby on her back. Who had never been lashed by a ten-year-old whiteboy as God knows they had. Who had not even escaped slavery—had, in fact, been *bought out* of it by a doting son and *driven* to the Ohio River in a wagon—free papers folded between her breasts (driven by the very man who had been her master, who also paid her resettlement fee—name of Garner), and rented a house with *two* floors *and* a well from the Bodwins" (137). These comparisons recall resentment between slaves who worked in the fields—who carried hundred pound sacks of cotton, picked okra, and were publicly whipped—and slaves who worked in the master's house cooking, cleaning, and serving and who were perceived to live in more privilege or protection. As numerous slave narratives have revealed, however, serving in the master's house may have entailed a great deal of suffering, including bodily and psychological risk. Further, such projections onto Baby Suggs ignore the realities of her past. Reflecting on Sweet Home, Baby Suggs observes that the farm is "tiny" compared to the "places she had been," but she appreciates her new situation because "there wasn't a rice field or tobacco patch in sight, and nobody, but nobody, knocked her down. Not once.... [N]obody said you-black-bitch-what's-the-matter-with-you and nobody knocked her down" (139). Baby Suggs also walks with a limp because of "the field work that broke her hip" and is grateful that the Garners didn't force their slaves to mate, "[n]ever brought them to her cabin with directions to 'lay down with her,' like they did in Carolina" (140). Although Baby Suggs eventually found a less arduous work experience at Sweet Home and was granted her freedom, she experienced similar forms of suffering. Further, her freedom was obtained at great cost, as she witnessed her son Halle give up his remaining life and labor to their white owners in order to buy her, accepting separation from the last child that remained to her.

By minimizing Baby Suggs's suffering in comparison to their own, members of the community establish differences that prevent them from feeling the sympathy they previously did. They grow angry at the appearance of Baby Suggs's lack of suffering, calling it arrogance: "It made them furious. They swallowed baking soda, the morning after, to calm the stomach violence caused by the bounty, the reckless generosity on display at 124. Whispered to each other in the yards about fat rats, doom and uncalled-for pride" (137). Baby Suggs, sensitive to the mood of community members, believes that she has incurred their resentment because she has "overstepped, given too much, offended them by excess" (138). Indeed, she has. But it is not the excess of the feast that offends; it is the excess of joy—the lack of suffering—on display. In a community that *requires* suffering for sympathetic inclusion, the visible presence of *continued* suffering is necessary.

It is this lack of sympathy that causes the community to fail Baby Suggs and Sethe when Schoolteacher and his nephews appear in town: "Not Ella, not John, not anybody ran down or to Bluestone Road, to say some new whitefolks with the Look just rode in.... Nobody warned them ... it wasn't the exhaustion from a long day's gorging that dulled them, but some other thing—like, well, like meanness—that let them stand aside, or not pay attention, or tell themselves somebody else was probably bearing the news already to the house" (157). Perceived differences in suffering result in emotional withholding rather than sympathetic support. This "meanness" is a misguided wish to bring a member of the community back into alignment by proving that they suffer in equal measure. Just as later, when "everybody in town was longing for Sethe to come on difficult times" because her "outrageous claims, her self-sufficiency seemed to demand it" (171), failing to act stems from a desire for the perceived non-sufferer to experience suffering that reminds them of the experiences of those in pain and returns them to a position within that sympathetic community—one cannot be a member of this community if one is not actively engaged with suffering. Sethe's past suffering does not engender sympathy because her self-sufficiency suggests that she no longer requires the group's support.

By choosing not to act, the community contributes to the events that culminate in Sethe's desperate, violent response to the prospect of being re-enslaved. As shocked as they are by Sethe's choices, these events place Baby Suggs and Sethe in sympathetic positions because Sethe is once again under the control of whites—although not returned to slavery, she is arrested and sent to jail—and Baby Suggs loses her reunited, happy family—one of her grandchildren is dead, two are injured, and her daughter-in-law and granddaughter are in jail. Thus, the community's initial response is to extend sympathy and support. However, Sethe refuses to demonstrate suffering:

> Outside a throng, now, of black faces stopped murmuring. Holding the living child, Sethe walked past them in their silence and hers. She climbed into the cart, her profile knife-clean against a cheery blue sky. A profile that shocked them with its clarity. Was her head a bit too high? Her back a little too straight? Probably. Otherwise the singing would have begun at once, the moment she appeared in the doorway of the house on Bluestone Road. Some cape of sound would have quickly been wrapped around her, like arms to hold and steady her on the way. As it was, they waited till the cart turned

about, headed west to town. And then no words. Humming. No words at all. (152)

It is clear that Sethe believes her actions are protective, not destructive. In attempting to kill her children, she radically claims her role as a mother and accomplishes her goal of keeping them out of slavery, for the second time. Although she mourns the loss of her daughter and clearly suffered under slavery, she does not demonstrate a form of suffering the community expects. Thus, they do not sing to her, do not offer groupsong to reach out "like arms to hold and steady her" because she does not appear to need steadying or their sympathy. Her refusal to demonstrate suffering makes her ineligible for their sympathy, and they respond with silence and emotional withholding. After these events, members of the community no longer visit 124, avoiding Baby Suggs and symbolically abandoning the family home and the extended, sympathetic family structure it represents.

Stamp Paid as a Transitional Catalyst to Sympathy

Stamp Paid, an influential and well-regarded community member, serves as a transitional figure who symbolizes the need to recognize differences in suffering and to find sympathy in healing after suffering. Although he is guilty of pushing Paul D to confront Sethe, he later serves as a catalyst in helping members of the community accept Sethe by allowing for the differences in suffering and acknowledging the prejudices that caused them to withhold their sympathy. Stamp Paid acquired his name from surviving the humiliation of being unable to prevent his wife, Vashti, from being forced to become a concubine in slavery: "Born Joshua, he renamed himself when he handed over his wife to his master's son. Handed her over in the sense that he did not kill anybody, thereby himself, because his wife demanded he stay alive. Otherwise, she reasoned, where and to whom could she return when the boy was through? With that gift, he decided that he didn't owe anybody anything. Whatever his obligations were, that act paid them off" (184–85). Stamp Paid considers his nonresistance, his acceptance of this humiliation, a price paid for his life and eventual freedom. Ferrying other fugitives across the Ohio River, Stamp Paid extends "this debtlessness to other people," proclaiming that their suffering in slavery was enough to balance out their choices and to cancel out any future suffering: "He ferried them and rendered them paid for; gave them their own bill of sale, so to speak. 'You paid it; now life owes you'" (185). Stamp Paid had been an integral part of each of the events leading to Sethe's bloody confrontation with Schoolteacher—he ferried her across the Ohio River, picked the blackberries that evolved into the feast, and saved Denver's life in the woodshed by grabbing her as Sethe swung her toward the wall. In the years that followed, Stamp Paid avoided 124 like the rest of the community, though he continued to love Baby Suggs and hoped that she would return to preaching in the Clearing. Although he chides Baby Suggs for her loss of faith and her decision to withdraw and study color, at her death his care allows him to serve as an intermediary between Sethe and the community. He goes into the house to carry out Baby Suggs's body—the first and only time he had been in the house since "the Misery"—because "nobody besides himself would enter 124" (171).

Stamp Paid's remorse after showing Paul D the newspaper clipping forces him to consider his motivations in interfering with Sethe, recognizing that his actions reveal a lack of sympathy: "Afterward—not before—he considered Sethe's feelings in the matter. And it was the lateness of this consideration that made him feel so bad" (170). His guilt causes him to wonder if he had "stopped the one shot she had of the happiness a good man could bring her" and if she was "vexed by the loss, the free and unasked-for revival of gossip by the man who had helped her cross the river and who was her friend as well as Baby Suggs'" (169). He also considers the impact of his actions upon Denver: "Maybe he should have thought of Denver, if not Sethe, before he gave Paul D the news that ran him off, the one normal somebody in the girl's life since Baby Suggs died" (170).

Although Stamp Paid has spent decades helping fugitives and promoting the view that slaves have paid their debt to life in suffering, his failure to think of Sethe and Denver is part of a personal history of failure to think beyond his own pain and feel sympathy for others' suffering. Even though Stamp Paid suffered in his humiliation (and possibly in the pain one feels watching a loved one be hurt), he fails to recognize his wife's suffering. The language he uses in telling the story of how he obtained his name focuses entirely on his own suffering and not on what his wife felt at being raped by her master's son: he "handed her over," he "did not kill anybody," and she "demanded he stay alive." Although Stamp Paid directs anger at the people who have power over the situation—stating that he "should have killed" his master's son and deliberately shaming his master's son's wife in the hope that she might find a way to put a stop to it (232)—he exhibits rage and violent fantasies toward the person he loves. Stamp Paid tells Paul D that while his wife was serving as a mistress, he "never touched her all that time," suggesting that he either sexually rejected her or, more likely, refrained from violence against her (233). Sexual rejection indicates that Stamp Paid views his wife's rape as interfering with his own sexual relationship to her body—he feels too angry, hurt, or disgusted to have intimate relations with her. Refraining from physical violence implies that Stamp Paid had considered and rejected directing his rage at her in this way, projecting his anger at his master's son onto her and revealing that he was angry at her for submitting to abuse that was beyond her control. When his wife is finally released from her sexual bondage, she says, "I'm back, Josh," signaling that she has returned to him both physically and emotionally, but as Stamp Paid explains: "I looked at the back of her neck. She had a real small neck. I decided to break it. You know, like a twig—just snap it." Although Stamp Paid doesn't actually harm his wife, his violent fantasies are a projection of his anger and reveal a lack of sympathy: he offers no consideration of the ways in which his wife suffers her prolonged period of rape, nor does his account show any awareness for the suffering she may have experienced from an emotional rift with a husband who blames her for complying.[5] In a novel whose main character is a woman who experiences sexual assault and goes to extreme lengths to reclaim her body and self, Stamp Paid's focus on his own suffering reveals a wide gulf between his proclaimed ideology and his lived practice.

In addition to feeling remorse over causing the breakup of Sethe's relationship with Paul D and pushing Denver into further isolation, Stamp Paid experiences another turning point when he discovers a piece of ribbon in the bottom of his boat. He is shocked to realize that what he had first mistaken for a bird feather was actually "a red ribbon knotted around a curl of wet woolly hair, clinging still to its bit of scalp" (180). In a time of violence and lynchings, "four colored schools burned to the ground; grown men whipped like children; children whipped like adults; black women raped by the crew; property taken, necks broken," Stamp Paid is more distressed by the implications of the object he has found because it touches him viscerally. Walking home, he feels dizzy and asks, "What *are* these people? You tell me, Jesus. What *are* they?" The physicality of this piece of ribbon, a woman's or a child's accessory, causes him to reflect on the abuses white people have inflicted on African Americans as a group and his love for Baby Suggs. Brought into physical and emotional connection with an anonymous woman's suffering, he recognizes a larger communal suffering that encompasses and surpasses his own. Stamp Paid thus develops a new understanding of Baby Suggs's pain and her withdrawal from the world, which motivates him to sympathize and reconnect with Sethe: "He kept the ribbon; the skin smell nagged him, and his weakened marrow made him dwell on Baby Suggs' wish to consider what in the world was harmless. . . . Mistaking her, upbraiding her, owing her, now he needed to let her know he knew, and to get right with her and her kin" (181). Stamp Paid's newfound sympathy motivates him to approach 124, which he does while "[f]ingering a ribbon and smelling skin" (176).

While Stamp Paid develops a new sympathetic awareness, his role as a transitional figure and catalyst means that his expression of sympathy alone is not sufficient to heal the breach with Sethe or to bring the community into sympathetic alignment with a larger history of suffering. Stamp Paid is unable to enter 124—finding it difficult to knock on the doors of a house that was once open to him and discovering that the residents don't hear his knock, once made. Stamp Paid doesn't at first understand the noise he hears outside the house on Bluestone Road—which the reader understands to be the voices of the women inside—thinking that it's "a conflagration of hasty voices" that he "couldn't describe or cipher" (172). But as he continues to return and knock on the door, he comes to believe "he knew who spoke them. The people of the broken necks, of fire-cooked blood and black girls who had lost their ribbons" (181). Finally, Stamp Paid looks through the window, sees the backs of Sethe and Beloved, and hurries away, believing "the undecipherable language clamoring around the house was the mumbling of the black and angry dead" (198). As Stamp Paid abandons his efforts—leaving the women inside the house "free at last to be what they liked, see whatever they saw and say whatever was on their minds" (199)—the past and the obsessive relationship that develops between Sethe and Beloved seems to have overwhelmed the family.

Reasserting Sympathetic Community

Critics have vigorously debated Beloved's identity, ranging from interpreting her literally as an anonymous slave woman who has escaped slavery (House), to Sethe's daughter returned in ghost form (Demetrakopoulos, Edwards, Trudier Harris, and Wyatt), to the embodiment of slave history (Clemons and Holden-Kirwan), to an amalgamation of the ghost of both Sethe's daughter and her mother (Horvitz), to the explanation that Morrison suggests in the text of a young woman who escaped from sexual captivity as Ella, Stamp Paid's sister, had done. What is clear, however, is that *Sethe believes* Beloved to be her daughter and wishes Beloved to participate in the "rememory" of her own past and to demonstrate understanding of her choices. It is also clear that Beloved is associated with more than Sethe's individual suffering. Beloved blends time ("All of it is now"), references experiences from the Middle Passage ("I am always crouching. . . . storms rock us and mix the men into the women and the women into the men"), and connects Sethe to those Middle Passage experiences ("the woman is there with the face I want. . . . The woman with my face is in the sea. . . . Sethe's is the face that left me") (210, 211, 213). The language in the "rememory" chapters is fractured and disconnected in a postmodern fashion, breaking the possibility of straightforward narrative of linear connection. It is associative and links Sethe's present to the larger suffering Beloved recalls.

Sethe believes that Beloved's return is an opportunity for personal healing, a signal that her actions have been viewed with sympathy and that she can move forward in the full realization of the relationship she had sacrificed so much to claim: "Now I can look at things again because she's here to see them too. After the shed, I stopped. . . . Because you mine and I have to show you these things, teach you what a mother should" (201). Because Beloved is connected to the larger, collective traumas of slavery, she also represents the potential for healing through sympathy from this past of suffering, as Sethe expresses: "Denver don't like for me to talk about it. She hates anything about Sweet Home except how she was born. But you was there and even if you too young to memory it, I can tell it to you" (202). Sethe believes that she "don't have to explain a thing" but that because she chooses to explain, Beloved will "understand, because she understands everything already. . . . [S]he'll understand. She my daughter" (200). Sethe expects Beloved to extend sympathetic understanding toward her because of their shared past, their emotional bond, and their blood ties. However, while the relationship at first seems to offer Sethe the affectional and sympathetic relationship she craves, as Beloved's power over her grows the sympathy evaporates. Rather than release Sethe from her memories and absolve her of guilt, trauma, and pain, Beloved—in reminding her of her failings—becomes selfish, violent, and vengeful. Beloved does not show sympathy to Sethe, nor does she share her suffering; in fact she forces her to dwell continuously in her painful past.

Finally, Sethe's relationship with Beloved becomes a destructive spiral that costs Sethe her physical and emotional health. Beloved appears to "feed" on Sethe's guilt and her desire to make up for past injuries, selfishly consuming all of her love, energy, and resources. Although the change occurs gradually, Beloved shifts from asking for stories from Sethe's past to accusing her of "leaving her behind," blaming Sethe for her suffering, and throwing tantrums to manipulate Sethe into giving her what she desires (241). Rather than find sympathy with a prodigal daughter who relates to Sethe's choices because she remembers her suffering, Beloved denies Sethe's explanations that she acted out of love, and Beloved's experiences from the "other side" are far greater than anything for which Sethe can atone. Thus, Sethe's health deteriorates as Beloved becomes a succubus, seducing her through the desire for sympathy rather than sex, draining Sethe of her selfhood and vitality while Sethe clings to the possibility of understanding and release.

The consumption of Sethe by her pain—by a suffering too great for any single person to overcome—prompts a recognition of the limits of a sympathy that requires its recipients to experience continuous and homogenous forms of suffering. Witnessing Sethe's struggle prompts Denver to feel sympathy for Sethe in new ways. Previously, Denver has felt cautious toward the mother who once tried to kill her and resentful of any memories from the Sweet Home past in which she cannot share. Thus, she has preferred to focus upon the story of her birth, the only story that allows her to understand Sethe's experiences and enables her in the retelling to feel "how it must have felt to her mother. Seeing how it must have looked" (78). Because Beloved appears to offer an affectional bond that Denver lacks—due to mistrust—with her mother as well as the opportunity, through storytelling, to share a common past, Denver is at first also drawn to Beloved. She is fearful that her mother might harm Beloved, but as she watches Sethe's decline, "The job she started out with, protecting Beloved from Sethe, changed to protecting her mother from Beloved" (243). Thus, Denver crosses the threshold of 124 for the first time to seek help from members of the community. After women in the community leave food gifts, Denver visits their homes to thank them, which allows her to talk with people who previously shunned her family: "[A] small conversation took place. All of them knew her grandmother and some had even danced with her in the Clearing" (249). In these exchanges, they share memories with her: "Others remembered the days when 124 was a way station, the place they assembled to catch news, taste oxtail soup, leave their children, cut out a skirt.... They remembered the party with twelve turkeys and tubs of strawberry smash. One said she wrapped Denver when she was a single day old and cut shoes to fit her mother's blasted feet" (249). By reaching out, Denver begins to reestablish affectional bonds and reform a sympathetic community through not only shared experience—the women relate memories of Baby Suggs and the home Denver lives in—but also unshared experience—times that Denver cannot remember because she was too young. In so doing, "the personal pride, the arrogant claim staked out at 124 seemed to them to have run its course. They whispered, naturally, wondered, shook their heads . . . but it didn't stop them caring whether she ate and it didn't stop the pleasure they took in her soft 'Thank you'" (249–50). Thus, the kinship structure of the community begins to reassert itself, as the women feel a protective care for Denver and want to provide for her needs. Furthermore, Denver's explanation of why she needs assistance reveals Beloved's presence in the house and Sethe's growing infirmity, prompting concern by women of the community.

Stamp Paid, who reminds community members of their former love for Baby Suggs and her family also shares the news about Beloved's existence and helps to motivate them toward a rediscovery of sympathy. He stands up against criticism of Sethe, reminding detractors of her connection to Baby Suggs as well as the unfairness of their judgment. Stamp Paid defends Sethe to his sister Ella when she criticizes Paul D for taking up with her, telling Ella, "You all was friends" and "You in deep water, girl" (187). Stamp Paid is the first to tell Ella about the unknown woman living at 124, and Ella thinks that she must be a spirit since Stamp Paid is sure the woman isn't Denver and one "[m]ight see anything at all at 124" (185). As news spreads of Beloved's presence, rumors fly among community members, but it is Ella who guides them into sympathy for Sethe despite their differences. The women "fell into three groups: those that believed the worst; those that believed none of it; and those, like Ella, who thought it through" (255).

Ella doesn't understand or sympathize with Sethe's choices, and there is a marked difference in their suffering. Ella, who had been held prisoner in a house where she was shared by a father and son, "understood Sethe's rage in the shed twenty years ago, but not her reaction to it, which Ella thought was prideful, misdirected, and Sethe herself too complicated" (256). Her past experiences with those men "gave her a disgust for sex," and she "measured all atrocities" against them. Significantly, Ella had also killed one of her own children, but in very different circumstances: she gave birth to, but refused to nurse, "a hairy white thing" that "lived five days never making a sound" (259). Ella's child was a product of rape and represented, to her, another violation. It was a "thing" rather than a child. Rather than claim her body and selfhood by claiming ownership of her child, Ella did the opposite of Sethe: she claimed her self by refusing to be forced to become a mother. She understands Sethe's anger in relation to her own assault, but she does not comprehend Sethe's radical mother-love or her violence against the children she loves. However, even though Ella finds Sethe's crime "staggering," she "didn't like the idea of past errors taking possession of the present. . . . Daily life took as much as she had. The future was sunset; the past something to leave behind. And if it didn't stay behind, well, you might have to stomp it out" (256). Thus, when a woman asserts that Sethe might deserve the punishment inflicted by Beloved, that "she had it coming," Ella counters, "Nobody got that coming." And when a woman protests that "[y]ou can't just up and kill your children," Ella points out, "No, and the children can't just up and kill the mama."

Ella leads the group of thirty women in approaching 124, their actions suggesting that they intend to confront, if not exorcise, Beloved from the house: "Some brought what they could and what they believed would work. Stuffed in apron pockets, strung around their necks, lying in the space between their breasts. Others brought Christian faith—as shield and sword. Most brought a little of both. They had no idea what they would do once they got there" (257). When the women arrive at the house, they are reminded of the sympathetic community that had existed before Baby Suggs's death and the way in which the house had functioned as a familial space: "[T]he first thing they saw was not Denver sitting on the steps, but themselves. Younger, stronger, even as little girls lying in the grass asleep. . . . They sat on the porch, ran down to the creek, teased the men, hoisted children on their hips, or, if they were the children, straddled the ankles of old men who held their little hands while giving them a horsey ride. Baby Suggs laughed and skipped among them, urging more. . . . [T]here they were, young and happy, playing in Baby Suggs' yard" (258). The women pray in front of the house. But when Ella hollers, the kneeling and standing women instantly join her, taking "a step back to the beginning. In the beginning there were no words. In the beginning was the sound, and they all knew what that sound sounded like" (259).

The gathering in front of the house begins to resemble the sympathetic blending of the Clearing, in which voices and movements join together, with Ella serving, like Baby Suggs, as their guide. Indeed, for Sethe, "it was as though the Clearing had come to her . . . where the voices of women searched for the right combination, the key, the code, the sound that broke the back of words.... It broke over Sethe and she trembled like the baptized in its wash" (261). The women breach the barrier of 124 with their sound, and Sethe sees "loving faces before her" (262). It is in that crucial moment that Bodwin appears and Sethe, mistaking him in her mind for Schoolteacher, runs from her porch to attack him. Beloved watches from the porch as Sethe runs "into the faces of the people out there, joining them and leaving Beloved behind... Then Denver, running, too. Away from her to the pile of people out there. They make a hill. A hill of black people, falling." Although Sethe's confused action stems from her fear of Bodwin and her desire to protect Beloved, it results in her reunion with a sympathetic group that, though struggling, literally embraces her and prevents her from further harming herself or others. Beloved disappears in this moment because Sethe has been reabsorbed by her community.

"A Friend of My Mind": Healing through Sympathy

The sympathy of Sethe's community saves her from the all-consuming suffering that results from daily inhabiting the trauma of slavery. But Sethe's personal road to healing begins with Paul D's return. Paul D initially seeks Sethe and finds support with her because of their shared past at Sweet Home, but he leaves because Sethe's radical claim of selfhood and motherhood displays a response to suffering that he cannot comprehend. Paul D, who has coped with pain by hiding his individual suffering deep within himself, cannot fully sympathize or connect with anyone else until he acknowledges that pain and learns to extend sympathy that is based on another's experience of suffering rather than his own. Even as Paul D attempts to share what happened at Sweet Home after Sethe escapes, he finds it difficult to explain: "I never have talked about it. Not to a soul" (71). Although he tells Sethe about being collared and his jealousy of a rooster's freedom in comparison to his own, he stops himself from going further: "Paul D had only begun, what he was telling her was only the beginning when her fingers on his knee, soft and reassuring, stopped him. Just as well. Just as well. Saying more might push them both to a place they couldn't get back from. He would keep the rest where it belonged: in that tobacco tin buried in his chest where a red heart used to be. Its lid rusted shut. He would not pry it loose now in front of this sweet sturdy woman, for if she got a whiff of the contents it would shame him" (72–73). Paul D not only prevents Sethe from understanding his suffering, but his withholding of his emotions inhibits him from understanding her. He maintains a view of Sethe formed from his memories and impressions in the past, a view that upholds his need to repress his suffering and does not allow him to understand her present-day self. This boundary, however, breaks down because of Beloved's controversial presence as well as the information that changes Paul D's perspective on Sethe. Beloved not only becomes a source of conflict between the pair, but, in her efforts to separate Paul D and Sethe, she acts again as succubus, seducing him and forcing him to confront the painful memories he has tried to lock away: "She moved closer with a footfall he didn't hear and he didn't hear the whisper that the flakes of rust made either as they fell away from the seams of his tobacco tin. So when the lid gave he didn't know it. What he knew was that when he reached the inside part he was saying, 'Red heart. Red heart,' over and over again" (117).

When Paul D's confrontation with Sethe reveals a person he doesn't recognize, he is devastated, unable to sympathize with her, and consumed by his suffering: "[H]e had nothing else to hold on to. His tobacco tin, blown open, spilled contents that floated freely and made him their play and prey. He couldn't figure out why it took so long. He may as well have jumped in the fire with Sixo and they both could have a good laugh. Surrender was bound to come anyway" (218–19). It is Stamp Paid, however, who reaches out to Paul D, despite having been a catalyst for separating them. He not only defends Sethe but also attempts to explain her actions and helps Paul D to understand that suffering is a part of everyone. Stamp Paid recognizes the love in Sethe's act and interprets her violence as an effort to outsmart the cause of suffering: "I was there. . . . She ain't crazy. She love those children. She was trying to out-hurt the hurter" (234). Stamp Paid's efforts to defend Sethe bring him and Paul D to a discussion of Beloved as the greater threat, and Paul D explains, "She reminds me of something. Something, look like, I'm supposed to remember." Given that Paul D has repressed, or "forgotten" suffering that is never truly left behind, he acknowledges that what truly frightens him and what separates him from Sethe is a larger history of slavery. Thus, Paul D is shaken by a "bone-cold spasm" that recalls a catalog of suffering: "[B]ad whiskey, nights in the cellar, pig fever, iron bits, smiling roosters, fired feet, laughing dead men, hissing grass, rain, apple blossoms, neck jewelry, Judy in the slaughterhouse, Halle in the butter, ghost-white stairs, chokecherry trees, cameo pins, aspens, Paul A's face, sausage, or the loss of a red, red heart" (235). But when he asks, "How much is a nigger supposed to take?" Stamp Paid responds, "All he can." By advocating for Sethe, sharing his own story, and acknowledging Paul

D's suffering, Stamp Paid provides a model for sympathy that acknowledges difference and allows space for healing.

Thus, Paul D's "coming is the reverse route of his going," as he gradually works his way back into the house and toward Sethe (263). After the attack on Bodwin, Paul D and Stamp Paid discuss Sethe's actions, making jokes about how "[t]hat woman is crazy" instead of seriously debating her sanity:

> "Every time a whiteman come to the door she got to kill somebody?"
> "For all she know, the man could be coming for the rent."
> "Wouldn't nobody get no letter."
> "Except the postman."
> "Be a mighty hard message."
> "And his last." (265)

Their conversation resembles the signifying of African American oral tradition that binds and bonds communities, using doublespeak and humor (akin to playing the dozens) to point out the underlying tensions and, in this case, diffuse them. When he returns to 124, Paul D examines the house, reviewing the bedroom he and Sethe once occupied, looking at the bed, which "seems to him a place he is not," and forcing himself to picture "himself lying there, and when he sees it, it lifts his spirit" (270). Imagining himself part of Sethe's house, part of Sethe's bed, Paul D projects a relationship between them, reconstructing the affectional bond they once held in preparation for the bond he hopes to reestablish.

But when Paul D finds Sethe lying in Baby Suggs's room singing lullabies, she appears ill and worn out. She is dwelling on the past. As Paul D considers her, he recalls Sixo's words about the woman he loved: "She is a friend of my mind. She gather me, man. The pieces I am, she gather them and give them back to me in the right order" (272–73). In this moment, Paul D realizes that his love for Sethe is not just because of their shared experiences. He accepts her differences, her individual qualities, extending sympathy that acknowledges differences in suffering while recognizing that she has been able to do the same for him: "He is staring at the quilt but he is thinking about her wrought-iron back; the delicious mouth still puffy at the corner from Ella's fist. The mean black eyes. The wet dress steaming before the fire. Her tenderness about his neck jewelry—its three wands, like attentive baby rattlers, curving two feet into the air. How she never mentioned or looked at it, so he did not have to feel the shame of being collared like a beast. Only this woman Sethe could have left him his manhood like that. He wants to put his story next to hers" (273). Paul D recognizes that this form of sympathy, of putting "his story next to hers," acknowledges the past and creates an opportunity for healing, telling Sethe: "[M]e and you, we got more yesterday than anybody. We need some kind of tomorrow." Thus, Paul D seeks to remind her of the selfhood she sought to claim in the first place, explaining that the loss of Beloved is not the loss of herself so much as a discovery of it: "You your best thing, Sethe. You are."

The novel ends on a hopeful note, suggesting that Paul D has recalled Sethe to herself and initiated a process of sympathy that will foster healing and complete her reintegration into a community that has fully accepted them both. Bruised and beaten but not yet defeated, Sethe needs the care of someone who understands her suffering and releases her from it, encouraging her to leave that pain in the past and define herself by the valuable qualities she still possesses, the qualities that enabled her to survive the trials of slavery in the first place. *Beloved* is a testament not only to power of self but also to the power of sympathy, so long as that sympathy accepts difference and allows the sufferer to move forward.

A Postmodern Sentimental Novel: Morrison's Deconstructed Neo-Slave Narrative

Beloved is considered a postmodern neo-slave narrative because of its blurring of the past and present and its questioning of grand historical metanarratives. Although it borrows many features from nineteenth-century slave narratives and focuses on the movement from bondage to freedom— literally, psychologically, and emotionally—Morrison's novel is a blend of genres. Stylistically, it employs typical features of the postmodern novel such as achronological narrative structure, shifts in perspective, polyvocal narration, use of the lyric, and incorporation of musical structures. Some chapters mimic free-verse poetry, with fractured narrative and no clear speaker. Unlike Walker's historical fiction, *Beloved* does not attempt to tell a straightforward account of the past, setting forth an alternative historical record that revises past perceptions and mirrors the rhetorical style of nineteenth-century slave narratives. Instead, it draws from that history in order to challenge the idea that any historical telling can be straightforward at all. As with many postmodern texts, *Beloved* pushes against the idea not only that the past can be narrated in a straight, cause-and-effect method but also that there is a single version of events that falls into a neatly contained story. *Beloved* highlights the polyvocality of history, the fact that millions of African Americans experienced slavery, and, while they suffered similar abuses, each person suffered individually and possesses a unique perspective on how it affected them. As a genre, neo-slave narratives already do some of this work by countering the grand narrative posited in a historical record written largely by whites, but *Beloved* goes further in fragmenting that metanarrative by giving voice to individuals from the past.

While the characters in Butler's *Kindred* jump back and forth in time, Morrison's characters experience the past and present as fluid, where memories—termed "rememory"—can occur as physical remnants, experiences that can be bumped into, that are "out there, in the world . . . waiting for you" (36). Morrison and Butler both emphasize the close links between past and present, but they differ on the manner of connection. Thus, Morrison's novel argues not so much, as Butler's does, that African Americans reacquaint themselves with their pasts in order to understand their present but that the past is already a part of present-day experience that must be understood as a living force. Morrison's work in editing *The Black Book* has often been cited in connection to *Beloved* because it was during that time that she came across the story of Margaret Garner. However, Morrison found more than just African American suffering in those centuries-old newspaper clippings. She found accounts of horrific abuses rendered in matter-of-fact language, but she also found instances of charity, love, and courage: "The two histories merge in the book, as in life, in a noon heat of brutality and compassion, outrage and satisfaction. Thus, it was that very mix that made editing the book so painful. Yet as the book suggests, pain, anger, befuddlement, melancholy and despair were not—are not—the only emotions defining the lives of black people in this country" ("Rediscovering"). Morrison recognized the mixture of suffering and compassion as an important part of African American culture that had significant meaning for contemporary conflicts: "There was a time, heretical as it sounds, when we knew who we were. One could see that knowledge, that coherence in our wide-spirited celebration of life and our infinite tolerance of differences. We thought little about 'unity' because we loved those differences among us."

In writing *Beloved*, Morrison sought to give voice to the multiple speakers of African American slave experience and, in many ways, to remind readers of the importance of hearing those voices. When Bonnie Angelo of *Time* praised Morrison in an interview for giving "new insight into the daily struggle of slaves," Morrison insisted that her goal was much larger, that she wished to bring readers into a personal, sympathetic relationship with those who had lived that history: "I was trying to make it a personal experience. The book was not about the institution—Slavery with a capital S. It was about these anonymous people called slaves. What they do to keep on, how they make a life, what they're willing to risk, however long it lasts, in order to relate to one another—that was incredible to me" ("Toni Morrison"). When Cecil Brown asked Morrison about Crouch's negative review of her novel and his assertion that Morrison was making inappropriate comparisons to the Holocaust, she reiterated that she was interested not in comparative suffering but in suffering itself, as exemplified in each individual: "The game of who suffered most? I'm not playing that game. That's a media argument. It's almost about quantity. One dead child is enough for me" ("Interview," 466).

Morrison has long resisted the label of magical realism for her work, despite incorporating fantastic elements like the ghost-figure of Beloved and Milkman's ability to fly in *Song of Solomon* (1977). Instead of magic, Morrison describes her use of fantastic elements as a blend of history, symbolism, and African American mythology designed to reach readers through familiar cultural signs. Just as sentimental novelists relied upon easily recognizable symbols and tropes to convey particular messages to their readers, Morrison incorporates African American cultural mythology to communicate with her intended audience: "I just tried to see what was already there, and to use that as a kind of well-spring for my own work. Instead of inventing myths... I was just interested in finding what myths already existed... I have too much respect for black people's imagination to suppose I can invent something for them. We have always done it. It's just the way in which I can employ them. You know, it's not unusual. Joyce uses the Ulysses myth and people use other things. I just use the ones that already exist, and I appropriate them for texts and characters" (Brown, "Interview," 462–63). Morrison appropriates both existing mythology and the voices of people from the past—fictionalizing not just Margaret Garner but her family and the millions of slaves who lived centuries ago—in order to revise the slave narrative genre, expanding it and making room for difference. This process brings readers in closer sympathy to the characters from the past. The sentimental novel extended sympathy across race, gender, and class boundaries; Morrison's novel does this while also extending sympathy through time, to bring African Americans of the past and present together. In revising the methods of sentimentalism, Morrison revises the methods of sympathy itself, offering new opportunities for a return to a time "when we knew who we were... [and] loved those differences among us."

8 / Conclusion

The selection of writers offered here demonstrates that together in a way they cannot alone sentimentalism continues to be an effective means by which contemporary texts argue for social change and instruct readers to identify and sympathize with individuals generally configured as Others. It also forces today's reader to wrestle with a nineteenth-century legacy of race, class, gender, and family ideologies that are still at the heart of American national identity. The individual family unit remains the defining metaphor of social organization for our society; therefore, the ability to extend the boundaries of that unit continues to be a powerful revolutionary tool. Yet because the family has become defined through biology, economics, and sympathy, it inherently requires that those seeking inclusion in the national family always perform an equation of likeness. In essence, the argument becomes: "I, and those like me, deserve sympathy, and therefore inclusion, because I am like the dominant social group in the following ways...." Thus, the argument for inclusion through sympathy becomes its own form of marginalization, as the specter of difference is required for the extension of sympathy from one group to another. Sympathy, that tool for eliding difference, ironically becomes a method for keeping difference in place.

Working-class and African American writers wrestle with these categories of marginalization in similar ways. Although the proletarian worker is not Othered through indelible racial difference, the rise of urbanization led to a wider gap between the middle and the working classes—a gap that is once again dramatically increasing with the twenty-first-century recession. Through a sentimental ideology that links social status with moral quality, members of the working class became coded as social outsiders whose class status was a result of a moral rather than economic failing. Therefore, members of the working class today prefer to identify themselves as middle-class, whether or not their economic circumstances support that identity—to be working-class is to admit a form of personal failing. Furthermore, many of the political attacks on social services designed to help the working class survive economic hardships—as demonstrated during the 2012 election—focus primarily on moral arguments rather than on a system that has left millions without access to work or the means to support their families. Meanwhile, African Americans, who as a group have historically been excluded by sentimental ideology and definitions of the American family at every level, face similar social criticism. African Americans continue to be drawn as Other with significant cultural attention paid to the relationship between moral quality and achievement, as opposed to systemic discrimination or white privilege.

There is a strong link between discussions of class, race, and sympathy, as evidenced by the links between the sentimental novel, the slave narrative, and abolition as well as the antiracist arguments exhibited in women's proletarian writing. In *To Make My Bread*, Lumpkin argues against the racism that divided working-class African Americans and whites, which was often a catalyst for social tension as well as a method for breaking worker solidarity in strikes. Through Bonnie's sympathy for Mary—both fellow worker and fellow mother—Lumpkin demonstrates that African American workers deserved inclusion both in the working class and in the national family, just as she argues that the working class as a whole deserves sympathy and inclusion in the national family. In Walker's *Jubilee*, Vyry and her family demonstrate the middle-class work ethic and a belief in hard work as the way toward economic success. As in proletarian novels, the African American family suffers setbacks at every turn despite their faith in the virtues of hard work. The novel demonstrates that a lack of economic progress is due not to moral failings or a lack of the middle-class work ethic but to a larger system that creates obstacles too large to overcome individually. However, in *Jubilee*, Vyry eventually achieves sympathetic identification with white neighbors who support her and, therefore, remove many of the obstacles that prevented economic success, enabling her family to carry forward with the middle-class dream of hard work and prosperity. Thus, Vyry demonstrates the potential for sentimental power through moral rightness, faith in hard work, and the sympathetic reform of the society that prevented success.

This emphasis on sympathetic identification as a tool for social improvement and cathartic healing can lead to a form of sentimentalism that actually reinforces rather than critiques racial barriers when it focuses on the power of sympathy in and of itself instead of using sympathy as a catalyst for social change. This form of sentimentalism—which extends sympathy across class, race, and gender barriers in a manner that is less about understanding the suffering of the Other and more about placing the Other within the context of the self—bolsters the very ideologies that the authors whose work this study previously examined so strongly critique. Kathryn Stockett's *The Help* (2009) is an example of a form of sentimentalism that at first appears to perform the function of extending sympathy and expanding the boundaries of the family. Although *The Help* is neither a neo-slave narrative nor a proletarian novel, it is helpful to discuss the text in comparison to these two genres because it appears at the cross section of the three genres under discussion in this book. Like the majority of nineteenth-century sentimental novels, it is written by a middle-class, white woman as a sympathy-driven social critique. Like proletarian literature and neo-slave narratives, *The Help* identifies working-class and African American women as people who have been excluded from the American national family, despite having a significant influence in raising it.

However, the sympathetic equations developed in the narrative are so superficial that instead of offering a cultural critique and promoting social reform, the novel recasts a volatile and violent racial history in a rosy glow and considers African American women's experience in the Jim Crow era within the context of a white girl's coming-of-age story so that the narrative is not about understanding African American experience so much as it is about understanding how their experience shaped her life. Such a sentimental positioning inspires social inertia, essentially arguing for white readers that the value of understanding African American experience is ultimately about understanding the white self, offering virtually no critique of the social dynamics enabling racial difference and discrimination in the past and present.

Published in February 2009, by September 2011, Stockett's novel had spent 106 weeks on the *New York Times* best-seller list. It remained ranked thirty-fifth on the paperback list a year later. It was made into a feature film that, upon its release, earned over $100 million. *The Help*'s racial politics have made it a target of controversy, and critics have accused it of a range of offenses, including downplaying the actual abuses and hardships experienced by domestic workers, ignoring the real dangers African Americans faced during the Jim Crow era, and glossing over the tumultuous struggles of the civil rights movement. Stockett herself has not openly commented on the controversy; instead, the popularity of the novel and film speaks for itself. People love this story, particularly white, middle-class, middle-aged women who claim that the novel nostalgically reminds them of their childhoods, that it is "the story of my growing up years" (Patty W., "This Book").[1] The primary critical commentary on the web is from African American scholars, columnists, and bloggers who critique *The Help*'s racial politics and are responding to the frustratingly uncritical nostalgia and sympathy they see in whites' everyday responses. For example, Janelle Harris writes in her essay "I Am Not *The Help*," for *Clutch* online magazine: "I can see some white lady now, giving me that tight-lipped, puppy dog look of empathy and saying, 'It's OK. I understand. I saw *The Help.*'"[2] *The Help*'s critical defenders have been few—a handful of commentators suggest that the film and novel deserve credit for starting a vigorous public debate about race, white privilege, and cultural memory.[3] So one question to ask is how this novel—about 1960s racism, about the abuses perpetuated by white women against black women—so thoroughly captured the attention and affection of contemporary white audiences.

The answer is that *The Help*'s sentimentalism operates as a salve to white, privileged audiences. While acknowledging the cruelties of one of America's deepest cultural hurts—the legacy of slavery and the racism that has literally relegated groups of people to subhuman status and divided our country against itself—it absolves the beneficiaries of that privilege from the advantages they receive from that racism and their participation in perpetuating it. It does so by allowing contemporary white audiences to cast racism as a problem only of the past, to emotionally identify with racial Others by focusing on their common suffering, and to redefine racism largely in terms of a violation of affection.

African American women have a history of working in domestic service, and it is no coincidence this 2009–11 blockbuster about domestic service is set in the Jim Crow era, contrasting today's complicated (supposedly "post-racial") racial conflicts to a time when racism appears more "real," overt, and intentional. Enslaved African American women and indentured servants have provided household labor throughout American history, and after the Civil War, African Americans in the South were mainly employed as sharecroppers, housekeepers, and caregivers, remaining in economic servitude. If Stockett's primary interest in *The Help* was to examine the hardships of housekeepers or the complex relationships between workers of color and white employers, she could easily have chosen to set her story in the present. According to a 2011 report by the Center for American Progress, an estimated 2.5 million people work every year in domestic service, and the racial demographics of this field have not changed much over the past century (Boyd, "The Color of Help"). Domestic Workers United and DataCenter together report that 95 percent of domestic workers in New York today are people of color, and 93 percent are women (*Home*, 10). Many are foreign-born. Numerous studies have been conducted on the physical, verbal, and sexual abuse committed against these women,[4] and domestic workers successfully organized to pass a Domestic Workers Bill of Rights in New York State, which went into effect on November 29, 2010. *The Help*, however, is not seeking to examine today's reality, nor does it question or critique the socioeconomic factors that have maintained domestic service as a field in which women of color serve white families. Instead, *The Help* nostalgically promotes the myth that those types of relationships are archaic—based on an institution of the past—thereby implying that the racist ideologies that supported them are also of the past.

Against a backdrop of bouffant hairdos and high waistlines, Ford Galaxy convertibles, Frankie Valli's "Sherry," and ladies' clubs, *The Help* only gestures at the harsh realities of racial segregation by telling stories of individual acts of cruelty and blasé assumptions that African Americans are lesser beings. Not only do readers witness the cutting remarks and degrading comments that African American workers had to tolerate as part of their daily jobs, but Hilly Holbrook, Jackson's leading socialite, heads a farcical Junior League initiative to force all white homes to build separate bathrooms for use by their domestic workers. The novel and film make only passing references to the violence perpetrated on African Americans during this period—including Medgar Evers's murder in the very same town—and the very real reasons the domestic workers are afraid to participate in Skeeter's project. In so doing, the narrative suggests that the racism and mistreatment these women suffer is a result of individual actions, of the deliberate meanness of their bad employers instead of the result of a larger social system that protects white power and privilege. As an aspiring writer who feels she doesn't fit in to her wealthy friendship groups, the single and independent-minded Skeeter is uncomfortable at home: she longs for a career and is bothered by the way her friends treat their domestic servants. In short, she is a vehicle for the contemporary reader/viewer engaging with this period—she is the lens for our current selves, for a perspective that understands and sympathizes with that past, but feels uncomfortable there. Because Skeeter, a white woman, disagrees with treating the housekeepers poorly, because she stands up to Hilly, because Hilly is humiliated and deposed from her social hierarchy, and because Skeeter helps the maids overcome their silence and share their stories, *The Help* suggests a kind of feel-good activism in which racism can be and has been defeated. It implies that because Skeeter wins and everybody feels good in the end, racism has ended and is—like Woolworth's soda shops—a relic of the past.

Despite suggesting that its major characters have triumphed over racism by socially humiliating their white employers, *The Help* closes well before the end of the civil rights movement. The novel ends in July 1963, before the March on Washington and Martin Luther King's "I Have a Dream" speech, before the Birmingham church bombing, before the Twenty-Fourth Amendment to the Constitution, before the Freedom Summer, and before the 1964 Civil Rights Act. Because *The Help* closes before the achievement of significant gains in racial equality, the novel suggests that its characters' personal struggles are part of the momentum leading to real-world social change. It also implies, by setting its action in the early 1960s, that because these kinds of struggles have since been eradicated, one must reach into the past beyond the civil rights movement to understand this kind of racism, to a pre–civil rights period in which white women could treat African American women with cruelty out of racial ignorance. That was then, this is now, the comparison suggests.

What is overlooked, however, is that very little changes for the domestic servants as a result of publishing their book. The process of sharing their stories is certainly cathartic because their voices are being heard for the first time (and they make a little money, too). However, while everyone feels better, only Skeeter's fundamental living circumstances change. Skeeter doesn't become a civil rights activist, and her mission to publish the stories of domestic workers is prompted by her desire for a New York career—an editor tells her, "Write about what disturbs you, particularly if it bothers no one else" (71). Although she becomes personally invested in these women, Skeeter is driven as much by the need to publish a book that matters to her career as she is by a book that matters. Despite taking a few precautionary measures, the maids know that participating in the project exposes them to possible retribution. Indeed, Aibileen, one of the book's narrators, is fired from her job, and she retires from domestic work entirely, knowing that she is now unemployable. But as she leaves her former employer's house, she thinks, "I'm free.... I head down the hot sidewalk at eight thirty in the morning wondering what I'm on do with the rest a my day. The rest a my life.... Maybe I ought to keep writing, not just for the paper, but something else, about all the people I know and the things I seen and done. Maybe I ain't too old to start over" (444).

Skeeter, meanwhile, achieves exactly what she had hoped; she is offered a job in New York and plans to leave Mississippi. Although she expresses some concern about what will happen to the women after she leaves, Minnie tells her: "I'm on take care a Aibileen and she gone take care a me. But you got nothing left here but enemies in the Junior League and a mama that's gone drive you to drink. You done burned ever bridge there is. And you ain't *never* gone get another boyfriend in this town and everbody know it. So don't walk your white butt to New York, *run* it" (424). By framing Aibileen's firing as a move toward freedom and closing with Skeeter's relocation, *The Help* suggests that the problems in Jackson have been functionally resolved. While there may be some residual social tension—resulting in a hit to Skeeter's social life—it glosses over Aibileen's serious economic quandary. It does not seriously explore any consequences that other maids who participated in the project may experience, ranging from firing to violent retribution when lynching is a real risk during this historical period. While it argues that African American women should not be mistreated, it does not examine the system that promotes inequality and enables this mistreatment on a broad scale, which means that it fails to advocate for systemic social change. In fact, one of the collaborators tells Aibileen that another maid was nearly fired but that her employer told her: "[I]f Hilly wasn't telling everybody it's not Jackson I'd fire you so quick your head would spin.... I can't fire you or people will know I'm Chapter Ten. You're stuck working here for the rest of your life" (434). Publishing the book has not led to an end to the bathroom segregation movement, domestic work reforms, or greater civil rights, nor does it push the characters or the reader to examine the social systems that create those oppressive circumstances. What the reader/viewer knows, instead, is that civil rights do eventually come, and because this feel-good story occurs before those events, this narrative is situated as though it participates in some way in the efforts to overturn entrenched racism. Thus, readers delight in Skeeter's happy ending and don't worry about the

African American women she leaves behind. The message is that "it all works out in the end, so there's no need to trouble yourself further."

One of the attractions of *The Help* for white audiences is that they emotionally identify with both Skeeter and the African American housekeepers. It is significant that readers and viewers do not primarily identify with the white, middle-class socialites and employers of the book and film with whom they may actually have the most in common in terms of race, gender, and class. Stockett achieves this sympathetic identification by emphasizing the common suffering between Skeeter and the maids, expanding that circle to include the audience. It is a move very similar to that conducted by Harriet Beecher Stowe in *Uncle Tom's Cabin*, whereby Stowe encouraged white, middle-class women to sympathize with the suffering of enslaved mothers by equating the loss of a child through sale to the loss of a child through death—the despair prompted by a mother's grief became a universal symbol of suffering that humanized African American women for white audiences and allowed them to relate to their suffering when families were forcibly separated. In *The Help*, Skeeter is cast as a perpetual outsider, the weak member of the "mean girl" herd. She's portrayed as the constant subject of her mother's (and, at times, her friends') criticism for being unpolished and unattractive, with bad hair, no boyfriend, and no real power within Jackson's social hierarchy. Her only source of comfort and support has been Constantine, the family maid who raised her and is now gone. Skeeter's ability to see the ways that Aibileen, Minnie, and the other maids are hurt and offended by their treatment is a result of her own sensitivity to outsider status. Her racial consciousness comes from her emotional identification with what it feels like to be treated as less than equal. However, as Skeeter slowly learns, racial Otherness is much more hurtful than what she has experienced personally. Yet because *The Help* creates this sympathy through Skeeter's identification with the "mean girl" paradigm, much of the racism in the book is cast in terms of high school–style exclusionary behavior. Racism, for Jackson housekeepers, is largely portrayed as a series of social slights, of public insults and degrading comments, and, rather than being forced to eat at the "losers" table in the cafeteria, maids must occupy segregated racial spaces. Contemporary audiences, well versed in modern iterations of "mean girl" and high school culture, relate to these kinds of social Othering, which transcend race but provide a metaphor for the social separations and hurt feelings that occur as a result of racism. Thus, *The Help* provides a mechanism by which audiences bypass emotional identification with those closest to themselves in the text, those whose race and class positions place them in power in both the past and present culture. Instead, the text invites audiences to emotionally identify with the struggles and apparent triumphs of the *The Help*'s underdogs.

Another way in which *The Help* encourages emotional identification is through its process of narration: Stockett appropriates the first-person voices of two African American characters in order to invite closer sympathetic identification by the reader. Skeeter, Aibileen, and Minnie take turns narrating the novel. With thirteen chapters totaling 184 pages of narration, Skeeter's voice dominates the novel and serves as the anchor for the text. She is the vehicle carrying contemporary audiences into the narrative.[5] Aibileen narrates eleven chapters (119 pages) and Minnie narrates nine chapters (97 pages), supplementing Skeeter's view of events and revealing another side of life in Jackson. Notably, Skeeter's chapters are written in Standard English with no indications of Southern dialect despite her Mississippi background, a convention that generally goes unremarked because Standard English, as the term suggests, is intended to serve as a universal norm. It is a kind of Everyman's rhetoric, used when the language isn't meant to call attention to itself. However, Stockett chose to write the Aibileen and Minnie chapters in an imitation of African American patois. For example: "I walk real slow through my yard, wondering what it's gone be now. Miss Skeeter stand up, holding her pocketbook tight like it might get snatched. White peoples don't come round my neighborhood less they toting the help to and fro, and that is just fine with me. I spend all day long tending to white peoples. I don't need em looking in on me at home" (101). Such rhetoric calls attention to the differences in the women's race and class, but not enough to make the diction unreadable. While Skeeter's speech, like her race, goes unremarked and assumes a universal experience, Aibileen's and Minnie's language is marked as different, just as their bodies indicate difference by the color of their skin.

Rather than obscure understanding or consistently call attention to the ways in which Aibileen, Minnie, and the African American women they represent are always different or Other, however, Stockett's appropriation of their voices invites reader identification and sympathy. By placing their narratives alongside Skeeter's, Stockett suggests that a parallel exists between the women's stories and perspectives. The African American "dialect" Stockett employs is only a mild variation upon Standard English; it is based upon Standard English, occasionally interspersing "Southernized" words or phrases but leaving the basic grammatical structure intact (altering "going" to "gone," using regional verbs like "toting" instead of "carrying" or "bringing"). It is easy for a reader of Standard English to figure out the intended meaning because it mimics familiar speech patterns. The style of narration also gestures at familiar "mammy language" from plantation films and novels, which is easily readable to general audiences and has been used to provide humor and "local color." It is a sympathetic connection in which the specter of difference always hovers. *The Help*'s first and last chapters are narrated by Aibileen, so that Skeeter's personal "growth" or the bildungsroman emphasis of the novel is framed by the warm, storytelling tone of a woman similar to the maid Skeeter credits with raising her. Thus, while nodding to the differences between Aibileen, Minnie, and Skeeter, Stockett's appropriation of Othered voices suggests that readers truly can cross racial boundaries, that they can "get inside" these women and see through their eyes. In the tradition of William Styron's *The Confessions of Nat Turner*, Stockett's gesture is a controversially imaginative exploration in which she tries not just to describe sympathetically the experiences of Others but to give voice to them.[6] As Stockett explains in her afterword:

> I don't presume to think that I know what it really felt like to be a black woman in Mississippi, especially in the 1960s.... I'm pretty sure I can say that no one in my family ever asked Demetrie [her family's housekeeper] what it felt like to be black in Mississippi, working for our white family. It never occurred to us to ask. It was everyday life. It wasn't something people felt compelled to examine. I have wished, for many years, that I'd been old enough and thoughtful enough to ask Demetrie that question. She died when I was sixteen. I've spent years imagining what her answer would be. And that is why I wrote this book. (451)

By imagining her way into the position of her fictional maids, Stockett invites contemporary audiences to imagine themselves in those positions as well. When Aibileen and Minnie express frustration, fear, uncertainty, and pain, their narration seems to offer a direct opportunity to the reader that is unmediated and untempered by white guilt or white response. The irony, of course, is that Stockett, a white woman, is the one writing the novel and imagining Aibileen and Minnie, so the entire experience is a product of white consciousness. But the effect of casting this perspective within the tenor of African American "voice" is to bring white readers in closer sympathy with a subjectivity that is usually inaccessible, foreign, or Other.

Following in the traditions of nineteenth-century sentimental fiction, *The Help* seeks to redefine the boundaries of the family according to affection, expanding beyond biological—and in this case racial—boundaries. In so doing, *The Help* also redefines the most deeply disturbing crime of racism as a violation of that familial affection. In Stockett's world, which builds upon plantation tradition and mythology, African American women raise white children and love them as their own, often loving them more deeply than the children's own biological mothers do. Those children eventually grow up to become adults who inherit the social power of white supremacy and disavow previous ties of affection with their nursemaids and housekeepers. The novel opens and closes with chapters narrated by Aibileen and focusing on the relationship she has developed with Mae Mobley, the daughter of her employer. In the opening paragraph, Aibileen explains: "Mae Mobley was born on a early Sunday morning in August, 1960. A church baby we like to call it. Taking care a white babies, that's what I do, along with all the cooking and cleaning. I done raised seventeen kids in my lifetime. I know how to get them babies to sleep, stop crying, and go in the toilet bowl before they mamas even get out a bed in the morning" (1). Rather than begin her narrative with statements about her own life, Aibileen immediately focuses on the white child (and past white children) she has raised and loved. Aibileen is portrayed as a more loving, more competent, more compassionate mother to Mae Mobley Leefolt than the disinterested, socially conscious "Miss" Leefolt is to her daughter.

Aware that Mae Mobley absorbs the unkind treatment of her biological mother, Aibileen worries that the little girl may grow up to forget compassion and turn her insecurity into abuse of others. Thus, Aibileen, who calls Mae Mobley "my special baby," tries to instill the idea that she is valued and loved: "I get to wondering, what would happen if I told her she something good, every day? ... I hold her tight and whisper, 'You a *smart* girl. You a *kind* girl, Mae Mobley. You hear me?' And I keep saying it till she repeat it back to me" (2, 92). These are the words of wisdom that Aibileen tries to impart to the toddler when she is fired at the end of the novel, saying good-bye in the final pages and the final scenes of the film. As both Mae Mobley and Aibileen cry over their forced separation, Aibileen sees a vision of the child grown up: "I look deep into her rich brown eyes and she look into mine. Law, she got old-soul eyes, like she done lived a thousand years. And I swear I see, down inside, the woman she gone grow up to be. A flash from the future. She is tall and straight. She is proud. She got a better haircut. And she is *remembering* the words

I put in her head. Remembering as a full-grown woman" (443). Aibileen and Mae Mobley enact the relationship cycle that had also occurred between Skeeter and the now-absent Constantine. Revealed through a series of flashbacks in the film and reminiscences in Skeeter's narrative, Constantine is clearly the mother figure that raised Skeeter, bolstered her confidence throughout her formative years, and triggered her racial awareness. When Skeeter returns home from college, she is shocked to find Constantine absent. Her mother refuses to provide clear answers about why Constantine is no longer there, and she can't understand how the woman who had raised her would have left suddenly without even writing a letter. As Skeeter grew up, Constantine provided her with affection and love, countering the barrage of criticism she received from her mother and others about her looks and her inability to fit in. Like Aibileen, Constantine urges Skeeter to consider her inward qualities; the first time Skeeter is called ugly, it is Constantine who discovers her weeping. She asks Skeeter, "Well? Is you?" and advises her that "[u]gly live up on the inside. Ugly be a hurtful, mean person. Is you one of them peoples?" (62). Thus, *The Help* suggests that it is this affectional bond that educates young women to look past racial difference and discover human similarity, prompting social change. By loving their charges and receiving love, Constantine and Aibileen teach through feeling. Skeeter's activism—if one can call it that—is prompted by her love of Constantine and her extended sympathy toward women in similar positions. By closing on Aibileen's vision of Mae Mobley, a version of Skeeter as a child, Stockett suggests that, through the power of their love, housekeepers and maids can educate a new generation of white children who will be stronger than their parents and not embrace racist ideologies.

Unfortunately, *The Help* does not address the fact that the mean, racist white employers who abuse these African American housekeepers were likely themselves raised in similar situations by women such as Aibileen and Constantine but did not absorb this message of love or grow up to become antiracist. By treating racism as a problem of affection and individual meanness, it suggests that it can be remedied through individual relationships and loving bonds but neglects to seriously consider the strength of existing power structures that place pressure on those relationships. One interesting illustration of the problem of casting racism in terms of a violation of affection occurs with the confrontation between Skeeter and her mother over Constantine.

The novel and the film adaption of *The Help* present this confrontation and its outcome a little differently. In the novel, Constantine's daughter

Lulabelle was given away at birth and lives in Chicago but comes to Jackson as an adult to be reunited with her mother. Light enough to pass for white, she nonchalantly interrupts a Daughters of the American Revolution (DAR) chapter at the house and chats with its members, offending Skeeter's mother with her brazenness: "A Negro in my home. Trying to act white" (363). Skeeter's mother not only forces Constantine to make her daughter leave, but she also confronts Lulabelle and reveals a hurtful secret about her past. Skeeter's mother, in later sharing this story, appears unrepentant and only saddened and surprised that Constantine left after the encounter to go back to Chicago with her daughter. However, she does cry when Skeeter begins to weep: "Mother sniffs, keeping her eyes straight ahead. She quickly wipes her eyes.... 'I knew you'd blame me when it—it wasn't my fault'" (365). In the film, however, Lulabelle is clearly African American and accidentally interrupts the DAR chapter. She is still bold, however, knocking on the front door and attempting to walk through the room instead of going around the house to the back entrance to wait for Constantine. Skeeter's mother is pained by the confrontation but pressured by the head of the DAR to dismiss Constantine on the spot.

When Skeeter confronts her mother in the film, she insists that she had no other choice but shows deep remorse for firing Constantine because she sees how deeply she has hurt Skeeter. In both instances, Skeeter's mother is subject to social pressure to maintain racial boundaries, as evidenced by the presence of the DAR. In the novel, she shows less affection for Constantine and less awareness of what she might have felt. In both versions, however, Skeeter's mother realizes that she has done something wrong because she has hurt her own daughter. What should be a moment of racial awakening is actually a moment of emotional sensitivity to her own daughter—her mother regrets hurting Skeeter but does not acknowledge the larger issues of racial inequality at the root of her treatment of Constantine and Lulabelle. The novel makes clear that Constantine died shortly after moving to Chicago, and the implication—which the film makes explicit—is that Constantine dies of a broken heart, as though the deepest hurt was not the years of racism or abuse, nor the physical toll of years of hard work upon her body, but that she had been cast out of her "white family."

The Help presents a potent combination of sympathy and sentimental ideals that draws upon recognizable cultural codes to reassure audiences composed of the dominant racial and class group that sympathy in and of itself is enough to remedy social problems. This soothing sentimentalism is unlike the sentimental rhetorical mode of proletarian literature, which argues that sympathy leads to a call for action and systemic social change. It also directly contrasts neo-slave narratives, which question the purpose and power of sympathy without cultural critique and demand for change. The key difference is in the mode of sympathy and the attempt to understand the suffering of the Other—whether an outward extension of sympathy from self to Other allows for understanding of the suffering of that Other and expands the boundaries of the family or whether, as in *The Help*, sympathizing with the suffering of the Other becomes a lens through which one focuses upon and understands the self.

Because of this inward focus *The Help* does not address systemic social issues, and it glorifies sympathy without engendering a motivation in the reader for a broader critique of social or power hierarchies, a criticism often levied against nineteenth-century sentimental novels perceived to be too focused on the pleasures of crying and not enough on the work of institutional reform. Stockett's novel acknowledges the emotional burden of white guilt but avoids examining or deconstructing the system that privileges whites and places them in positions of higher social power, even as they struggle within that system and against each other. *The Help* allows well-meaning white readers to feel terrible about race and class inequalities without recognizing the ways in which they have directly benefited from that system or need to change it. As such, the novel works to generate sympathy across race and class boundaries, but by refusing a systemic critique, it maintains and reinforces those very same lines.

Sentimentalism is a complex rhetorical mode, and twentieth-century authors have struggled with the ways in which its use comes with inherent risks. Authors who relied on sympathy risked the reinforcement of hierarchies or power structures because of the inertia that can be created when feeling itself becomes substituted for critique, when feeling feels like enough. Each of the novelists in this study appropriates sentimentalism in order to cast an analytical lens upon the class and race systems that injure certain groups of people. However, Lumpkin, Johnson, and Steinbeck demonstrate the need for action by casting their characters in literal life-or-death struggles and showing that sympathetic connection and the creation of extended families is the only way that humans literally can survive. Walker suggests a similar idea when the white community accepts Vyry for her ability to serve as a midwife—literally bringing them life—as well as *Jubilee*'s biblical structure. The family's trials and wanderings allude to the Hebrews wandering in the desert, an implication that promotes a message not only of endurance but also of journeying toward a better life. In *Kindred*, Butler strongly argues that addressing present-day struggles requires a deeper, sympathetic understanding of the past. Finally, concerns about the complex nature of sympathy are at the heart of the sentimental skepticism explicitly expressed by Morrison in *Beloved*. She draws upon both its power to heal and its potential to divide when communities seek to reinforce suffering instead of expanding its boundaries to allow for difference.

More work remains to be done in the field of contemporary sentimentalism. While race and class are primary subjects for exploration because of nineteenth-century sentimental ideals and definitions of the family, the appeals of sympathy and the sentimental mode are not limited to these subjects. Because of the way in which sentimentalism touches readers and audiences on a personal level and because it redefines the most intimate unit that organizes our lives—the family—it is an infinitely flexible mode. Furthermore, the twentieth century has seen different Othered groups demanding visibility and social recognition that previously were ignored or invisible social categories. One such way in which sentimentalism has been adapted is to expand beyond the assumption that the family is defined just by race and class or that the recipients of sympathy are either female or heterosexual. With broader visibility of gay, lesbian, bisexual, transgender, and queer issues, twentieth- and twenty-first century authors have adopted sentimentalism to capture the experiences of and to extend sympathy to these marginalized groups. Although Eve Kosofsky Sedgwick warns against "a sentimental appropriation by the large culture of male homosexuality as spectacle," many authors have appropriated the sentimental tradition for their own uses (*Epistemology*, 144).

James Baldwin—who resisted the label of sentimentalism because of its feminized and spectacularized associations—still drew upon its sympathetic powers, portraying the struggle of a gay man to accept himself and his refusal to be a part of any family—blood-related, affectional, or associational—in *Giovanni's Room* (1956). The AIDS crisis, particularly in the 1980s, also offered new opportunities to draw gays as deserving of sympathy and as part of the national family. As Robert J. Corber argues in "Nationalizing the Gay Body: AIDS and Sentimental Pedagogy in *Philadelphia*," AIDS activists mobilized a form of sentimentality that borrowed from ongoing civil rights efforts "to focus attention on the persistence of racism and sexism without alienating mainstream

Americans. These groups have emphasized the pain and suffering caused by their marginalization from national life so as to avoid appearing to engage in identity politics. Rather than antidiscrimination legislation and affirmative action programs, they have sought the 'healing' and 'closure' promised by the mass witnessing of their suffering" (109). Thus, Tony Kushner's *Angels in America: A Gay Fantasia on National Themes* (1993) presents the struggles of gay men facing the AIDS crisis during the Reagan era.[7] The plays make gay men's suffering visible by revealing the ways that AIDS devastates the gay community, destroying relationships and decimating extended networks of "chosen families." However, after retroviral treatments became more effective, sentimental gay and lesbian fiction began again to focus on suffering that was produced by marginalization. Annie Proulx's "Brokeback Mountain," which was published in the *New Yorker* in 1997 and made into an Oscar-winning film in 2005, signaled a popular shift away from the threat of AIDS to focusing on gay men's emotional lives and their inability to live openly as well as on their struggles to choose—as in *Giovanni's Room*—to which family they belong when the impact of that choice is a perceived negation of masculinity and a potential risk to their lives.

Contemporary sentimentalism is a powerful and complex mode that draws from a historical legacy and builds upon modern structures of thought and feeling. Despite continued public and critical resistance against its perceived feminine associations, sentimentalism enables authors to reach readers on an intimate level in ways that push them to make connections across social boundaries. As scholars and critical theorists continue to deconstruct associations between gender and the biological body, and as feminists continue to push against cultural validation of the masculine and de-validation of the feminine, the uses of sentimentalism will grow even more broad and complex. Sentimentalism as an ideal is about human connection, about forging sympathetic links between groups originally perceived as unalterably different in order to show that they are connected. However, sentimentalism is also about finding new ways to define social groups and determining who is ultimately in charge of making those designations. Let us hope that Morrison is right, and that by critiquing sentimentalism's foundational assumptions, new forms of sympathy that accept difference will emerge.

Notes

1 / Introduction

1. Edward Said, in *Orientalism* (1978), theorized that Western beliefs about the Orient were constructed entirely from Western perspectives and assumptions, leading to a dominant worldview based on "The West" and "The Other." Said's ideas have since influenced literary, social, gender, and race theories that posit that white privilege and heteronormative society also follows this pattern, creating Others out of individuals who are not members of the dominant, hegemonic group.

2. Famous examples of sentimental novels include Susan Warner's *The Wide, Wide World* (1850), Harriet Beecher Stowe's *Uncle Tom's Cabin* (1852), Fanny Fern's *Fern Leaves from Fanny's Portfolio* (1854), Maria Susanna Cummins's *The Lamplighter* (1854), and Fanny Fern's *Ruth Hall* (1855).

3. For more thorough examinations of the cultural work of nineteenth-century sentimental literature, see Jane Tompkins, *Sensational Designs* (1985); Philip Fisher, *Hard Facts* (1985); Cathy N. Davidson, *Revolution and the Word* (2004); Gillian Brown, *Domestic Individualism* (1990); Shirley Samuels, *The Culture of Sentiment* (1992); Markman Ellis, *The Politics of Sensibility* (1996); Elizabeth Barnes, *States of Sympathy* (1997) and *Love's Whipping Boy: Violence and Sentimentality in the American Imagination* (2011); Julia A. Stern, *The Plight of Feeling* (1997); Julie Ellison, *Cato's Tears* (1999); Lori Merish, *Sentimental Materialism* (2000); Paula Bennett, *Poets in the Public Sphere* (2003); and Laurent Berlant, *Female Complaint* (2008).

4. Building upon Weinstein's argument, Carol J. Singley proposes that adoption—one method by which families are legally and officially expanded—is also a significant social construction in sentimental texts. In *Adopting America* (2011), Singley argues that adoption both redefines the family and reaffirms its importance as a social unit because "adoption may be represented openly as an alternative to biological kinship, or it may be designed as an elaborate fiction that replicates the biologically intact family structure it replaces" (6). The project of redefining the family, according to Singley,

occurs on both an individual and a national level. The sentimental novel, with its frequent use of the adoption plot, fostered "a new republican conception of the family as a nonhierarchical group of individuals whose will to be together is at least as important as blood ties" (83).

5. In *Sentimental Modernism* (1991), Suzanne Clark effectively counters that sentimentalism was an integral part of modernism's development that could never wholly be left behind: "Modernism rejected the sentimental, because modernism was sentimental. Modernism was still caught in a gendered dialectic which enclosed literature, making the text the object of a naturalized critical gaze" (7). Clark argues that modernism's attack on sentimentalism enabled the movement to establish a new form of literary criticism that was intrinsically gendered and heavily dependent on the very thing it denigrated. However, in order to define itself as a significant literary movement, modernism required something significant to define itself against; it needed the sentimental to provide an opposing system of values even as it held up true expression of human feeling as a test of its authenticity and the efficacy of the aesthetics endorsed. The sentimental became "a shorthand for everything modernism would exclude, the other of its literary/nonliterary dualism" (9). Michael Bell, in *Sentimentalism, Ethics, and the Culture of Feeling* (2000), observes that despite its criticism of the sentimental, "the modernist generation also continued the transformation of sentiment into an implicit criterion of true feeling, a development which even now largely escapes recognition whether in the common language of feeling or in the specialist practice of literary criticism" (160).

6. The quotation used in the heading is from Meridel Le Sueur, "They Follow Us Girls" (1935), 7.

7. "The Negro Family: The Case for National Action" is the title of a report written and released in 1965 by Daniel Patrick Moynihan, assistant secretary of labor (and later a U.S. senator), and known more commonly as "the Moynihan Report." In this report, Moynihan urged the U.S. government to adopt a national policy for the reconstruction of the African American family, arguing that the real cause of the deep roots of black poverty arises not from segregation, discrimination, or a lack of voting power but from unemployment and the lack of a nuclear family structure. According to Moynihan, the structure of the African American family is unstable and "approaching complete breakdown." Moynihan cites increasingly matriarchal African American family culture, where more than 25 percent of women are divorced, separated, or living apart from their husbands and in which approximately 25 percent of all births are illegitimate. Furthermore, Moynihan argues that African American children, particularly boys, raised by mothers in fatherless homes experience stunted academic and employment potential as well as a higher likelihood of delinquency and crime.

8. The most active period of slave narrative publication occurred in the mid-nineteenth century, presumably as part of increasing abolitionist agitation leading up to the Civil War and in response to the passage of the 1850 Fugitive Slave Law. It is difficult, if not impossible, to ascertain the exact number of slave narratives that were published; scholarly estimates place the total number of published slave narratives still in existence between 85 and 142, while other accounts number between 2,000 and more than 6,000 if court records, broadsides, and interviews are included (Foster, *Witnessing*, 21). Frances Smith Foster observes, however, that the estimates of slave narratives that are still in existence likely represent only "a small portion of those

which were written" (22). It is useful to consider the number of editions printed and copies sold during the mid-nineteenth century to gauge the genre's popular appeal. According to Foster, Moses Roper's 1838 narrative went through eleven editions; Frederick Douglass's 1845 narrative published seven editions in four years; William Wells Brown's 1847 narrative sold four editions in its first year; and Josiah Henson's 1849 narrative experienced a jump in sales after it was revealed that he was a model for Harriet Beecher Stowe's Uncle Tom, going from sales of 6,000 copies in its first three years to over 100,000 copies.

9. Although not the only sentimental novel to take slavery as its subject, *Uncle Tom's Cabin* firmly convinced abolitionists of the power of sentimental fiction to persuade readers. After its publication and dramatic sales success in 1852, antislavery novels as well as slave narratives were all compared to *Uncle Tom's Cabin* in their ability to move readers. When Richard Hildreth published an expanded edition of his antislavery novel *The Slave; or, Memoirs of Archy Moore* (1836) as *The White Slave* in 1852, a reviewer in *Frederick Douglass' Paper* observed that "readers of *Uncle Tom's Cabin* will take it as the highest style of recommendation to say of this book, that it will be read with as deep an interest and as ineffeaceable [*sic*] an impression as that masterly work" and that "[w]e hope it may be as extensively read as Mrs. Stowe's great work; it will do invaluable service in intensifying the hostility to slavery that exists, and may perhaps open the eyes of some of the friends or apologists of the system, to some of its enormities" (*The White Slave*, n.p.). When the narrative of Solomon Northup was published in 1853 under the title *Twelve Years a Slave*, amanuensis David Wilson claimed to present "a faithful history of Solomon Northup's life, as [I] received it from his lips" (xvi). Northup's narrative is dedicated to Harriet Beecher Stowe and introduced as "another Key to Uncle Tom's Cabin" on its frontispiece. Because the narrative itself invites immediate comparison, a reviewer from the 1853 *Detroit Tribune* judged the autobiographical quality of Northup's narrative against the fictional impact of Stowe's novel: "Next to 'Uncle Tom's Cabin,' the extraordinary Narrative of Solomon Northup is the most remarkable book that was ever issued from the American press. Indeed, it is a more extraordinary work than that, because it is only a simple unvarnished tale of the experience of an American freeman of the 'blessings' of Slavery, while Mrs. Stowe's Uncle Tom is only an ingenious and powerfully wrought novel, intended to illustrate what Solomon saw and experienced—Southern Slavery, in its various phases."

10. Although the presence of novelistic features raised debate over the "authenticity" of slave narratives that do not follow a strictly autobiographical writing style, more recent critical assessments of fictionalized slave narratives have explored the ways such authors critique contemporary social ideologies that are promulgated in sentimental literature and antebellum culture. Women's narratives such as Harriet Jacobs's *Incidents in the Life of a Slave Girl* (1861) and Sojourner Truth's *Narrative of Sojourner Truth* (1850) have been noted by Hazel V. Carby and Lori Merish for their use of sentimental conventions to interest a white, middle-class, female readership while also "engag[ling] with the codes of gendered identity that measure black women's exclusion from full (civil) subjectivity in nineteenth-century America" (Merish, *Materialism*, 193). African American women's narratives expose "the ways in which sentimentalism both constitutes and delimits forms of female political agency, subjectivity, and desire in liberal political culture" (193). Examinations of slave narratives written by women have generally focused on the ways women writers undercut the marginalization

created by sentimental ideology, whereas examinations of men's fictionalized slave narratives have focused on their use of sentimental conventions to increase identification with white masculine agency. Interestingly, while women's fictionalized slave narratives are thought to "demystify sentimental fictions of white male protection, sentimental ownership, and 'civilized' masculine authority" (193), narratives written by men are often shown to use those conventions in the development of tension between individuality and community. Men's narratives also critique the ideological marginalization preventing African Americans from performing the masculine role of self-governing actor, protector, provider, and property owner. While slave narratives written by men may depict sentimentalized emotional scenes and emphasize family or community connection, they often represent the male author as an independent, self-made man in order to counter feminized associations with family, community, and victimhood. Few slave narratives written by men, if any, are credited with openly critiquing sentimental fiction's gender ideology, and most uses of such conventions in male writing are thought to associate sentimentality with the promotion of African American manhood through the attainment of racially privileged technologies such as literacy and property ownership. Thus, nineteenth-century slave narratives show active engagement with the sentimental novel, as many adopted its techniques in order to win "to anti-slavery many hearts which else would have remained cold and indifferent" (Douglass, *Life and Times*, 572).

11. For more on the genre of neo-slave narratives, see Ashraf H. A. Rushdy, *Neo-Slave Narratives: Studies in the Social Logic of a Literary Form* (1999) and *Remembering Generations: Race and Family in Contemporary African American Fiction* (2001); Caroline Rody, *The Daughter's Return: African-American and Caribbean Women's Fictions of History* (2001); Angelyn Mitchell, *The Freedom to Remember: Narrative, Slavery, and Gender in Contemporary Black Women's Fiction* (2002); and Arlene R. Keizer, *Black Subjects: Identity Formation in the Contemporary Narrative of Slavery* (2004).

12. As with nineteenth-century sentimental texts, I must use the term *genre* loosely. These texts are connected through their use of the sentimental mode, but other methods by which we define *genre*—such as specific plot conventions or stylistic features—do not capture all of the works that are germane to this category.

2 / Grace Lumpkin's *To Make My Bread*

1. In what is more commonly known as the Loray Mill Strike, the National Textile Workers Union (NTWU), a communist union, had hoped to establish a southern stronghold and worked to organize several mills in Gaston County, North Carolina. The strikes lasted from April 1, 1929, to the end of September 1929. The strike began at Loray Mill in Gastonia and grew to include the American Textile Mills in nearby Bessemer City. Clashes between strikers and law enforcement included mass violence at rallies and in the tent cities that had been established when mill owners evicted striking workers from their company-owned housing. The strikes resulted in two prominent deaths: Police Chief Orville F. Aderholt and Ella May Wiggins, a white single mother of five who worked in the American Textile Mill, wrote protest ballads, and helped organize female and African American workers to participate in the strike. For more historical background, see John A. Salmond, *Gastonia, 1929: The Story of the Loray Mill Strike* (1995).

2. Reportage became a significant genre during this period, "creating a rapport between the direct experiences of those who suffered and struggled and the writers who came into contact with them" (Rabinowitz, *Labor and Desire*, 2). Reportage was the "direct rendering of (class) struggle through carefully detailed (individual) analysis" (2), and many proletarian authors—including Meridel Le Sueur, Josephine Herbst, and John Steinbeck—not only were known for this writing but based much of their later fiction upon it.

3. *To Make My Bread* reveals that women are not protected from sexual danger even within the home. Young Frank, Ora's son, sexually harasses and molests Bonnie while the two families are living in a mill house. After Frank is forced to leave school and begin working in the mill, he swears that he will go "to the devil as fast as [he] can" (208). Shortly thereafter, he begins following Bonnie around: "Sometimes he found her in a room by herself, and backing her into a corner, would try to touch her leg under her dress. And even in the dark when she was undressing for bed in the room [they shared] she felt his eyes staring at her trying to make her out.... Whatever it was he made the whole place uncomfortable for her" (228).

4. There is not a large body of scholarship on *To Make My Bread*, but scholars have maintained an interest in the novel because of its depiction of the 1929 Gastonia mill strikes and their unique gender dynamics. Examinations have primarily focused on the novel as an important example of strike fiction (Rideout and Blake), as an example of women's radical fiction (Urgo), as radical fiction focused on Southern women workers (Cook), and as an illustration of the use of the maternal figure as a radical symbol and a trope for female activism (Campbell, Kirby, and Schreibersdorf). Suzanne Sowinska provides an analysis of *To Make My Bread*'s race dynamics in "Writing across the Color Line," arguing that the women form a cross-racial alliance based on mutual understanding and need and noting that women workers also have lower wages than white male workers and are in the "last hired, first fired" category of mill workers.

5. Emma's and Ora's families initially live together until Granpap buys a farm off company property and asks Emma to move her family there with him. Ora and Frank move into a different mill house, and one of their older daughters stays home from school to care for the young children. Bonnie marries Jim Calhoun, and they live in Granpap's farmhouse until Jim leaves for the war and the walk between the farm and mill grow too far for Bonnie, so she moves back to a house in the village with her brother John and Emma. Granpap eventually loses the farm, Jim returns home and works in the mill, Emma dies of pellagra, and John marries Zinie Martin—the daughter of Jennie Martin, a friend and neighbor from Swain's Crossing who had also moved with her family to work in the mills—and they live with Bonnie and Jim. Granpap passes away, and Zinie's brother-in-law is killed in an accident, which "forced John and Zinie to break up the house with Bonnie, for Jennie needed them to help with money" (316–17). Jim leaves Bonnie, who can no longer afford her company house, so she moves her children to a cabin off company property that had "been lived in by colored people" (317).

6. George Lipsitz, in *The Possessive Investment in Whiteness: How White People Profit from Identity Politics*, outlines the ways that policies adopted long after Emancipation economically and socially advantaged whites by pitting minorities against each other, specifically reserving benefits and work protections for whites, destroying affordable minority housing, and maintaining de facto segregation. Lipsitz points to

policies such as the New Deal Era Wagner Act and Social Security Act, which excluded farmworkers and domestics from coverage, "effectively denying those disproportionately minority sectors of the work force protections and benefits routinely afforded whites" (5). The 1934 Federal Housing Act brought home ownership within reach of millions of citizens, "but overtly racist categories in the Federal House Agency's (FHA) 'confidential' city surveys and appraisers' manuals channeled almost all of the loan money toward whites and away from communities of color." Similarly, northern trade unions were segregated, so gains in pensions, insurance, and job security were awarded to whites, "who formed the overwhelming majority of the unionized work force." For additional studies on the economic impact of segregation and race policy in the United States, see Gary M. Anderson and Dennis Halcoussis, "The Political Economy of Legal Segregation: Jim Crow and Racial Employment Patterns" (1996); Sherry Cable and Tamara L. Mix, "Economic Imperatives and Race Relations: The Rise and Fall of the American Apartheid System" (2003); and Donald Tomaskovic-Devey and Vincent J. Roscigno, "Racial Economic Subordination and White Gain in the U.S. South" (1996).

7. Lumpkin does not address whether the fictional mill in *To Make My Bread* is an all-white mill, as she does not portray African Americans at work in spooling or weaving rooms in equivalent jobs to whites. She includes Mary Allen, who sweeps floors, and African Americans who live in Stumptown and are recruited to fill the positions vacated by the striking workers.

8. The doctor shames Bonnie in a context, as well, of a faith in the social and medical power of physicians, who hold an elevated status. Although the McClures had received advice from a neighboring friend's doctor that Emma "needs plenty of good food, and no doctor," they felt obligated to call for the company doctor when Emma's health began to fail: "[W]ith people advising that they get Doctor Foley, and with their own uncertainty, they found it the only thing to do" (276). The McClures and the laboring community rely on the company doctor because they do not know how to treat severe illness and because doctors possess knowledge. However, *To Make My Bread* emphasizes the participation of figures such as doctors in the system that prevents the working class from achieving economic stability. The doctor's social power is, therefore, set in light of his own complicity in the capitalist system, de-emphasizing his ability to shame working mothers like Emma and Bonnie because of the ways he is tainted by the capitalist profit system. A doctor holds a position of respect; he is a figure who does not suffer from the same ills as his patients, is educated, and espouses the ideals of the middle class. He is, therefore, able to enforce traditional cultural standards and shame his patients for their inability to provide proper food and rest—which they can readily see the doctor himself has no problem obtaining. His services are expensive, which makes them exclusive and valuable; it also makes them difficult for the working class to afford.

9. The elderly Granma Wesley owns a spinning wheel, a loom that had been passed down from the earliest generations of Wesleys to settle in the mountains, and two sheep. Her ambition had been to finish a coverlet from their wool before she died, and each year "she sheared the animals herself, combed the wool and spun it into thread for the loom. In the summer on a clear day anyone passing through Possum Hollow near enough to the cabin could hear the loom" (27). "Everyone" in the community knows of Granma Wesley's "great wish to finish the coverlet before she died." Thus, it

becomes both a community tragedy and salvation when her family must slaughter and eat the sheep in order to survive a particularly harsh winter.

4 / Caretaking, Domesticity, and Gender in John Steinbeck's *The Grapes of Wrath*

1. Throughout his career, Bristol continued to link his work from California's Central Valley with *The Grapes of Wrath*, renaming many of the photographs after the characters in Steinbeck's novel. After retiring to Ojai, California, in 1976, Bristol reconsidered his early career. He renamed his 1937–38 photographs of migrant camps after characters in the novel and titled the series *The Grapes of Wrath*.

2. See Sandra Beatty, "A Study of Female Characterization in Steinbeck's Fiction" (1979); Warren Motley, "From Patriarchy to Matriarchy: Ma Joad's Role in *The Grapes of Wrath*" (1982); Nellie McKay, "'Happy[?]-Wife-and-Motherdom': The Portrayal of Ma Joad in John Steinbeck's *The Grapes of Wrath*" (1990); Mimi R. Gladstein, "Deletions from the *Battle*; Gaps in the *Grapes*" (1992); Lorelei Cederstrom, "The 'Great Mother' in *The Grapes of Wrath*" (1997); and Vivyan C. Adair, "Of Home-Makers and Home-Breakers: The Deserving and the Undeserving Poor Mother in Depression Era Literature" (2007).

3. See Richard Astro, *John Steinbeck and Edward F. Ricketts: The Shaping of a Novelist* (1973); Robert Briffault, *The Mothers: A Study of the Origins of Sentiments and Institutions* (1927); Nellie McKay, "'Happy[?]-Wife-and-Motherdom': The Portrayal of Ma Joad in John Steinbeck's *The Grapes of Wrath*" (1990); and Warren Motley, "From Patriarchy to Matriarchy: Ma Joad's Role in *The Grapes of Wrath*" (1982).

4. See Meridel Le Sueur, *The Girl* (1930s) and *Salute to Spring* (1940); Grace Lumpkin, *To Make My Bread* (1932); and Tillie Lerner Olsen, *Yonnondio: From the Thirties* (1930s).

5. Nancy Armstrong argues in *Desire and Domestic Fiction: A Political History of the Novel* (1987) that texts including eighteenth-century conduct books and novels about women's home life, social customs, romantic entanglements, and marital arrangements created new forms of social power. She contends that writers ranging from Samuel Richardson to the Brontës, Jane Austen, and Virginia Woolf focused on new forms of female identity as a central component to an emerging middle class based on economic status, social behavior, and moral quality. Nina Baym extends this examination to women's writing in nineteenth-century American literature in *Woman's Fiction: A Guide to Novels by and about Women in America, 1820–70* (1993), where she shows that women's writing developed from the domestic tradition and was inaugurated by Catharine Maria Sedgwick's *A New-England Tale* (1822). These texts continued to draw on the nineteenth-century American culture of Sentiment and relied on the inherent goodness of human nature and the power of feelings as a guide to right conduct for the vulnerable female protagonist as well as for the reader.

6. When a con-rod bearing blows in the Wilsons' car, which Al had worked on, Al "felt his failure" (166). While he is glad that Tom has the knowledge to fix the car, his perceived failure makes him angry and defensive: "Al's face went red with anger. He throttled down his motor. 'Goddamn it,' he yelled, 'I didn't burn that bearin' out! What d'ya mean, I'll bust a spring too?'" The implication, Al knows and defends himself against, is that a failure to maintain the car is a failure of his masculine ability to provide for the family.

7. Tom earns Knowles's respect by grinding a car valve: "You can do her," he said. "Damn good thing. You'll need to" (246). Knowles offers insight into the dire work situation, advising them and providing a tip on possible work because Al helps him repair the car: "Floyd said patiently, "I know ya jus' got here. They's stuff ya got to learn. If you'd let me tell ya, it'd save ya somepin. If ya don' let me tell ya, then ya got to learn the hard way"" (260).

5 / Margaret Walker's *Jubilee*

1. Psalm 22:11–18 reads: "Be not far from me; for trouble is near; for there is none to help. Many bulls have compassed me: strong bulls of Bashan have beset me round. They gaped upon me with their mouths, as a ravening and a roaring lion. I am poured out like water, and all my bones are out of joint: my heart is like wax; it is melted in the midst of my bowels. My strength is dried up like a potsherd; and my tongue cleaveth to my jaws; and thou hast brought me into the dust of death. For dogs have compassed me: the assembly of the wicked have inclosed me: they pierced my hands and my feet. I may tell all my bones: they look and stare upon me. They part my garments among them, and cast lots upon my vesture" (King James Version).

2. Jesus prays in the garden of Gethsemane, the night after the Feast of the Passover, knowing of the pain, suffering, and humiliation to come before his crucifixion and death.

7 / Toni Morrison's *Beloved*

1. Indeed, the danger of witnessing is exemplified through Halle, who hides in the hayloft while Schoolteacher's nephews assault his wife. Unable to reveal himself and knowing that he could do nothing to stop the abuse, Halle is forced to watch his wife's mammary rape. The trauma of this event breaks him, and Paul D later finds him babbling incoherently, with butter slathered over his face.

2. In "Rediscovering Black History," Morrison describes the experience of gathering materials for what eventually became *The Black Book* (Harris et al., 1974): it was "as though I were experiencing once again the barbarity visited upon my people as I sat in Spike Harris's apartment reading 17th-century through 19th-century newspapers with a magnifying glass." She came across a clipping from 1854 titled "A Visit to the Slave Mother Who Killed Her Child," which described the Margaret Garner case that eventually became the foundation for *Beloved*. Morrison noted, "Such accounts jammed the pages of early American newspapers."

3. Baby Suggs has been so hurt by the loss of her children that she is better prepared for news of Halle's death "than she had [been] for his life" and "barely glanced" at him when he was born because "it wasn't worth the trouble to try to learn features you would never see change into adulthood anyway. Seven times she had done that" (139).

4. During their reunion, Paul D inquires about Halle, and Sethe tells him, "I think he's dead. It's not being sure that keeps him alive" (8). When Paul D asks what Baby Suggs believed, Sethe asserts, "Same, but to listen to her, all her children is dead. Claimed she felt each one go the very day and hour."

5. Although Morrison makes it clear that Stamp Paid didn't murder his wife in that moment, she leaves Vashti's fate ambiguous. Paul D asks, "Did you? Snap it?" and Stamp Paid replies, "Uh uh. I changed my name" (233). However, when Stamp Paid

explains that he escaped by boating up the Mississippi and walking the rest of the way, he only says that Vashti died and offers no further details.

8 / Conclusion

1. A 2012 survey of 4,530 five-star reviews on Amazon.com reveals a high number of white reviewers who acknowledge their race identity and not only argue against criticism of the novel's historical distortions but claim that the text is the story of their own lives or provides new insights into their memories of life in that period. For just a sampling, see Mitzi Aldridge, "She Speaks the Truth" (2009); Avid Reader, "I Was Blown Away by This Book—WOW!" (2009); M. S. Clay, "What a Read!" (2009); N. Gargano, "I Wish I Could Give More than Five!!" (2009); Harriet, "'Helps' Blur the Lines We've Drawn—a Book I'll Never Forget!" (2009); Kelly Phillips, "I Don't Have All the Words to Say How Much I Loved This Book" (2009); Katherine H. Steele, "My Life, Revisited" (2010); and S. D. Sawyer, "So THAT'S What 'The Help' was Thinking" (2012).

2. See also Amy Biancolli, "'The Help' Review: A Heaping Helping of Bigotry" (2011); Association of Black Women Historians, "An Open Statement to the Fans of *The Help*" (2011); Douglas A. Blackmon and Cameron McWhirter, "Plaintiff Says 'Help' Humiliated Her" (2011); Manohla Dargis, "'The Maids' Now Have Their Say" (2011); Roger Ebert, Review of *The Help* (2011); David Edelstein, "Movie Review: Viola Davis Gives the Too-Soft *The Help* a Spine" (2011); Marshall Fine, "Huffpost Review: *The Help*" (2011); Roxane Gay, "The Solace of Preparing Fried Foods and Other Quaint Remembrances from 1960s Mississippi: Thoughts on *The Help*" (2011); Linda Holmes, "Actor Wendell Pierce Takes to Twitter to Talk about 'The Help'" (2011); Ann Hornaday, "Black and White, and Not Enough 'Help'" (2011); Jamilah Lemieux, "I Don't Need Kathryn Stockett's 'Help'" (2011); Karina Longworth, "*The Help* Review" (2011); Laura Miller, "The Dirty Secrets of 'The Help': A Black Maid Sues a White Author for Stealing Her Story, but Is That What's Really Going On?" (2011); Wesley Morris, Review of *The Help* (2011); Ann Oldenburg, "'Help' Author Kathryn Stockett Responds to Lawsuit" (2011); Peter Rainer, Review of *The Help* (2011); Campbell Robertson, "A Victory in Court for the Author of 'The Help'" (2011); Ujala Sehgal, "Even Emma Stone Can't Save 'The Help' from Heat for 'Fake' History" (2011); Rinku Sen, "'The Help' Today Still Don't Have Rights, Actually" (2011); Sergio, "Actor Wendell Pierce Isn't Exactly Thrilled with 'The Help'" (2011); Julianne Escobedo Shepherd, "New Film *The Help* Whitewashes the Civil Rights Struggle into a Heartstring-Tugging Hallmark Card" (2011); Akiba Solomon, "Why I'm Just Saying No to 'The Help' and Its Historical Whitewash" (2011); Tami, "This Is Why I Worry about 'The Help'" (2011); Patricia A. Turner, "Dangerous White Stereotypes" (2011); Rebecca Wanzo, "Love 'The Help,' but Please Stop Asking Me to Do the Same" (2011); and Zerlina, "Professor Melissa Harris-Perry Calls 'The Help' Movie 'Ahistorical and Deeply Troubling'" (2011).

3. See, e.g., Jamia Wilson, "The Upside of *The Help* Controversy: It Made Us Talk about Race" (2011).

4. See *Hidden in the Home: Abuse of Domestic Workers with Special Visas in the United States* (Human Rights Watch, 2001); *Home Is Where the Work Is: Inside New York's Domestic Work Industry* (Domestic Workers United and DataCenter, 2006); "Domestic Workers: Human Rights Abuses and Discrimination in the Workforce" (Beach, 2008); *Domestic Workers' Rights in the United States: A Report Prepared for the*

U.N. Human Rights Committee in Response to the Second and Third Periodic Report of the United States (Andolan Organizing South Asian Workers et al., n.d.); "The Color of Help: Workers of Color Dominate Domestic Services but Lack Union Rights" (Boyd, 2011).

5. The film adapts this technique by primarily focusing on Skeeter's perspective while interspersing her storyline with scenes of Aibileen and Minnie at work and at home.

6. Stanley Crouch, in his essay "Segregated Fiction Blues" (2004), explores the criticism Styron received for writing *The Confessions of Nat Turner* as well as the ways in which American writers can write effectively beyond their own racial categories. Crouch contends that "Hemingway's dictum of writing about what you know has become an excuse for avoiding risks" and that the results of breaking up "the big sweep of American life" into ethnic, religious, sexual, class, and regional divisions that can only be written about from personal experience is "dull and dismal" (25, 18). Although Crouch agrees that Styron wrote an "unconvincing Freudian mess of self-hatred" and "sexual confusion," he is concerned that the "impact of the controversy was that white writers at large opted for folding instead of holding, convinced that the challenge of writing across the color line was too big a risk to their careers and their reputations" (21, 23).

7. *Angels in America* is a two-play series. Part 1, *Millennium Approaches*, was first performed in May 1990, receiving its world premiere in 1991. Part 2, *Perestroika*, premiered in 1992.

Works Cited

Adair, Vivyan C. "Of Home-Makers and Home-Breakers: The Deserving and the Undeserving Poor Mother in Depression Era Literature." *The Literary Mother: Essays on Representations of Maternity and Child Care.* Ed. Susan Staub. Jefferson, NC: McFarland, 2007. 48–66.

Aldridge, Mitzi. "She Speaks the Truth." Review of *The Help: A Novel*, by Kathryn Stockett. Amazon.com, 16 Aug. 2009. http://www.amazon.com/review/R1R4NHK2PFL2E.

Anderson, Gary M., and Dennis Halcoussis. "The Political Economy of Legal Segregation: Jim Crow and Racial Employment Patterns." *Economics and Politics* 8.1 (1996): 1–15. doi: 10.1111/j.1468-0343.1996.tb00117.x.

Andolan Organizing South Asian Workers et al. *Domestic Workers' Rights in the United States: A Report Prepared for the U.N. Human Rights Committee in Response to the Second and Third Periodic Report of the United States.* University of North Carolina School of Law, n.d. (accessed 7 Sept. 2011). http://www.law.unc.edu/documents/clinicalprograms/domesticworkersreport.pdf.

Andrews, William L. *To Tell a Free Story: The First Century of Afro-American Autobiography, 1760–1865.* Urbana: University of Illinois Press, 1986.

Angelo, Bonnie. "Toni Morrison: The Pain of Being Black." *Time*, 22 May 1989. http://www.time.com/time/magazine/article/0,9171,957724,00.html.

Armstrong, Nancy. *Desire and Domestic Fiction: A Political History of the Novel.* New York: Oxford University Press, 1987.

———. "Introduction: The Politics of Domesticating Culture, Then and Now." *The Novel: An Anthology of Criticism and Theory, 1900–2000.* Ed. Dorothy J. Hale. Malden, MA: Blackwell, 2006. 622–43.

Association of Black Women Historians. "An Open Statement to the Fans of *The Help.*" 2011. http://www.abwh.org/index.php?option=com_content&view=article&id=2%3Aopen-statement-the-help.

Astro, Richard. *John Steinbeck and Edward F. Ricketts: The Shaping of a Novelist.* Minneapolis: University of Minnesota Press, 1973.

Austen, Jane. *Pride and Prejudice: A Novel. In Three Volumes.* London: Printed for T. Egerton, Military Library, Whitehall, 1813.

Avid Reader. "I Was Blown Away by This Book—WOW!" Review of *The Help: A Novel,* by Kathryn Stockett. Amazon.com, 2 June 2009. http://www.amazon.com/review/R2324B53EEBYQP.

Baldwin, James. *Giovanni's Room.* New York: Dial, 1956.

Barnes, Elizabeth. *Love's Whipping Boy: Violence and Sentimentality in the American Imagination.* Chapel Hill: University of North Carolina Press, 2011.

———. *States of Sympathy: Seduction and Democracy in the American Novel.* New York: Columbia University Press, 1997.

Baskind, Samantha. "The 'True' Story: *Life* Magazine, Horace Bristol, and John Steinbeck's *The Grapes of Wrath.*" *Steinbeck Studies* 15.2 (2004): 39–74. doi: 10.1353/stn.2004.0029.

Baym, Nina. *Woman's Fiction: A Guide to Novels by and about Women in America, 1820–70.* 1978. Urbana: University of Illinois Press, 1993.

Beach, Marissa. "Domestic Workers: Human Rights Abuses and Discrimination in the Workforce." Report to the Commissioners of Washington State Human Rights Commission (WSHRC), 10 Dec. 2008.

Beatty, Sandra. "A Study of Female Characterization in Steinbeck's Fiction." *Steinbeck's Women: Essays in Criticism.* Ed. Tetsumaro Hayashi. Muncie, IN: Steinbeck Society of America, 1979. 1–6.

Beaulieu, Elizabeth Ann. *Black Women Writers and the American Neo-Slave Narrative: Femininity Unfettered.* Westport, CT: Greenwood, 1999.

Bell, Bernard W. *The Afro-American Novel and Its Tradition.* 1987. Amherst: University of Massachusetts Press, 1989.

Bell, Michael. *Sentimentalism, Ethics, and the Culture of Feeling.* Houndmills, Basingstoke, Hampshire: Palgrave Macmillan, 2000.

Bennett, Paula. *Poets in the Public Sphere: The Emancipatory Project of American Women's Poetry, 1800–1900.* Princeton, NJ: Princeton University Press, 2003.

Berger, James. "Ghosts of Liberalism: Morrison's *Beloved* and the Moynihan Report." *PMLA* 111.3 (1996): 408–20. http://www.jstor.org/stable/463165.

Berlant, Lauren. *Female Complaint: The Unfinished Business of Sentimentality in American Culture.* Durham, NC: Duke University Press, 2008.

Biancolli, Amy. "'The Help' Review: A Heaping Helping of Bigotry." Dir. Tate Taylor. *San Francisco Chronicle,* 10 Aug. 2011. http://www.sfgate.com/

movies/article/The-Help-review-A-heaping-helping-of-bigotry-2335343.php.
Blackmon, Douglas A., and Cameron McWhirter. "Plaintiff Says 'Help' Humiliated Her." *Wall Street Journal*, 18 Feb. 2011.
Blake, Fay M. *The Strike in the American Novel*. Metuchen, NJ: Scarecrow Press, 1972.
Boyd, Kyle. "The Color of Help: Workers of Color Dominate Domestic Services but Lack Union Rights." Center for American Progress, 17 June 2011. http://www.americanprogress.org/issues/race/news/2011/06/17/9783/the-color-of-help.
Briffault, Robert. *The Mothers: A Study of the Origins of Sentiments and Institutions*. New York: Macmillan, 1927.
Bristol, Horace. "The Grapes of Wrath: Horace Bristol's California Photographs." J. Paul Getty Museum, Past Exhibitions and Installations, 15 Oct. 2002. http://www.getty.edu/art/exhibitions/bristol.
Brontë, Charlotte. *Jane Eyre*. London: Smith, Elder and Co., Cornhill, 1847.
Brontë, Emily. *Wuthering Heights*. London: Thomas Cautley Newby, 1847.
Brown, Cecil. "Interview with Toni Morrison." *Massachusetts Review* 35.3 (1995): 455–73. http://www.jstor.org/stable/25090662.
Brown, Gillian. *Domestic Individualism: Imagining Self in Nineteenth-Century America*. Berkeley: University of California Press, 1990.
Brown, William Wells. *Narrative of William W. Brown, a Fugitive Slave. Written by Himself*. Boston: Anti-Slavery Office, 1847.
Butler, Octavia. *Kindred*. 1979. Boston: Beacon, 1988.
Cable, Sherry, and Tamara L. Mix. "Economic Imperatives and Race Relations: The Rise and Fall of the American Apartheid System." *Journal of Black Studies* 34.2 (2003): 183–203. doi: 10.1177/0021934703254098.
Campbell, Patricia R. "Portraits of Gastonia: 1930s Maternal Activism and the Protest Novel." PhD dissertation. University of Florida, 2006.
Cantwell, Robert. *The Land of Plenty*. New York: Farrar and Rinehart, 1934.
——. Review of "To Make My Bread," by Grace Lumpkin. *Nation* 135 (1932): 372.
Carby, Hazel V. *Reconstructing Womanhood: The Emergence of the Afro-American Woman Novelist*. New York: Oxford University Press, 1987.
Casey, Janet Galligani. "Agrarian Landscapes, the Depression, and Women's Progressive Fiction." *The Novel and the American Left: Critical Essays on Depression-Era Fiction*. Ed. Janet Galligani Casey. Iowa City: University of Iowa Press, 2004. 96–117.
——. "Radial Ruralities." *A New Heartland: Women, Modernity, and the Agrarian Ideal in America*. New York: Oxford University Press, 2009. 123–56.
Cederstrom, Lorelei. "The 'Great Mother' in *The Grapes of Wrath*." *Steinbeck and the Environment: Interdisciplinary Approaches*. Ed. Susan F. Beegel,

Susan Shillinglaw, and Wesley N. Tiffany. Tuscaloosa: University of Alabama Press, 1997. 76–91.

Chapman, Abraham. "Negro Folksong: Review of *Jubilee*." *Saturday Review* 24 Sept. 1966, 43–44.

Clark, Suzanne. *Sentimental Modernism: Women Writers and the Revolution of the Word*. Bloomington: Indiana University Press, 1991.

Clay, M. S. "What a Read!" Review of *The Help: A Novel*, by Kathryn Stockett. Amazon.com, 6 Mar. 2009. http://www.amazon.com/review/RL4GQ3SHVXW50.

Clemons, Walter. "A Gravestone of Memories." *Newsweek*, 28 Sept. 1987, 74–75.

Coiner, Constance. *Better Red: The Writing and Resistance of Tillie Olsen and Meridel Le Sueur*. New York: Oxford University Press, 1995.

Conroy, Jack. *The Disinherited*. [New York]: Covici-Friede, 1933.

Cook, Sylvia J. *From Tobacco Road to Route 66: The Southern Poor White in Fiction*. Chapel Hill: University of North Carolina Press, 1976.

———. "Gastonia: The Literary Reverberations of the Strike." *Southern Literary Journal* 7.1 (1974): 49–66. http://www.jstor.org/stable/20077503.

Corber, Robert J. "Nationalizing the Gay Body: AIDS and Sentimental Pedagogy in *Philadelphia*." *American Literary History* 15.1 (2003): 107–33.

Crouch, Stanley. "Aunt Medea." *Critical Essays on Toni Morrison's "Beloved."* Ed. Barbara H. Solomon. New York: G. K. Hall, 1998. 64–71.

———. "Segregated Fiction Blues." *Artificial White Man: Essays on Authenticity*. New York: Basic Civitas Books, 2004: 15–50.

Cullinan, Colleen Carpenter. "A Maternal Discourse of Redemption: Speech and Suffering in Morrison's *Beloved*." *Religion and Literature* 34.2 (2002): 77–104. http://www.jstor.org/stable/40059820.

Cummins, Maria Susanna. *The Lamplighter*. Boston: J. P. Hewett and Company; Cleveland: Jewett, Proctor and Worthington, 1854.

Dargis, Manohla. "'The Maids' Now Have Their Say." *New York Times*, 9 Aug. 2011.

Davidson, Cathy N. *Revolution and the Word: The Rise of the Novel in America*. 1986. New York: Oxford University Press, 2004.

Davis, Rebecca Harding. *Life in the Iron Mills, and Other Stories*. 1861.

Demetrakopoulos, Stephanie A. "Maternal Bonds as Devourers of Women's Individuation in Toni Morrison's *Beloved*." *African American Review* 26.1 (1992): 51–59. http://www.jstor.org/stable/3042076.

DeMott, Robert. Introduction. *The Grapes of Wrath*. By John Steinbeck. New York: Penguin, 2006. ix–xlv.

DiChario, Nick. "A Conversation with Octavia Butler." *Conversations with Octavia Butler*. Ed. Conseula Francis. Jackson: University Press of Mississippi, 2010. 206–12.

Dieng, Babacar. "Reclamation in Walker's *Jubilee*: The Context of Development of the Historical Novel." *Journal of Pan African Studies* 2.4 (2008): 117–27.

Dillon, Elizabeth Maddock. "Sentimental Aesthetics." *American Literature* 76.3 (2004): 495–523. doi: 10.1215/00029831-76-3-495.
Dobson, Joanne. "The American Renaissance Reenvisioned." *The (Other) American Traditions: Nineteenth-Century Women Writers*. Ed. Joyce W. Warren. New Brunswick, NJ: Rutgers University Press, 1993. 164–82.
———. "Reclaiming Sentimental Literature." *American Literature* 69.2 (1997): 263–88. http://www.jstor.org/stable/2928271.
Domestic Workers United and DataCenter. *Home Is Where the Work Is: Inside New York's Domestic Work Industry*. DataCenter, 14 July 2006. http://www.datacenter.org/reports/homeiswheretheworkis.pdf.
Douglas, Ann. *The Feminization of American Culture*. 1977. New York: Noonday Press / Farrar, Straus and Giroux, 1998.
Douglass, Frederick. *The Life and Times of Frederick Douglass, Written by Himself*. Boston: De Wolfe and Fiske Co., 1892.
———. *My Bondage and My Freedom*. New York: Miller, Orton and Mulligan, 1855.
———. *Narrative of the Life of Frederick Douglass, an American Slave. Written by Himself*. Boston: Anti-Slavery Office, 1845.
Du Bois, W. E. B. *The Souls of Black Folk*. *Writings*. 1903. New York: Library of America, 1986. 357–547.
Ebert, Roger. Review of *The Help*, dir. Tate Taylor. *Chicago Sun-Times*, 9 Aug. 2011.
Edelstein, David. "Movie Review: Viola Davis Gives the Too-Soft *The Help* a Spine." Dir. Tate Taylor. *New York Magazine*, 9 Aug. 2011.
Edwards, Thomas. "Ghost Story." Review of *Beloved*, by Toni Morrison. *New York Review of Books*, 5 Nov. 1987, 18–19.
Eliot, George. *Middlemarch. A Study of Provincial Life*. Edinburgh and London: William Blackwood and Sons, 1871.
Ellis, Markman. *The Politics of Sensibility: Race, Gender, and Commerce in the Sentimental Novel*. New York: Cambridge University Press, 1996.
Ellison, Julie. *Cato's Tears and the Making of Anglo-American Emotion*. Chicago: University of Chicago Press, 1999.
Farrell, James T. *The Young Manhood of Studs Lonigan*. New York: Vanguard Press, 1934.
Fiedler, Leslie A. "Looking Back after Fifty Years." *San José Studies* 16.1 (1990): 54–64.
Fine, Marshall. "Huffpost Review: *The Help*." Dir. Tate Taylor. *Huffington Post*, 8 Aug. 2011. http://www.huffingtonpost.com/marshall-fine/huffpost-review-ithe-help_b_923082.html.
Fisher, Philip. *Hard Facts: Setting and Form in the American Novel*. New York: Oxford University Press, 1985.
Fitzgerald, F. Scott. *Tender is the Night*. New York: Scribner, 1934.
Flanagan, Roy. Review of *To Make My Bread*, by Grace Lumpkin. *Survey Midmonthly* 68 (1932): 560.

Foley, Barbara. "Women and the Left in the 1930s." *American Literary History* 2.1 (1990): 150–69. http://www.jstor.org/stable/489816.

Foster, Frances Smith. *Witnessing Slavery: The Development of Ante-Bellum Slave Narratives*. 2nd ed. Madison: University of Wisconsin Press, 1994.

Foster, Hannah Webster. *The Coquette; or, The History of Eliza Wharton*. Boston: Ebenezer Larkin, 1787.

Freibert, Lucy. "Southern Song: An Interview with Margaret Walker." *Frontiers: A Journal of Women Studies* 9.3 (1987): 50–56. http://www.jstor.org/stable/3346261.

Friend, Beverly. "Time Travel as a Feminist Didactic in Works by Phyllis Eisenstein, Marlys Millhiser, and Octavia Butler." *Extrapolation* 23.1 (1982): 50–55.

Gaines, Ernest. *The Autobiography of Miss Jane Pittman*. New York: Dial Press, 1971.

Gargano, N. "I Wish I Could Give More than Five!!" Review of *The Help: A Novel*, by Kathryn Stockett. Amazon.com, 23 Feb. 2009. http://www.amazon.com/review/R3T4ZIUQUYR9Z8.

Gay, Roxane. "The Solace of Preparing Fried Foods and Other Quaint Remembrances from 1960s Mississippi: Thoughts on *The Help*." *Rumpus*, 17 Aug. 2011.

Gibson, Ellen. "What's Selling? The Great Depression." *Business Week* 4108 (2008): 19.

Gladstein, Mimi R. "Deletions from the *Battle*; Gaps in the *Grapes*." *San José Studies* 18 (1992): 43–51.

Graham, Maryemma. "The Fusion of Ideas: An Interview with Margaret Walker Alexander." *African American Review* 27.2 (1993): 279–86. http://www.jstor.org/stable/3042022.

Hall, Jacquelyn Dowd. "Women Writers, the 'Southern Front,' and the Dialectical Imagination." *Journal of Southern History* 69.1 (2003): 3–38. http://www.jstor.org/stable/30039839.

Halper, Albert. *The Foundry*. New York: Viking Press, 1934.

The Hand That Feeds U.S. "The Grapes of Wrath. Part II?" n.d. (accessed 12 Oct. 2011). http://www.thehandthatfeedsus.org/farming_america_Grapes-of-Wrath-part2.cfm.

Harriet. "'Helps' Blur the Lines We've Drawn—a Book I'll Never Forget!" Review of *The Help: A Novel*, by Kathryn Stockett. Amazon.com, 22 July 2009. http://www.amazon.com/review/R39HMET7USFYE7.

Harris, Cheryl I. "Whiteness as Property." *Harvard Law Review* 106.8 (1993): 1707–91. http://www.jstor.org/stable/1341787.

Harris, Janelle. "I Am Not *The Help*." *Clutch Magazine*, 15 Aug. 2011.

Harris, Middleton A., et al., eds. *The Black Book*. 1974. New York: Random House, 2009.

Harris, Trudier. "*Beloved*: 'Woman, Thy Name Is Demon.'" *Critical Essays on Toni Morrison's Beloved*. Ed. Barbara H. Solomon. New York: G. K. Hall, 1998. 127–37.

———. *The Scary Mason-Dixon Line*. Baton Rouge: Louisiana State University Press, 2009.
Haytock, Jennifer. *At Home, At War: Domesticity and World War I in American Literature*. Columbus: Ohio State University Press, 2003.
Henson, Josiah. *The Life of Josiah Henson, Formerly a Slave, Now an Inhabitant of Canada, as Narrated by Himself*. Boston: A. D. Phelps, 1849.
Hentz, Caroline Lee. *The Planter's Northern Bride*. Philadelphia: T. B. Peterson Ltd., 1854.
Hildreth, Richard. *The Slave; or, Memoirs of Archy Moore*. 2 vols. Boston: John H. Eastburn, printer, 1836.
———. *The White Slave; or, Memoirs of a Fugitive*. 8th ed. Boston: Tappan and Whittemore, 1852.
Hoffman, Nancy. Afterword. *Now in November*. By Josephine Johnson. New York: Feminist Press at the City University of New York, 1991. 233–74.
Holden-Kirwan, Jennifer L. "Looking into the Self That Is No Self: An Examination of Subjectivity in *Beloved*." *African American Review* 32.3 (1998): 415–26. http://www.jstor.org/stable/3042242.
Holmes, Linda. "Actor Wendell Pierce Takes to Twitter to Talk about 'The Help.'" *Monkey See*, National Public Radio, 16 Aug. 2011.
Hornaday, Ann. "Black and White, and Not Enough 'Help.'" *Washington Post*, 10 Aug. 2011.
Horvitz, Deborah. "Nameless Ghosts: Possession and Dispossession in *Beloved*." *Studies in American Fiction* 17.2 (1989): 157–67.
House, Elizabeth B. "Toni Morrison's Ghost: The Beloved Who Is Not Beloved." *Studies in American Fiction* 18.1 (1990): 17–25.
Human Rights Watch. *Hidden in the Home: Abuse of Domestic Workers with Special Visas in the United States*. New York: Human Rights Watch, 2001.
Jacobs, Harriet. *Incidents in the Life of a Slave Girl. Written by Herself*. Ed. L. Maria Child. Boston: Published for the author, 1861.
Johnson, Josephine. *Jordanstown: A Novel*. New York: Simon and Schuster, 1937.
———. *Now in November*. New York: Simon and Schuster, 1934.
———. *Seven Houses: A Memoir of Time and Places*. New York: Simon and Schuster, 1973.
Jones, Gayl. *Corregidora*. New York: Random House, 1975.
Keizer, Arlene R. *Black Subject: Identity Formation in the Contemporary Narrative of Slavery*. Ithaca, NY: Cornell University Press, 2004.
Kenan, Randall. "An Interview with Octavia E. Butler." *Callaloo* 14.2 (1991): 495–504. http://www.jstor.org/stable/2931654.
King James Bible. Cambridge: Chadwyck-Healey, 1996.
Kirby, Lisa A. "'How It Grieves the Heart of a Mother [. . .]': The Intersections of Gender, Class, and Politics in Grace Lumpkin's *To Make My Bread*." *Women's Studies* 37 (2008): 661–77. doi: 10.1080/00497870802205191.

Klein, Ezra. "Amazon.com and the Grapes of Wrath." *Washington Post*, 20 Sept. 2011. http://www.washingtonpost.com/blogs/wonkblog/post/amazoncom-and-the-grapes-of-wrath/2011/08/25/gIQAvLSz9K_blog.html.

Klotman, Phyllis Rauch. "'Oh Freedom'—Women and History in Margaret Walker's *Jubilee*." *Black American Literature Forum* 11.4 (1977): 139–45. http://www.jstor.org/stable/3041649.

Kushner, Tony. *Angels in America: A Gay Fantasia on National Themes*. 1993. New York: Theatre Communications Group, 2003.

Landon, Brooks. *Science Fiction after 1900: From the Steam Man to the Stars*. New York: Routledge, 2002.

Langdon, Mary [Mary Hayden Green Pike]. *Ida May: A Story of Things Actual and Possible*. Boston: Phillips, Sampson and Co., 1854.

Lemieux, Jamilah. "I Don't Need Kathryn Stockett's 'Help.'" *Jezebel*, 26 Apr. 2011.

Le Sueur, Meridel. *The Girl*. 1930s. London: Women's Press, 1978.

——. *Ripening: Selected Work, 1927–1980*. Old Westbury, NY: Feminist Press, 1982.

——. *Salute to Spring*. New York: International Publishers, 1940.

——. "They Follow Us Girls." *Anvil*, July/Aug. 1935, 5–7.

Lipsitz, George. *The Possessive Investment in Whiteness: How White People Profit from Identity Politics*. Philadelphia: Temple University Press, 2006.

Longworth, Karina. "*The Help* Review." Dir. Tate Taylor. *Los Angeles Weekly*, 11 Aug. 2011.

Lumpkin, Grace. *Full Circle*. Boston: Western Islands, 1962.

——. *A Sign for Cain*. New York: Lee Furman, 1935.

——. *To Make My Bread*. 1932. Ed. Suzanne Sowinska. Urbana: University of Illinois Press, 1995.

——. *The Wedding*. New York: L. Furman, 1939.

Lumpkin, Katharine Du Pre. *The Making of a Southerner*. 1947. Athens: University of Georgia Press, 1981.

Martis, Holly. "Lineages of American Fascism: A Study of Margaret Walker's Historical Novel *Jubilee*." *Socialism and Democracy* 22.2 (2008): 49–72.

Mason, Paul. "In Steinbeck's Footsteps: America's Middle-Class Underclass." *BBC News*, 28 July 2011. http://www.bbc.co.uk/news/world-us-canada-14296682.

Mathieson, Barbara Offutt. "Memory and Mother Love in Morrison's *Beloved*." *American Imago* 47.1 (1990): 1–21.

McElderry, B. R., Jr. "*The Grapes of Wrath*: In the Light of Modern Critical Theory." *College English* 5.4 (1944): 308–13.

McGreal, Chris. "From Dust to Bust, America's Poor Take on a New Type of Monster." *Guardian*, 27 Aug. 2009.

McKay, Nellie. "'Happy[?]-Wife-and-Motherdom': The Portrayal of Ma Joad in John Steinbeck's *The Grapes of Wrath*." *New Essays on the Grapes of Wrath*. Ed. David Wyatt. New York: Cambridge University Press, 1990. 47–69.

———. "An Interview with Toni Morrison." *Contemporary Literature* 24.4 (1983): 413–29. http://www.jstor.org/stable/1208128.

Merish, Lori. *Sentimental Materialism: Gender, Commodity Culture, and Nineteenth-Century American Literature*. Durham, NC: Duke University Press, 2000.

Miller, Laura. "The Dirty Secrets of 'The Help': A Black Maid Sues a White Author for Stealing Her Story, but Is That What's Really Going On?" *Salon*, 22 Feb. 2011.

"Miscellaneous." *Frederick Douglass' Paper*, 21 Sept. 1855.

Mitchell, Angelyn. *The Freedom to Remember: Narrative, Slavery, and Gender in Contemporary Black Women's Fiction*. New Brunswick, NJ: Rutgers University Press, 2002.

Mitchell, Margaret. *Gone with the Wind*. New York: MacMillan, 1936.

Morris, Wesley. Review of *The Help*, dir. Tate Taylor. *Boston Globe*, 10 Aug. 2011.

Morrison, Toni. *Beloved*. New York: Plume, 1987.

———. "Memory, Creation, and Writing." *Thought* 59 (1984): 385–90.

———. "Person to Person: Toni Morrison." *Black Seeds: Black World Monthly*, 1980, 28–29.

———. "Rediscovering Black History." *New York Times*, 11 Aug. 1974.

———. *Song of Solomon*. New York: Alfred Knopf, 1977.

Motley, Warren. "From Patriarchy to Matriarchy: Ma Joad's Role in *The Grapes of Wrath*." *American Literature* 54 (1982): 397–412.

Moynihan, Daniel Patrick. "The Negro Family: The Case for National Action." US Department of Labor, Office of Policy Planning and Research, Mar. 1965. http://www.dol.gov/oasam/programs/history/webid-meynihan.htm.

Muchnic, Suzanne. "Travels with Steinbeck: Horace Bristol's Remarkable Depression-Era Photographs Are on Display for the First Time." *Los Angeles Times*, 22 Jan. 1989.

Naylor, Gloria, and Toni Morrison. "A Conversation." *Southern Review* 21 (1985): 567–93.

Nekola, Charlotte, and Paula Rabinowitz, eds. *Writing Red: An Anthology of American Women Writers, 1930–1940*. New York: Feminist Press at the City University of New York, 1987.

Northup, Solomon, and David Wilson. *Twelve Years a Slave: Narrative of Solomon Northup, a Citizen of New-York, Kidnapped in Washington City in 1841, and Rescued in 1853*. Auburn, NY: Derby and Miller, 1853.

"A Novel of the Southern Mills." Review of *To Make My Bread*, by Grace Lumpkin. *New York Times*, Sept. 25, 1932, BR7.

Oldenburg, Ann. "'Help' Author Kathryn Stockett Responds to Lawsuit." *USA Today*, 23 Feb. 2011.

Olsen, Tillie Lerner. "A Biographical Interpretation." *Life in the Iron Mills, and Other Stories*, by Rebecca Harding Davis. Ed. Tillie Lerner Olsen. Old Westbury, NY: Feminist Press, 1972. 67–174.

———. *Yonnondio: From the Thirties*. 1974. Lincoln: University of Nebraska Press, 2004.
Oppenheim, Jane E. Review of *Jubilee*, by Margaret Walker. *Best Sellers* 26.13 (1966): 229–30.
Osborne, Kevin. "Better Late than Never: Americans Target Corporate Greed." *Cincinnati CityBeat*, 5 Oct. 2011.
"Other 2—No Title." *National Era*, 25 Aug. 1853, sec. 7 (347): 135.
Person, Leland S. *The Cambridge Introduction to Nathaniel Hawthorne*. Cambridge: Cambridge University Press, 2007.
Phillips, Kelly. "I Don't Have All the Words to Say How Much I Loved This Book." Review of *The Help: A Novel*, by Kathryn Stockett. Amazon.com, 16 Feb. 2009. http://www.amazon.com/review/RXITPPBVO0B3U.
Potts, Stephen W. "'We Keep Playing the Same Record': A Conversation with Octavia E. Butler." *Science Fiction Studies* 23.3 (1996): 331–38. http://www.jstor.org/stable/4240538.
Proulx, Annie. *Close Range: Wyoming Stories*. New York: Scribner, 1999.
Rabinowitz, Paula. *Labor and Desire: Women's Revolutionary Fiction in Depression America*. Chapel Hill: University of North Carolina Press, 1991.
Rainer, Peter. Review of *The Help*, dir. Tate Taylor. *Christian Science Monitor*, 9 Aug. 2011.
Rattray, Laura. "Editing the 1930s: The Lost Work of Josephine Johnson." *Women* 16.2 (2005): 189–202.
———. "Josephine Johnson and Clifton Fadiman at Simon and Schuster: The Genesis of a Pulitzer." *Papers of the Bibliographical Society of America* 98.2 (2004): 209–27.
Richardson, Samuel. *Clarissa; or, The History of a Young Lady*. London: Printed for S. Richardson, 1747–48.
———. *Pamela; or, Virtue Rewarded*. London: Printed for C. Rivington and J. Osborn, 1740.
Rideout, Walter B. *The Radical Novel in the United States, 1900–1954: Some Interrelations of Literature and Society*. New York: Hill and Wang, 1956.
Risley, Ford. *Abolition and the Press: The Moral Struggle against Slavery*. Evanston, IL: Northwestern University Press, 2008.
Robertson, Campbell. "A Victory in Court for the Author of 'The Help.'" *New York Times*, 16 Aug. 2011.
Rody, Caroline. *The Daughter's Return: African-American and Caribbean Women's Fictions of History*. New York: Oxford University Press, 2001.
Romines, Ann. *The Home Plot: Women, Writing, and Domestic Ritual*. Amherst: University of Massachusetts Press, 1992.
Roper, Moses. *A Narrative of the Adventures and Escape of Moses Roper from American Slavery*. Philadelphia: Merrihew and Gun, 1838.
Rowell, Charles. "An Interview with Octavia Butler." *Callaloo* 20.1 (1997): 47–66.

Rowson, Susanna. *Charlotte Temple; or, A Tale of Truth*. London: Minerva Press, 1791.
Rushdy, Ashraf H. A. "The Neo-Slave Narrative." *Cambridge Companion to the African American Novel*. Ed. Maryemma Graham. Cambridge: Cambridge University Press, 2004. 87–105.
———. *Neo-Slave Narratives: Studies in the Social Logic of a Literary Form*. New York: Oxford University Press, 1999.
———. *Remembering Generations: Race and Family in Contemporary African American Fiction*. Chapel Hill: University of North Carolina Press, 2001.
Said, Edward. *Orientalism*. New York: Pantheon Books, 1978.
Salmond, John A. *Gastonia, 1929: The Story of the Loray Mill Strike*. Chapel Hill: University of North Carolina Press, 1995.
Samuels, Shirley, ed. *The Culture of Sentiment: Race, Gender, and Sentimentality in Nineteenth Century America*. New York: Oxford University Press, 1992.
Sawyer, S. D. "So THAT'S What 'The Help' Was Thinking." Review of *The Help: A Novel*, by Kathryn Stockett. Amazon.com, 8 July 2012. http://www.amazon.com/review/R3CRGAERQC12F9.
Schreibersdorf, Lisa. "Radical Mothers: Maternal Testimony and Metaphor in Four Novels of the Gastonia Strike." *Journal of Narrative Theory* 29.3 (1999): 303–22. http://www.jstor.org/stable/30225736.
Sedgwick, Catharine Maria. *A New-England Tale; or, Sketches of New-England Character and Manners*. New York: E. Bliss and E. White, 1822.
Sedgwick, Eve Kosofsky. *Epistemology of the Closet*. Berkeley: University of California Press, 1990.
Seelye, John. "Come Back to the Boxcar, Leslie Honey; or, Don't Cry for Me, Madonna, Just Pass the Milk: Steinbeck and Sentimentality." *Beyond Boundaries: Rereading John Steinbeck*. Ed. Susan Shillinglaw and Kevin Hearle. Tuscaloosa: University of Alabama Press, 2002. 11–33.
Sehgal, Ujala. "Even Emma Stone Can't Save 'The Help' from Heat for 'Fake' History." Dir. Tate Taylor. *Atlantic Wire*, 14 Aug. 2011.
Sen, Rinku. "'The Help' Today Still Don't Have Rights, Actually." *ColorLines: News for Action*, 11 Aug. 2011.
Sergio. "Actor Wendell Pierce Isn't Exactly Thrilled with 'The Help.'" *Shadow and Act: On Cinema of the African Diaspora* (blog), *Indiewire*, 18 Aug. 2011. http://blogs.indiewire.com/shadowandact/actor_wendell_pierce_isnt_exactly_thrilled_with_the_help.
Shepherd, Julianne Escobedo. "New Film *The Help* Whitewashes the Civil Rights Struggle into a Heartstring-Tugging Hallmark Card." Dir. Tate Taylor. *Guernica: A Magazine of Art and Politics*, 15 Aug. 2011.
Shillinglaw, Susan. "Biography in Depth: John Steinbeck, American Writer." Martha Heasley Cox Center for Steinbeck Studies, San Jose State University, San Jose, CA, n.d.

Singley, Carol J. *Adopting America: Childhood, Kinship, and National Identity in Literature*. New York: Oxford University Press, 2011.

Smith, Adam. *A Theory of Moral Sentiments*. London: A. Millar, 1759.

Smith, Valerie. "Neo-Slave Narratives." *The Cambridge Companion to the African American Slave Narrative*. Ed. Audrey Fisch. Cambridge: Cambridge University Press, 2007. 168–87.

Solomon, Akiba. "Why I'm Just Saying No to 'The Help' and Its Historical Whitewash." *ColorLines: News for Action*, 10 Aug. 2011. http://colorlines.com/archives/2011/08/why_im_just_saying_no_to_the_help.html.

Sowinska, Suzanne. Introduction. *To Make My Bread*. By Grace Lumpkin. Urbana: University of Illinois Press, 1995. vii–xliii.

———. "Writing across the Color Line: White Women Writers and the 'Negro Question' in the Gastonia Novels." *Radical Revisions: Rereading 1930s Culture*. Ed. Bill Mullen and Sherry Lee Linkon. Urbana: University of Illinois Press, 1996. 120–43.

Spillers, Hortense J. "A Hateful Passion, a Lost Love." *Feminist Studies* 9.2 (1983): 293–323. http://www.jstor.org/stable/3177494.

Steadman, R. W. "A Critique of Proletarian Literature." *North American Review* 247.1 (1939): 142–52. http://www.jstor.org/stable/25115083.

Steele, Katherine H. "My Life, Revisited." Review of *The Help: A Novel*, by Kathryn Stockett. Amazon.com, 13 Apr. 2010. http://www.amazon.com/review/R3HC72OPHXJ9YO.

Steinbeck, John. *Cannery Row*. New York: Viking Press, 1945.

———. *The Grapes of Wrath*. 1939. New York: Penguin, 2006.

———. *In Dubious Battle*. New York: Covici-Friede, 1936.

———. *Of Mice and Men*. New York: Covici-Friede, 1937.

———. *Tortilla Flat*. New York: Covici-Friede, 1935.

Steinberg, Marc. "Inverting History in Octavia Butler's Postmodern Slave Narrative." *African American Review* 38.3 (2004): 467–76. http://www.jstor.org/stable/1512447.

Stepto, Robert. "'Intimate Things in Place': A Conversation with Toni Morrison." *Massachusetts Review* 18.3 (1977): 473–89. http://www.jstor.org/stable/25088764.

Stern, Julia A. *The Plight of Feeling: Sympathy and Dissent in the Early American Novel*. Chicago: University of Chicago Press, 1997.

Stockett, Kathryn. *The Help: A Novel*. New York: Amy Einhorn Books, 2009.

Stowe, Harriet Beecher. *Uncle Tom's Cabin*. Cleveland: John P. Jewett and Company, 1852.

Tami. "This Is Why I Worry about 'The Help.'" *What Tami Said* (blog), 9 Aug. 2011. http://www.whattamisaid.com/2011/08/this-is-why-i-worry-about-help.html.

Tate, Claudia. "Black Women Writers at Work: An Interview with Margaret Walker." *Fields Watered with Blood: Critical Essays on Margaret*

Walker. Ed. Maryemma Graham. Athens: University of Georgia Press, 2001. 28–43.

Thackeray, William Makepeace. *Vanity Fair: A Novel without a Hero.* London: Bradbury and Evans, 1848.

Tomaskovic-Devey, Donald, and Vincent J. Roscigno. "Racial Economic Subordination and White Gain in the U.S. South." *American Sociological Review* 61.4 (1996): 565–89. http://www.jstor.org/stable/2096394.

Tompkins, Jane. *Sensational Designs: The Cultural Work of American Fiction, 1790–1860.* New York: Oxford University Press, 1985.

Truth, Sojourner. *The Narrative of Sojourner Truth.* Ed. Olive Gilbert. Boston: Printed for the author, 1850.

Turner, Patricia A. "Dangerous White Stereotypes." *New York Times,* 28 Aug. 2011.

Urgo, Joseph R. "Proletarian Literature and Feminism: The Gastonia Novels and Feminist Protest." *Minnesota Review* 24 (Spring 1985): 64–84.

Vorse, M. H. Review of *To Make My Bread,* by Grace Lumpkin. *New Republic* 73 (1932): 104.

W., Patty. "This Book Was Really about My Young Years." Review of *The Help: A Novel,* by Kathryn Stockett. Amazon.com, Dec. 2010. http://www.amazon.com/review/R3IQGK1N5CH678.

Walker, Margaret. "How I Wrote *Jubilee*." *How I Wrote "Jubilee," and Other Essays on Life and Literature.* Ed. Maryemma Graham. Old Westbury, NY: Feminist Press, 1990. 50–66.

———. *Jubilee.* 1966. Boston: Mariner Books, 1999.

Wanzo, Rebecca. "Love 'The Help,' but Please Stop Asking Me to Do the Same." *Huffington Post,* 12 Aug. 2011. http://www.huffingtonpost.com/rebecca-wanzo/the-help-movie_b_925550.html.

———, *The Suffering Will Not Be Televised: African American Women and Sentimental Political Storytelling.* Albany: State University of New York Press, 2009.

Warner, Susan [Elizabeth Wetherell]. *The Wide, Wide World.* New York: George P. Putnam, 1850.

Weatherwax, Clara. *Marching! Marching!* New York: J. Day, 1935.

Weinstein, Cindy. *Family, Kinship, and Sympathy in Nineteenth-Century American Literature.* Cambridge: Cambridge University Press, 2004.

Westerman, Jennifer H. "Landscapes of Labor: Nature, Work, and Environmental Justice in Depression-Era Fiction." PhD dissertation. University of Nevada, Reno, 2009. DA3342624.

"The White Slave." *Frederick Douglass' Paper,* 10 Sept. 1852.

Willis, Sara Payson [Fanny Fern]. *Fern Leaves from Fanny's Portfolio.* Auburn, NY: Miller, Orton and Mulligan, 1854.

———. *Ruth Hall.* New York: Mason Brothers, 1855.

Wilson, Harriet E. *Our Nig; or, Sketches from the Life of a Free Black.* Boston: Printed for Geo. C. Rand and Avery, 1859.

Wilson, Jamia. "The Upside of *The Help* Controversy: It Made Us Talk about Race." *Good*, 23 Aug. 2011.

Wolfe, Tom. *A Man in Full: A Novel*. New York: Farrar, Straus and Giroux, 1998.

Wyatt, Jean. "Giving Body to the Word: The Maternal Symbolic in Toni Morrison's *Beloved*." *Critical Essays on Toni Morrison's Beloved*. Ed. Barbara H. Solomon. New York: G. K. Hall, 1998. 211–32.

Zerlina. "Professor Melissa Harris-Perry Calls 'The Help' Movie 'Ahistorical and Deeply Troubling.'" *Feministing* (blog), 11 Aug. 2011.

Index

abolition, 15, 187
Aderholt, Orville F., 206n1
African American women: control over bodies, 16, 155–59, 167, 174, 179; discourses about motherhood, 12, 126, 149–50, 152–53, 155, 158–59, 193; discourses about womanhood, 12–13, 16–17, 38, 127; female lineage, 115–16, 120; marginalization of, 1, 19; and middle class, 12–13; negotiating sentimental conventions, 12–13, 15–17, 113, 151–53, 158–59. *See also* mothers
agrarianism, 61
AIDS crisis, 200–201
American Communist Party. *See* Communist Party [American]
American Dream, 19, 69, 79, 111
American Individualism, 21, 53. *See also* capitalism
Andrews, William L., 13–14
Angelo, Bonnie, 184
Armstrong, Nancy, 94–95, 209n5
Astro, Richard, 92, 209n3
Austen, Jane, 60, 209n5; *Pride and Prejudice*, 60

Baldwin, James, 200–1; *Giovanni's Room*, 200–201
Barnes, Elizabeth, 14, 203n3
Baskind, Samantha, 90
Baym, Nina, 8–9, 95–96, 209n5

Beaulieu, Elizabeth Ann, 114, 132
Bell, Bernard W., 15–16
Bell, Michael, 204n5
Beloved. *See under* Morrison, Toni
Bennett, Paula, 203n3
Berger, James, 159–60
Berlant, Lauren, 152–53, 203n3
bildungsroman, 26, 60, 64, 81
Black Book, The. *See under* Harris, Middleton
black women. *See* African American women
Blake, Fay M., 207n4
Boyd, Kyle, 190, 211n4
Briffault, Robert, 91–92, 94, 102, 209n3
Bristol, Horace, 89–91, 209n1
Brontë, Charlotte, 94, 209n5; *Jane Eyre*, 94
Brontë, Emily, 59, 94, 209n5; *Wuthering Heights*, 94
Brown, Cecil, 185
Brown, Gillian, 41, 203n3
Brown, William Wells, 205n8; *Narrative of William W. Brown*, 205n8
Butler, Octavia, 2, 127–46; connecting the present to the past, 17, 21–22, 184, 200; *Kindred*, 17, 21–22, 126, 127–46, 184, 200; showing when sympathy is lost

Campbell, Patricia R., 207n4
Cantwell, Robert, 23, 60; *The Land of Plenty*, 60

capitalism: abuses or failures of, 8–9, 12, 21, 37, 39–40, 41, 53–54, 76–77; and the American Dream, 111; and belief in landownership, 37, 61, 65–68, 77; capitalist mythologies, 20, 37, 40–41, 62, 64–70, 76–77, 85–86, 96, 111, 208n8; critiques of, 53, 40, 60, 61–62, 76–77, 93, 110; cycle of failure, 33, 62, 208n8; dehumanization, 54; enforcing individualism, 40–41, 53–54, 91–93, 102; fracturing community, 36, 38, 50–51, 86; and gender, 25, 27, 40, 50–51, 61–62, 66–70, 70–76, 91, 93, 95–97, 110; and hard work, 32–33, 40–41, 48, 53, 62, 69, 111, 187–88; and race, 12–13, 28–29, 79–80
Carby, Hazel V., 205n10
caregiving, 1, 2, 21, 35, 39, 41, 110, 119, 166–67; activism as caregiving, 57; exercising agency through caregiving, 103–104, 109–10; extending sympathy through caregiving, 169; failure to meet caregiving ideals, 35, 50–51; group caretaking, 55, 88, 102, 178; male caregiving, 39, 49, 86, 87–111. *See also* domestic work
Casey, Janet Galligani, 61
Center for American Progress, 190
Chapman, Abraham, 112
children: abuse of, 34–35, 66–67; death or loss of, 41–42, 44, 58, 140–41, 152, 153, 154–56, 165–67, 210n3; inspiring sympathy, 26–27, 38, 41–42, 44, 103, 153, 161; orphans, 5, 159; passing on learned prejudices, 43–44, 196–97; protection of, 22, 32–33, 36, 39, 123, 149, 153, 155, 160, 172; and sentimental tropes, 5, 38–39; vulnerable, 5, 62, 69. *See also* mothers
Christianity: Bible, the, 38, 47, 133; biblical references, 52, 119, 200, 210n1; Christ figure, 45, 119; Christian destiny [divine purpose], 21, 113, 119–20, 123, 125; Christlike sacrifice, 1, 45, 57, 71, 99–100, 117; comparison to Jewish slaves, 125; creating community, 45, 46, 51; divine consolation, 4; Jesus Christ, 100, 119, 123, 152, 174, 210n2; Moses, 21, 125; theonomy, 120
Civil Rights era [Civil Rights movement], 12–13, 18, 127, 189, 191–92, 200; Civil Rights Act, 191

Civil War, 30, 67, 112–15, 120, 189, 204n8; Civil War fiction, 112; Union army, 122
Clark, Suzanne, 204n5
Clemons, Walter, 175
Coiner, Constance, 24
Communist Party [American], 8–9, 11, 24, 26, 31, 206n1
Conroy, Jack, 60; *The Disinherited*, 60
Cook, Sylvia J., 207n4
Corber, Robert J., 200–201
Crash of 1929, 19, 63
Crouch, Stanley, 147–48, 150, 185, 212n6
Cullinan, Colleen Carpenter, 152
Cult of True Womanhood, 38
Culture of Sentiment, 3, 15, 209n5
Cummins, Maria Susanna, 203n2; Gertrude Flint [Gerty], 152; *The Lamplighter*, 117, 152, 203n2

Daughters of the American Revolution [DAR], 198
Davidson, Cathy N., 14, 203n3
Davis, Rebecca Harding, 25–26; *Life in the Iron Mills*, 25–26
Delany, Samuel R., 127
Demetrakopoulos, Stephanie A., 151
DeMott, Robert, 107
Depression, The. *See* Great Depression, The
DiChario, Nick, 130–31
Dickinson, Emily, 59
Dieng, Babacar, 114
Dillon, Elizabeth Maddock, 37, 54
Dobson, Joanne, 4, 56
domestic fiction, 28, 94–95, 209n5
domestic labor, 51; child care, 25, 56, 149, 196, 207n5; housework, 25, 39, 49, 51, 56, 93, 102–3, 110; managing household resources, 40, 72–73, 93. *See also* caregiving
domestic novel. *See* domestic fiction
domestic sphere: challenging beliefs about home and safety, 33–38; and class, 9, 38; expanding, 10, 21, 29, 38–39, 51–52, 58, 87–110; and race, 38; and sentimental ideals, 28, 38–39, 95–96. *See also* family
double consciousness, 159–60
Douglas, Ann, 6
Douglass, Frederick, 15, 133, 142, 206n10; *Frederick Douglass' Paper*, 205; *The Life and Times of Frederick Douglass*, 206n10; *My Bondage and My Freedom*,

15; *Narrative of the Life of Frederick Douglass*, 133
Dozier, Elvira Ware, 115
Du Bois, W. E. B., 159–60; *The Souls of Black Folk*, 159–60

Edwards, Thomas, 175
Eliot, George, 60; *Middlemarch*, 60
Ellis, Markman, 203n3
Ellison, Julie, 203n3
Emancipation, 38, 120
Enlightenment, The, 7, 152; philosophy about sympathy, 152. *See also* sensibility
Evers, Medgar, 190

family: African American family, 11–13, 16, 20, 22, 77, 111, 187; consanguinity, 158–59; defined by affection, 2, 5, 22, 32, 158–59, 196; defined by biology, 22; expanded through adoption, 5, 158, 203n4; expanded through affection, 2, 4–5, 22; 32, 155–59, 164, 168, 196; expanded through domestic space, 21, 29, 87–111; expanded through marriage, 158; expanding cultural family, 2, 10–11, 55–56, 76, 77–79, 86, 110–11, 178; failures to extend family through sympathy or affection, 53, 69–70, 81–86, 168, 171–72, 198, 199; gay community as family, 200–201; matriarchal family structure, 91–93; national family, 1–2, 5, 10, 12–13, 17–18, 61–62, 77, 86, 110, 159, 186–88, 200, 203n4; other ways to define, 200; proletarian ideals, 10; realigned around women, 20, 70–76, 113, 120, 125–26; sentimental ideals, 4–5, 12, 17–18, 28–29, 41–42, 47, 65, 185; separation of, 2–4, 29, 37–38, 41, 57–58, 108, 139–42, 145, 149, 152–53, 166, 170, 196. *See also* mothers
Farrell, James T., 60; *The Young Manhood of Studs Lonigan*, 60
Feminist Movement, The, 12; anti-feminist response, 147; feminist interpretation, 60, 132, 150; feminist recovery, 25, 60
Fern, Fanny [Sara Payson Willis], 3, 203n2; *Fern Leaves from Fanny's Portfolio*, 203n2; *Ruth Hall*, 3, 203n2; Ruth Hall, 152
Fiedler, Leslie A., 95
Fisher, Philip, 3–4, 54, 203n3

Fitzgerald, F. Scott, 59; *Tender is the Night*, 59
Flanagan, Roy, 23
Foley, Barbara, 24–25
Foster, Frances Smith, 205n8
Foster, Hannah Webster, 117; *The Coquette*, 117
Freedman's Bureau, 122
Freibert, Lucy, 116
Friend, Beverly, 131–32
Fugitive Slave Law, 204n8

Gaines, Ernest, 113; *The Autobiography of Miss Jane Pittman*, 113
Garner, Margaret, 148–49, 184–85, 210n2
Gastonia Mill strikes, 23, 24, 29, 31, 32, 57, 206n1, 207n4. *See also* Loray Mill strikes
Gibson, Ellen, 88
Graham, Maryemma, 116
Grapes of Wrath, The. *See under* Steinbeck, John
Great Depression, The, 8, 19, 62, 65, 69, 87–88

Hall, Jacquelyn Dowd, 24, 26
Halper, Albert, 60; *The Foundry*, 60
Harris, Cheryl I., 165
Harris, Janelle, 189
Harris, Middleton A., 184, 210n2; *The Black Book*, 184, 210n2
Harris, Spike. *See* Harris, Middleton, A.
Harris, Trudier, 175
Hawthorne, Nathaniel, 5–6
Haytock, Jennifer, 98
Henning, Carol, 89
Henson, Josiah, 205n8; *Life of Josiah Henson*, 205n8
Hentz, Caroline Lee, 14; *The Planter's Northern Bride*, 14
Herbst, Josephine, 207n2
Hildreth, Richard, 205n9; *The Slave; or, Memoirs of Archy Moore*, 205n9; *The White Slave*, 205n9
Hoffman, Nancy, 60–61, 63
Holden-Kirwan, Jennifer L., 175
Holocaust, 185
Horvitz, Deborah, 175
House, Elizabeth B., 175

industrialization, 7, 10, 18, 67. *See also* urbanization

Jacobs, Harriet, 148, 205n10; *Incidents in the Life of a Slave Girl*, 148, 205n10

Jesus Christ. *See under* Christianity
Jim Crow era, 16, 38, 188–89, 207n6
John Reed Clubs, 89
Johnson, Josephine, 2, 59–86; connecting home and public space, 20–21, 58; creation of extended families, 199; extending sympathy to working class, 10–11; focus on both class and gender, 96; focus on both class and race, 79–80; *Jordanstown*, 62; *Now in November*, 20–21, 59–86, 96; *Seven Houses*, 63
Jones, Gayl, 113; *Corregidora*, 113
Joyce, James, 185
Jubilee. See under Walker, Margaret
Jung, C. G., 151

Kenan, Randall, 129, 130–31
Kindred. See under Butler, Octavia
King, Martin Luther, Jr., 191; "I Have a Dream," 191
kinship. *See* family
Kirby, Lisa A., 207n4
Klotman, Phyllis Rauch, 114
Ku Klux Klan, 115, 121–24
Kushner, Tony, 201; *Angels in America*, 201, 212n7

Landon, Brooks, 131
Langdon, Mary [Mary Haydon Green Pike], 14; *Ida May*, 14
Le Sueur, Meridel, 93, 204n6, 207n2, 209n4; *The Girl*, 209n4; *Salute to Spring*, 209n4; "They Follow Us Girls," 204n6
Lipsitz, George, 207n6
literacy, 16; connection between literacy and whiteness, 137, 151, 206n10
Loray Mill strikes. *See* Gastonia Mill strikes
Lumpkin, Grace, 2, 23–58; connecting home and public space, 20–21, 69, 86, 93; creation of extended families, 199; extending sympathy to working class, 10–11; focus on both class and gender, 62–63; focus on both class and race, 27, 42–45; 187, 208n7; *Full Circle*, 31; portrayal of women's roles, 72, 93; *A Sign for Cain*, 31; *To Make My Bread*, 20, 23–58, 62–63, 187, 208n7; *The Wedding*, 31
Lumpkin, Katharine Du Pre, 30–31; *The Making of a Southerner*, 30–31

marginalization *See* Others
Martis, Holly, 114
Marxist literature. *See* proletarian literature
masculinity, 92, 104, 105–11, 133, 152; black masculinity, 16, 120, 206n10; failures of, 40, 209n6; and land, 94, 97; and proletarian writing, 9, 24–25, 28, 29, 63; and providership/labor, 12, 29, 34, 39–40, 69–70, 94, 97, 110; as universal norm, 150; and violence, 34–35, 91, 98, 108–9; white masculinity, 90
Mason, Paul, 87
Mathieson, Barbara Offutt, 151
matriarchy, 12, 17, 92–94, 97, 102, 107–8, 110, 126, 204n7. *See also* mothers
McElderry, B. R., Jr., 95
McGreal, Chris, 87
McKay, Nellie, 92, 94, 102, 110, 209n2
Merish, Lori, 203n3, 205n10
middle class: appeals to, 10, 50; feminized associations, 7, 9, 24; formation of, 8–9, 209n5; ideals, 33, 50, 208n8; misperceptions about the working class, 46, 48–49; in sentimental fiction, 8–9; and separate spheres ideology, 28
Middle Passage. *See under* slavery
Mitchell, Margaret, 112, 114, 133; *Gone with the Wind*, 112, 114
modernism, 1, 6–10, 18, 46, 204n5
moral suasion, 14–15
Morrison, Toni, 2, 147–85; *Beloved*, 17, 85, 146, 147–85; and critique of sympathy, 17, 22, 85, 146, 201; and motherhood, 17, 22; *Song of Solomon*, 185. *See also* postmodern
mothers: African American, 11–12, 21, 22, 116, 126, 129–30, 147–85, 204n7; creating sympathy for others, 32–33, 38–42, 44, 56, 111, 152–53, 193; discourse about in sentimental novels, 5, 10, 17–18, 32, 40, 134, 158–59; and grief, 42, 48, 165–66, 193; inspiring revolutionary consciousness, 36, 38–42; mother-child relationship, 22, 149, 154–55; mothering beyond biological family, 103–4, 168–69, 158, 196–97; as moral center of the family, 21, 62, 70–76, 123, 126, 158; redefining beliefs about, 40; refusing to mother, 178–79; struggles of, 20, 28, 35–36, 38–42, 48–49, 208n8; and white,

middle-class domesticity, 17–18, 50–51. *See also* African American women
Motley, Warren, 92, 94, 102, 209n2
Moynihan, Daniel Patrick, 11–12, 16–17, 204n7; "The Negro Family: The Case for National Action" [Moynihan Report], 11–12, 16, 204n7. *See also* African American women
Muchnic, Suzanne, 90

naturalism, 6–7, 9, 46
Nekola, Charlotte, 24
neo-slave narratives, 2, 15–17, 113; and historical narrative, 113, 114–15, 129–30, 183–95; and the Moynihan era, 17; and readership, 11; relationship to sentimental novels, 13–15, 19–20, 111, 148–49, 188. *See also* Moynihan, Daniel Patrick
Northup, Solomon, 205n9; *Twelve Years a Slave*, 205n9
Now in November. See under Johnson, Josephine

Olsen, Tillie Lerner, 25–26, 93, 96, 209n4; *Yonnondio*, 25–26, 96, 209n4
Oppenheim, Jane E., 112
oral history, 20, 21, 113, 115, 133
oral tradition [African American], 182
Osborne, Kevin, 87
Others: appropriation of Othered perspectives, 24, 58, 195; and class, 186–87; definitions of, 18–19, 200–201, 203n1; and definitions of family, 5; extending sympathy for, 1–2, 18–19, 88, 134, 145–46, 186–88; and race, 17, 19–20, 193–95, 159–60; white sympathy for, 145–46, 153, 188, 189, 195

pastoral novel, 60–61
Person, Leland S., 6
Pilgrim's Progress, 4, 21
postmodernism, 6, 16; *Beloved* as postmodern, 22, 148, 176, 183–84
privilege: class, 47, 63, 134; male, 133–35, 145, 150; white, 12, 16, 45, 133–35, 145, 150, 153, 187, 189–90, 199, 203n1, 205n10
Proletarian literature, 8–10, 18, 21, 24, 27–28, 31, 66, 111, 123, 188, 199. *See also* realism

Proulx, Annie, 201; "Brokeback Mountain," 201
public sphere, 10, 25, 27–29, 58, 91, 152

Rabinowitz, Paula, 24–25, 27–28, 207n2
Rattray, Laura, 59, 62
realism, 6–7, 9, 18, 94, 148; Proletarian realism, 9, 25, 28, 60, 63; Magical realism, 185
Reconstruction, 16, 38, 120
reportage, 9, 11, 19, 62, 89, 207n2
revolutionary consciousness, 28, 51, 64, 76, 100, 111; inspired by separation or loss, 41, 57–58
Richardson, Samuel, 209n5
Rideout, Walter B., 207n4
Risley, Ford, 15
Romines, Ann, 95, 102–3
Roper, Moses, 205n8; *A Narrative of the Adventures and Escape*, 205n8
Rowell, Charles, 127–29
Rowson, Susanna, 119; *Charlotte Temple*, 119
Rushdy, Ashraf H. A., 113, 206n11

Said, Edward, 203n1; *Orientalism*, 203n1
Salmond, John A., 206n1
Samuels, Shirley, 3, 95, 203n3
Schreibersdorf, Lisa, 207n4
Sedgwick, Catherine Maria, 209n5; *A New-England Tale*, 209n5
Sedgwick, Eve Kosofsky, 200
Seelye, John, 95
segregation, 12, 190, 192, 204n7, 207n6; overcoming through sympathy, 44–45
sensibility, 7, 62–64, 152; novels of, 60–61
sentimental novels, 3–7; adoption within abolitionist writing, 15, 187, 205n9; affection as driving force, 4–5; and association with white, middle-class domesticity, 13, 19, 151, 188; creation of the middle class, 5, 8–9; criticisms of, 5–7, 9, 199; and men, 4, 29, 69, 159; reorganizing family, 4–5, 62, 95, 116, 126, 151, 158–59, 196, 203n4; and rhetorical style, 3–4, 14; slave narrative engagement, 14–15, 148, 187, 205n10; and spiritual organization, 70–71, 117; sympathy in, 4, 134, 139, 152. *See also* family

sentimentality: African American literary tradition and, 12–13, 16–18, 150–51, 205n10; criticism of, 1, 6–8, 9–10, 95, 147–48; definition, 2–3. *See also* Culture of Sentiment; sentimental novels

shame: and gender roles, 108–9, 182–83; as response to Othering and suffering, 29, 46–50, 58, 77, 128–30, 180, 208n8

Shillinglaw, Susan, 89

Singley, Carol J., 203n4

slave narratives, 14–16, 20, 115, 131, 185, 187, 204n8; female-authored, 116; male-authored, 205n10

slavery: African American literary tradition and, 2, 3, 13–22, 113–15, 147–48, 150–53, 205n9, 205n10; cultural legacy of, 12, 38, 119, 123, 128–30, 134, 183–85, 189; Middle Passage, 176. *See also Beloved*; neo-slave narratives; *Jubilee*; *Kindred*

Smith, Adam, 152

Smith, Valerie, 16

Sowinska, Suzanne, 30–31

Spillers, Hortense J., 117, 120

Steadman, R. W., 9

Steinbeck, John, 2, 87–111; *Cannery Row*, 88; creation of extended families, 86, 199; expanding the domestic space, 21; extending sympathy to working class, 10–11, 207n2; film version of *The Grapes of Wrath*, 88, 90; *The Grapes of Wrath*, 21, 87–111; *In Dubious Battle*, 88–89; *Of Mice and Men*, 88; *Tortilla Flat*, 88, 89. *See also* Bristol, Horace; reportage

stereotype, 3–4, 38, 112, 127, 138, 149, 153

Stern, Julia A., 203n2

Stockett, Kathryn, 188–99, 211n1, 211n2; *The Help*, 188–99, 211n1, 211n2

Stowe, Harriet Beecher, 3, 14, 74, 149, 152–53, 193, 205n8; comparisons to *Uncle Tom's Cabin*, 15, 95, 205n9; Eliza, 152; Little Eva, 74; Uncle Tom, 305n8; *Uncle Tom's Cabin*, 3, 14, 152–53, 193, 205n8, 205n9. *See also* Henson, Josiah

Styron, William, 195, 212n6; *The Confessions of Nat Turner*, 195, 212n6

Thackeray, William Makepeace, 94; *Vanity Fair*, 94

Tillich, Paul, 120

To Make My Bread. See under Lumpkin, Grace

Tompkins, Jane, 3, 7–8, 95, 203n3

trauma, 16, 22, 123, 148–49, 156, 162, 176, 180, 210n1; traumatic recurrence, 16, 180

Truth, Sojourner, 142, 205; *Narrative of Sojourner Truth*, 205

Tubman, Harriet, 142

Uncle Tom's Cabin See under Stowe, Harriet Beecher

Updike, John, 159

urbanization, 6–7, 18, 46, 67, 186–87. *See also* industrialization

Urgo, Joseph R., 207n4

veracity, 13–14, 21, 116

Vorse, M. H., 23

Walker, Margaret, 2, 112–26; connection to history, 21, 112–15, 183; *Jubilee*, 17, 21, 112–26, 155, 187–88, 199; and legacy of slavery, 17, 21, 132; and middle-class work ethic, 187–88; reorganizing the family, 21, 199–200

Walton, Edith, 59

Wanzo, Rebecca, 150, 152–53, 211n2

Warner, Susan [Elizabeth Wetherell], 203n2; Ellen Montgomery, 21, 152; *The Wide, Wide World*, 21, 117, 203n2

Weatherwax, Clara, 60; *Marching! Marching!*, 60

Weinstein, Cindy, 5, 158–59, 203n4

Wiggins, Ella May, 30, 42, 56–57, 206n1; *Mill Mother's Lament*, 42, 56

Wilson, David, 205n9

Wilson, Harriet E., 148; *Our Nig*, 148

Wolfe, Tom, 150; *A Man in Full*, 150

women writers, 10; African American women writers, 16–17, 117, 127, 150–51, 205n10; Proletarian women writers, 24–28, 29, 38, 58, 90–91, 95–96. *See also* domestic fiction

Woolf, Virginia, 209n5

Wyatt, Jean, 151–52, 175

About the Author

Jennifer A. Williamson is a gender specialist at a Washington D.C. area global development organization, and a former instructor of English and Women's Studies at the University of North Carolina at Chapel Hill. She has previously taught at the University of Maryland–College Park. She is the author of numerous articles and the editor of *The Sentimental Mode: Essays in Literature, Film and Television* (McFarland, forthcoming). Her research and publications focus on gender, women's writing, domesticity, the sentimental tradition, and slave narratives and constructions of race.

www.ingramcontent.com/pod-product-compliance
Lightning Source LLC
Chambersburg PA
CBHW021848300426
44115CB00005B/66